MW00789106

The New York Times

WEEKENDS WITH WILL

The New York Times

WEEKENDS WITH WILL
A Year of Saturday and Sunday *New York Times* Crosswords

Edited by Will Shortz

ST. MARTIN'S GRIFFIN ❧ NEW YORK

THE NEW YORK TIMES WEEKENDS WITH WILL.
Copyright © 2010 by The New York Times Company. All rights reserved.
Printed in the United States of America. For information, address
St. Martin's Press, 175 Fifth Avenue, New York, N.Y. 10010.

www.stmartins.com

All of the puzzles that appear in this work were originally published
in *The New York Times* from January 1, 2006, to December 30, 2006.
Copyright © 2006 by The New York Times Company.
All Rights Reserved. Reprinted by permission.

ISBN 978-0-312-65668-3

10   9   8   7   6   5   4   3

The New York Times

SATURDAY

by Jim Hyres

ACROSS

1 Some pizza slices, e.g.
8 They employ speakers
15 Army E-7
17 One good at making faces
18 Moved like molasses
19 Plant holder?
20 Needles
21 1971 U.S. Open winner __ Smith
22 Launch
24 It's sold in bars
25 A abroad
26 Modern company category
28 A abroad
29 Modified
31 Like British bishops
33 Time to attack
34 2004 P.G.A. Player of the Year
35 Dreamliner developer
37 Miss Gulch miffed her
40 Ovidian openings
41 Contact lens solutions
43 N.L. West team, on scoreboards
44 Home on the range: Var.
46 Moselle feeder, to Moselle natives
47 South-of-the-border spouses: Abbr.
48 End of __
50 36-Down, por ejemplo
51 Island in the East China Sea
52 1995 Annie Lennox hit
55 "Maybe yes, maybe no"
56 Be made up
57 Worried about, slangily

DOWN

1 Anti
2 Satan, to Scots
3 Fictional swinger
4 When some people retire
5 Sud's opposite
6 __ T
7 Whiny one
8 Infected
9 Chorus bit
10 Sponsorship
11 Lessor's list
12 Gloater's remark
13 Narrow, in a way
14 Lineate
16 Not impromptu
22 Caviar fish
23 Potential vote-getter
26 Pluto and others
27 Change places?
30 "__ get it!"
32 __ Friday's
34 Auto options
35 Like some gardens
36 Ciudad Bolívar is on it
37 With lightness
38 Wipeout?
39 Bullyragged
42 Driving aid, of sorts
45 Hotel room amenities
47 __ lot (is telling)
49 First drawing class, perhaps
51 Only
53 Mountain road section
54 Binding declaration

2

SATURDAY

by David Quarfoot

ACROSS

1 Soup line
9 Erased
14 One might request help getting started
16 Inclined . . . or flat
17 Makes something up
18 Roman land
19 Company once taken over by Carl Icahn
20 "So sorry"
22 Mr., abroad
24 Southwestern sign-off
25 Reminds a bit too much
26 Like Indians
28 Suffix with jardin
29 Irish Sea feeder
30 Jazz fan, most likely
32 Rubens painted her
35 Decor finish?
37 Figs. in identity theft
38 Goes off
42 Like a lottery winner, typically
46 Boomer's kid
47 He played J-Bone in "Johnny Mnemonic"
49 Quaint schoolroom item
50 "No ___!"
52 Beau's belle
54 Carmaker since 1949
55 Layabouts
58 Opposite of always, in Augsburg
59 Round window
60 Tender shoot?
62 First name in TV talk
63 Whip snapper
64 They're perfect
65 Cross the line?

DOWN

1 Best Supporting Actor for "The Fortune Cookie," 1966
2 She served eight days in jail for public obscenity
3 Sub-Saharan scourge
4 Year for Super Bowl LXXXIV
5 Exploit
6 Where the Enola Gay plane was built
7 Start of a Beatles title
8 Olympic team?
9 Vision: Prefix
10 DuPont trademark
11 Made impossible
12 Steams up
13 Hypersaline spot
15 In places
21 Sub-Saharan scourge
23 1986 Indy 500 winner
27 ___ forces
31 "Ixnay"
33 Italian province
34 Gets back to, quickly
36 Foosball locale
38 Look into
39 Like some copies
40 Mentor's companion
41 Manager's terse order
43 It's a short walk from Copacabana
44 Celebrity-spotting eatery
45 "A diamond is forever" sloganeer
48 "Key Largo" Oscar winner
51 Fee to enter a poker game
53 Daughter of Zeus
56 Period in sch.
57 Out-of-commission cruisers
61 Feather holder?

SATURDAY

by Brendan Emmett Quigley

ACROSS

1 Accusatory words
5 Certain red algae
12 Potting materials
14 Clicker
15 Native up north
16 Essayist whose motto was "Que sais-je?"
17 10 kilogauss
18 It has many soap slots
19 Plans to get back at
21 "Dog Barking at the Moon" painter, 1926
22 Comes back
23 Name on some briefs
24 Provide with new squares, perhaps
25 Insults wittily
26 It isn't repeated
28 Land at an Italian airport?
31 Captain of the Ghost, in Jack London's "The Sea Wolf"
34 William ___, secretary of commerce under Clinton
35 Casserole dishes
37 Day before a Jewish holiday
38 Passing legend
40 Go
42 They're treated by veterinarios
43 Turned over
44 Floor coverings, to a Brit
45 Pronunciation considerations
46 Cousin of Jane Eyre
47 One singled out before drinking
48 It's full of slots, briefly

DOWN

1 Martyred Carmelite nun ___ Stein
2 Music critic's bane
3 One tying up a turkey, say
4 Exercise, in Exeter
5 Brazilian port known for coffee
6 Artificial flavor base
7 Petal product: Var.
8 Number one
9 Not stopped
10 Many Madrileños
11 They're good at taking things down
13 Legally punishable
14 Starbucks slip-ons
16 Make a mess of
20 Woman in Chekhov's "The Sea-Gull"
23 Chart climber
25 Literary character who debuted in "The Curse of Capistrano"
27 Beat up
28 City on the Salentine Peninsula
29 Warner Music Group label
30 Looks up to
32 Involves
33 Order lover
34 Not be able to take
35 One way of fitting
36 Big bore
38 Pop singer McCartney
39 Leader of a 1970 military coup
41 Theme of Nabokov's "Lolita"

SATURDAY

ACROSS

1 Easily swindled sort
5 Baby with big eyes
10 They're not good
14 Like some hurricanes
15 ___ Island
16 Secluded spot
17 Fine-tuner
18 Midlevel math course
20 Some important decisions
22 Really let have it
23 Wreathes
24 Loud succession of sounds
25 It's debatable
26 Mouth burner
29 Goes over
32 Fictional mariner and others
34 Dam, e.g.
35 You might get into it before going under
37 Jet pump for fluid withdrawal
39 Carrier with Tokyo hdqrs.
40 George ___, German-American artist known for vitriolic caricature
42 Some wines
43 13-Down creator
45 Old empire member
47 Singer Cantrell
48 Leaves in the kitchen
52 Academy offering
54 Picture tube
55 Historic ship that sank on Christmas Day

by Dana Motley

57 Ned Beatty's role in "Superman"
58 Bureau: Abbr.
59 River through Newark, England
60 1955 Tony winner for "Quadrille"
61 Source of some pressure, maybe
62 Go (along)
63 Lummoxes

DOWN

1 It may hang on a pot
2 Like Filipinos
3 Not inadvertent
4 Some pianos
5 Appendixes, e.g.
6 For what purpose
7 Quick survey
8 Teachers' degs.
9 It's ball-bearing
10 Advance
11 Stalwarts
12 Two-time Newbery winner ___ Lowry
13 Funny number
19 Ones keeping a firm balance?
21 African beauty
24 Get going
27 Place for a tap
28 "___ to Hold" (1943 film musical)
29 Spoils
30 1990s transportation secretary
31 Just by scanning
33 Department store area
36 Soap opera creator ___ Phillips
38 Corporation whose stock symbol is KO
41 They send things up
44 Real bitter-ender
46 Compact
49 Mustered
50 Imagine
51 Animal shelters
52 Order ender
53 Carry on
54 Syrup brand
56 Big inits. in 1970s TV

SATURDAY

ACROSS

1 Sheets
7 Rub
15 Flowering plant with prickly leaves
16 Funnelform flora
17 Like part of the heart
18 Periods of decline
19 Garage sale?
20 Neighbors of Indians
21 Breadwinner
22 Circus pioneer Ringling and others
23 Magazine contents
25 "___ Secretary," Madeleine Albright's 2003 autobiography
30 Lie very, very still
35 Wolfish
36 Be on the take
38 Throws off
39 Secret
40 Slaves
41 Bullied baby, maybe
42 Mouse manipulator?
43 It might hold the solution
49 Having the same concentration of salt as mammalian blood
54 Pounded
55 Cousin of a sego
56 "Fighting" collegiate team
57 Is older than
58 ___ Sea between Ireland and England
59 Concurring comment
60 O.K.

by Philip C. Ordway

DOWN

1 Put on
2 Prefix with syllabic
3 Like rhinos vis-à-vis elephants
4 Like some elephants
5 Ride
6 They can cause eruptions
7 It's simple to solve
8 Inclines
9 Recipe parts
10 Kind of steak
11 Shrub of the genus Indigofera
12 Film
13 Trails
14 Latin infinitive
24 Its currency is the dirham: Abbr.
25 Number associated with a boom
26 Emblem of life
27 Prayer addressee, in Paris
28 Unwelcome dining discovery
29 Work well together
30 Surveyor's map
31 Italian island reef
32 Follower of myself
33 Cry
34 Travels at a speed of
35 Home of San José
37 It may involve a homophone
41 Yeast, e.g.
42 "Benjamin"
44 Drones, say
45 Dispensary stock
46 Pool
47 "The State and Revolution" writer
48 A famous one was issued at Nantes
49 Parenting challenges
50 1980's Geena Davis sitcom
51 City once named Provo Bench
52 Tendency, as of events
53 Moonfish

6

SATURDAY

ACROSS

1 You may pretend to pick one
10 Chewed stimulant
14 He had a 2004 #1 hit "Drop It Like It's Hot"
15 Capital 12,000 feet above sea level
16 Willful ones?
17 "Take ___" (office order)
18 NPR reporter Shapiro
19 Title boy genius of a 1991 film
20 It might be neutral
21 Gets hot
23 "Who'da thunk it?!"
24 One of Bolivia's official languages
26 Campus grps.
28 Surprises with a call
30 Adenauer's successor as German chancellor
32 Word of admonishment
33 Native New Yorkers
35 Taker of two tablets
36 No-parking area
39 Preferably
42 "Kiss Hollywood Good-by" memoirist
44 Introduction to chemistry?
45 Virtuoso
46 Idyllic spot
48 Keypad locales
49 Dickens
50 Middle-of-the-roaders: Abbr.
52 Multiple of VI

53 Baked, in Bologna
54 Erroneous claim about a superhero
56 Fatty liquid
57 Hoi polloi
58 Sable or Montego, for short
59 It's graded subjectively

DOWN

1 "Shall We Dance" co-star
2 Not right
3 W.W. II icon on a 1999 stamp
4 Landed
5 "___ Oxford" (Ved Mehta memoir)
6 Name holder

7 Blew the whistle
8 Yes-men
9 QB protectors
10 Twinings offering
11 It gets little consideration
12 Best Director of 1997
13 Kind of dye
15 Dinner spinner?
22 Bluff, maybe
24 "That's ___ excuse for . . ."
25 Word with white, red or black
27 Rupee earner
29 Volt per ampere
31 Gave out
34 ___-Off (windshield cover brand)

36 Fourth steps in some sequences
37 Stuck
38 Prehistoric stone chips
40 Some royal coats
41 Like the best outlook
43 They can be overloaded
47 "Battlestar Galactica" commander
51 Fix
53 Modern address part
54 Rock suffix
55 E.T.O. transport

by David Quarfoot

SATURDAY

by Eric Berlin

ACROSS

1 2005's "Bad News Bears" and the like
14 Firm up-and-comers
15 Saw about frugality
16 Wildcats' sch.
17 TV Guide listings: Abbr.
18 Johnny Cash's "___ Picture of Mother"
19 Pauperize
21 Resting places
24 They're game
25 Something rattled
27 Identi-Kit options
29 Church with elders: Abbr.
30 Commander at the Alamo
32 Brings in
34 Modern inhabitants of ancient Aram
36 Fast movement
40 Have bad posture
42 Material for some sheets
43 Legal V.I.P.'s
46 "That's ___!"
48 Woman with une nièce
49 It might be stuck to a dish
51 Longtime first name in South Carolina politics
53 Peter Gunn's girlfriend
54 Megalopolis with about 30 million people, for short
56 Pianist Maisenberg
58 It may finish second

59 Realize there will be no resolution
63 "Don't put words in my mouth"
64 Not here

DOWN

1 Place to get rolls
2 Letters of discharge
3 Turnabouts, slangily
4 Proscriptions
5 Like some transfers
6 Picks
7 Damp and chilly
8 Great time
9 People may take a pass on them: Abbr.
10 Chose to play
11 Lab locale
12 Like badlands
13 Cool red giants

14 When many resolutions are broken
15 Certain links
20 One of the Leeward Islands
22 Unable to get one's feet on the ground?
23 Makes an impression on?
26 It's twirled on a trail
28 Smash production?
31 Puts one over on
33 Caterpillar features
35 Breed
37 French copper
38 Many a senior
39 King of diamonds feature
41 Like Mad
43 Tests

44 Loving, as eyes
45 Backbone part
47 Gentlemanly
50 Bel ___
52 Intervening, legally
55 Proceed impulsively
57 Canterbury can
60 Up to
61 Ladies' room
62 Some racecars

8

SATURDAY

ACROSS
1 Boarders' spots
9 Excites, with "up"
13 Declaration from Mama Rose in "Gypsy"
15 Seethe
16 Resolution phrase
17 Nitwit
18 Italian TV channel
19 Sleuth's outburst
20 Richard's longtime partner on Broadway
22 Down-home entertainment
24 High, in a way
26 Served as
28 Drop off
29 Shade of bleu
30 Kind of infection
32 One and the same
34 Bygone epidemic cause
35 Asian peppers
38 Shared sleeping accommodations
39 Serengeti creature
40 Some are made with chocolate
43 Pie chart dividers
44 Pardner's mount
45 Proves otherwise, briefly
49 Sugar amt.
50 Tell off in no uncertain terms
52 Burrow
53 Letter opener
55 Series of articles, maybe
57 "Give ___ hug"
58 Bannister's length
59 Overhead
62 Big hearts?
63 Bums
64 "Over here"
65 "Not necessarily"

DOWN
1 Guide
2 Bar
3 Vitamin C provider
4 1999 best seller "___ Road"
5 208 people
6 Dress material
7 Supportive org. since 1965
8 Bluejackets
9 Lane with smooth curves
10 Michael Jackson autobiography
11 Can you top this? Why, yes!
12 Mo preceder
13 Following
14 L train
21 Like the "Wheel of Fortune" wheel, again and again
23 Mocha native
25 Turkey
27 Booted, maybe
31 Renal : kidney :: amygdaline : ___
33 Getting up there
35 Q*___ (vintage video game)
36 Office holders
37 Larval amphibians
38 Split
40 Flex, for example
41 Squirt
42 One-named singer with the 2002 #1 hit "Foolish"
46 One known for a bad hair day
47 Phil who was a five-time Gold Glove winner
48 Photocopier selections
51 Feat
54 Cold war faction
56 In and out, quickly
58 "The Amazing Race" prop
60 -esque
61 Hamburger's one

by Henry Hook

SATURDAY

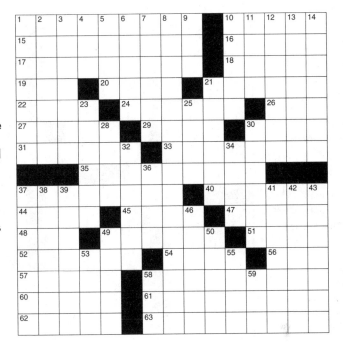

by Bob Peoples

ACROSS

1 Working together
10 Level connectors
15 Ready to take off
16 Arita porcelain
17 Dig in one's heels
18 Risk
19 N.Y.C. subway line
20 "The X-Files" org.
21 The "R" in Edward R. Murrow
22 Cleaner
24 Item with a long spout
26 It follows directions
27 Plains natives
29 Schedule
30 Sheet of matted fabric used in quilting
31 Staging area for the Crusades
33 Post-accident inquiry
35 Dated database
37 Rare occasion
40 King's bane
44 Abu ___, first Muslim caliph, 632–34
45 Turns down
47 Drug agent
48 Part of the sch. year
49 Tick off
51 Stage lead
52 Vegetable holder
54 Depilation brand
56 Common gift of welcome
57 Newswoman Gwen
58 Frequent raid target
60 View
61 Green light
62 Beginnings
63 Really big job

DOWN

1 1994 literary autobiography whose first chapter is titled "Infant Prodigy?"
2 River pollutant
3 Meal replaced by M.R.E.'s
4 Grass part
5 Bricklayers' equipment
6 Monteverdi opera
7 Common childhood malady
8 Epic 1975 showdown, popularly
9 N, O or P, in chem.
10 Bad-mouth
11 Rachel of "General Hospital"
12 "Art of silence" performer
13 Ahead of
14 Start to knit
21 Very violent, say
23 Ethylene glycol product
25 Chip ingredient
28 Hustle
30 Railyard sight
32 Lost ground
34 Birth
36 "Act!"
37 Grill sites, briefly
38 Visa charge
39 Largest country wholly in Europe
41 Ignis fatuus, the fair maid of ___
42 Learning
43 Handle
46 Don who directed "Invasion of the Body Snatchers," 1956
49 Idiots
50 Copier setting
53 Responded in court
55 Trainee
58 Loan figure: Abbr.
59 Except for

SATURDAY

ACROSS
1 Fair trade
11 Words with "move on" or "life"
15 Baby shower
16 Draft choices?
17 Spaghetti sauce slogan
18 Actively trading
19 Through
20 Its highest possible score is 180: Abbr.
21 Inflict upon
22 Many are trained in childbirth: Abbr.
24 Slugger Williams and others
25 Looking frightened
26 It was uncommon at the Forum
27 Way to direct a helm
28 They might offer support in prayer
29 Unité politique
30 Ready for mounting
32 Characterize
34 "The nerve!"
38 Love, e.g.
42 First of a noted trio
43 First name in 19th-century outlawry
46 Grandson of Leah
47 Philadelphia's Franklin ___: Abbr.
48 Asian au pair
49 Plagues, with "at"
50 "Breezy" star, 1973
51 Ram home?
52 Pituitary hormone
53 Historic Thor Heyerdahl craft
54 Little Thief, for one

by David Quarfoot

55 Snubbed person's comeback
59 Kids' TV character with a thick unibrow
60 Wipes out
61 Goddess who wed her brother
62 Physical component

DOWN
1 Shook
2 Last
3 Heads-up cry
4 Abbr. after Sen. Jack Reed's name
5 Label a bomb, perhaps
6 Letter run
7 "So-o-o sexy!"
8 Searched a trail, as a dog
9 Like some advertised films
10 "The Country Girl" playwright
11 Sides in an age-old battle
12 Smoke out
13 Go from 0 to 20 in three years?
14 Gets to
23 Luxury items for a king or queen
24 Pair from a deck, maybe
28 Knowledge
31 Property lawyers' concerns
33 Iowa college since 1851
35 More than look up to
36 Catches
37 Superlatively swank
39 Music critic's assignment
40 Raising Cain
41 Whip material
43 Star of the 1976 miniseries "I, Claudius"
44 Cries too easily, say
45 Zen enlightenment
49 Some cause laughter
56 Hi-___
57 Suffix with robot
58 Habitual scratcher

SATURDAY

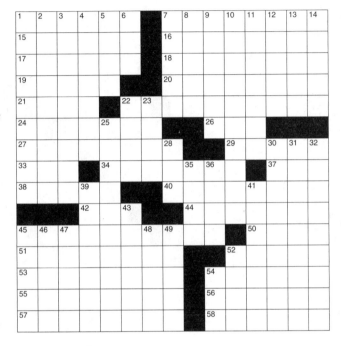

by Patrick Berry

ACROSS

1 Get close to
7 Shantytown shack material
15 Inuit garment
16 Singer of the 2002 #2 hit "Beautiful"
17 The silent treatment?
18 They take stock
19 Put on a lousy show, say
20 Common vending machine site
21 Snow in Nashville
22 Manual laborers in a convent
24 Mesopotamia dweller
26 Grp. concerned with defense
27 Luxury items
29 Strongly suggested
33 Middle square, say
34 1988 Bush campaign adviser
37 1951 play by Literature Nobelist Nelly Sachs
38 Three-time Masters winner
40 Theater lobby purchases
42 Author of the story collection "Little Birds"
44 Was naturally present
45 Manhunt assistants
50 Variable star in Cetus
51 Aria from "Otello"
52 "L'Évolution créatrice" author Bergson
53 Fairy tale parent
54 Signaled, on a quiz show
55 Screenplay skeleton
56 Axis nickname
57 How some medicines are administered
58 Reacted to a sudden pain, say

DOWN

1 Auto engine parts
2 Christian who does not believe in the Trinity
3 Unquestioned #1 status
4 Label obeyed by Alice
5 Lacking any curl
6 Spiky readout: Abbr.
7 Be reluctant to go
8 Fits
9 Efrem Zimbalist's birthplace
10 Home of the H. J. Heinz Co.
11 Overflowing with talent
12 Quarterback Rodney
13 Bug
14 Woodworking tools
22 Café addition
23 In a different way
25 Not permanent
28 Gull
30 Preparing (for)
31 "Dream Girl" playwright, 1945
32 Refused to recognize
35 Smart-looking, in British lingo
36 Great times
39 Inspirit
41 Puts another patch on
43 One of Poseidon's attendants
45 Argentine grassland
46 Toilet seats, e.g.
47 Dud
48 Title girl in a 1982 #1 John Cougar hit
49 Used a blade
52 ___ Bowl
54 Oil company facility

SATURDAY

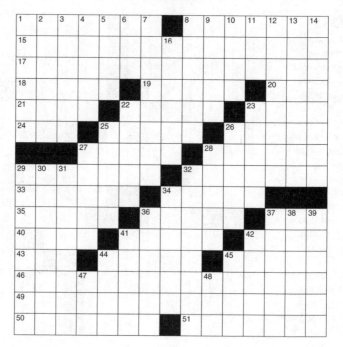

by Byron Walden

ACROSS
1 Flirts with
8 Trying experiences
15 Eastbound waves?
17 "You and your conspiracy theories!"
18 Hera turned Antigone into one
19 Like the newspaper Al Shabiba
20 Main contents
21 Prefix with flop
22 Sea of ___, south of the Cyclades
23 Death to le roi
24 Space ball?
25 Six layers of a song?
26 Met number, maybe
27 Like arctic winds
28 Lenny Bruce, famously
29 Adjusts, as a magazine photo
32 Neckwear
33 Can't contain
34 Flock
35 Setting for Edward Hopper's "Nighthawks"
36 Paley's successor at CBS
37 Michelin guide no.?
40 E.P.A. output: Abbr.
41 Speed ___
42 Duster, for one
43 "The Story ___" (Pauline Réage novel)
44 "32 Flavors" singer Davis
45 Dog topper
46 Subjects of metaphysical research
49 "Picture Perfect" star
50 Permission slips, e.g.
51 Astrolabe alternative

DOWN
1 El Greco's "Bautismo de ___"
2 Milliner
3 Act on like a carbon filter
4 Barbie accessory
5 Buffet
6 Tabloid subj.
7 One of Chaucer's Canterbury pilgrims
8 Mexican beer named for its hometown
9 Marie, par exemple
10 Cabriolet maker
11 Portrait finish?
12 Ferretlike carnivore
13 Patriarch of the "First Family of Country Music"
14 Reel
16 Trammel
22 The biggest part of a large belt
23 Not pellucid
25 Person with a crystal ball
26 It was uttered in the past
27 Trapper's stock
28 Fashions
29 1985 Arnold Schwarzenegger film
30 Going rates?
31 Regular settings
32 Plants that are a natural source of cyanide
34 One who holds a note
36 "Sweet ___, run softly, till I end my song": Spenser
37 Where to begin
38 ___ Sea of California's Sonoran Desert
39 Terse demurral
41 Like the Rock of Ages
42 Focus of many an X-ray
44 Predisposed to fightin'
45 Multiple of CI
47 Georges Perec's 1969 novel "La Disparition" is written entirely without this
48 Compass dir.

SATURDAY

ACROSS

1 Request made while pointing at a display case
5 Little bit
8 Kind of patch
14 Ups
15 #4, once, in Boston
16 Appear that way
17 Ltrs. may be written in them
18 One of 100 positions
20 What some of the letters in this puzzle seemingly have
22 Link
23 Sound at a spa
24 Sound
30 Zoom
32 Nickname for young Skywalker
34 Words of concurrence
35 An old Warner Bros. production?
37 Carried away
39 How you have to think to solve this puzzle
42 Volunteered
43 Sleeveless Arab garment
44 Go this way and that
45 Where Billy the Kid was born, believe it or not: Abbr.
47 River that rises in Monte Falterona
50 Argentine writer ___ Sábato
52 It's well-regulated
54 Drop
56 Spills out, in the Bible
59 Universal competitor
64 Language from which shawl and divan come
65 Astronaut Collins
66 Start of an apology
67 Not stick out
68 Feedback
69 Suffix with planet
70 Performed terribly, slangily

DOWN

1 Try to pick up
2 Striped animals
3 Do business with
4 She, in Venice
5 Words repeated at the start of the "Sailor's Song"
6 Hit 1986–87 R & B album
7 Movie with the opening line "I admire your courage, Miss . . . ?"
8 Reply in a juvenile spat
9 Elder, e.g.
10 Row makers
11 "Trust ___" (1937 hit)
12 Do, re or mi, in Italy
13 Tough problem
19 Sparkling
21 Nice brushes
25 Super Bowl souvenir
26 Map line
27 Robert who wrote "The Power Broker"
28 Kind of card
29 Coffee-to-go necessity
31 In eruption
33 Disadvantaged
36 Bombed
38 Opposite of "duh!"
39 Humdinger
40 ___-Ude, Russia
41 Afresh
42 Milk source
46 Really good one
48 "Hold on!"
49 Mario Puzo best seller
51 Dots on a map
53 "Suppose . . ."
55 "___ the bag!"
57 First name in humor
58 Whacks
59 Insect repellent ingredient
60 Delicious but fattening
61 Precollege
62 Ages and ages
63 Deferential

by Kevan Choset and David Kwong

SATURDAY

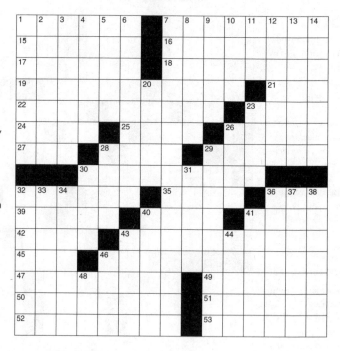

by Patrick Berry

ACROSS

1 Appear briefly, as a parade float
7 Spanish priest who famously opposed the conquistadors
15 Unbroken
16 She played a jilted wife in "Intermezzo," 1939
17 Note takers
18 Handyman's kit
19 TV, unflatteringly
21 Wrinkle-faced pooch
22 Went through the motions on stage, perhaps
23 Reaction to bad news
24 W shelfmate
25 Poor marks
26 Margin
27 Like Fagin
28 The ravages of time
29 King's card
30 She won the 1983 Oscar for Best Song
32 Went over the line?
35 Southeastern Conf. powerhouse
36 Memory unit, for short
39 Mantle's jersey number
40 ___ Lachaise (Paris's largest cemetery)
41 Builders at Uxmal
42 Underground treasures
43 Big moments
45 Land on the Arctic Cir.
46 Star of a "CSI" spinoff
47 Animal that's often exempt from "no pets" restrictions
49 Author of the Three Laws of Robotics
50 How chatterboxes talk
51 Togs
52 Diagnostic administered at home
53 Put in order

DOWN

1 Apothecaries' tools
2 Colonial home?
3 With a high grade
4 Star of a "CSI" spinoff
5 Watts's "King Kong" co-star, 2005
6 "I should say so!"
7 Famous first words
8 Desert dwellings
9 Hair confiner
10 Metal oxide
11 "The Lone Ranger" airer, 1949–57
12 City on the water
13 Soften
14 "Angle of Repose" author
20 Current location?
23 City founded by Mormon pioneers
26 Aloe additive?
28 Small-but-loud songbird
29 Actor originally slated to play Michael Corleone in "The Godfather"
30 Seals, in a way
31 Minded
32 Massachusetts senator succeeded by Kerry
33 Send another way
34 Earl in the Baseball Hall of Fame
36 Release from slavery
37 Blight
38 Flame-based cooker
40 Revolves
41 Akio ___, co-founder of Sony
43 Daughter in Inge's "Picnic"
44 Discrimination
46 Small bit of progress
48 Absolutely, in slang

SATURDAY

by Bob Peoples

ACROSS

1 Electrical connectors
10 League parts
15 Sweet little thing
16 Lumberjack
17 Worked up
18 "The Name Above the Title" autobiographer, 1971
19 Volcano feature
20 Look that may include thick-rimmed glasses
22 Small goose
24 Seedy joint
25 Gossip
26 Lean on
27 ___ League
28 Try to get in
30 1980s sitcom starring Geena Davis
31 Large track
34 Jellied delicacy
35 Clutch
37 It may be sympathetic
38 Have ___ to pick
40 Herbal drink
43 Actress Louise
44 2001 winner of the Israel Prize
45 Bond girl in "Octopussy"
49 Some modern icons
51 Assaulted
52 Entrance area
53 "Ronzoni ___ buoni" (old ad slogan)
54 Earthen jar
55 Cause for exclaiming "That's it!"
59 Extraterrestrial
60 Usually
61 Played out
62 Person with a line?

DOWN

1 Passed without notice
2 Poe subject
3 1965 Yardbirds hit
4 Cornmeal concoction
5 H.S. biology topic
6 Old telecom inits.
7 "Uh-uh!"
8 One of 16 popes
9 Reinforces
10 Cheap
11 Big bets
12 Ancient Greek storage vessels
13 Pasta topper
14 Cineplex feature
21 Barely get
23 Bind
24 Stink
29 Currency replaced by the euro
31 Grinds
32 Worker's advocate, for short
33 Pharmacy solution
36 Stuff
39 Hornswoggles
41 Literary miscellany
42 Official magazine of the National Space Society
46 Yupik outerwear
47 Get by
48 Longshoreman, at times
50 Part of many a Halloween costume
56 Sorry
57 Sets
58 Two qtrs.

SATURDAY

by Brendan Emmett Quigley

ACROSS

1 Brilliant thinkers they're not
12 Some fallout
15 Hookup spot
16 Part of R.R.: Abbr.
17 Some tape-recorded interviews
18 Family V.I.P.'s
19 Deliver crosses, e.g.
20 It's next to nothing
21 They line some streets
23 Barron's reader, slangily
25 Creator of Genesis
27 Concerto component
28 Mideastern royal family name
30 NASA craft
32 Mil. list
33 Period in India's history
35 Hydrotherapy option
37 Vostok 1 passenger
41 Place for seeds
42 "Me? Harrumph!"
44 Org. in which decisions are awarded
45 You might tear it up
46 Some dairy stock
48 Abbr. in the real estate section
51 Choisy-___ (Paris suburb)
53 Employer of TV's Nash Bridges, briefly
55 1997 Bond girl Michelle
57 "ER" actress Freeman
59 100 sen
61 Miracle-___
62 Kind of student, for short
63 Versatile restaurant style
66 Neighbor of Telescopium
67 Song with the lyric "When you kiss me heaven sighs"
68 Turner of a page in history
69 Big top worker

DOWN

1 Unfriendly sorts
2 Like Swiss cheese
3 Muscular disorder
4 Picture within a picture?
5 Like some textbook publishers
6 Spot announcements?
7 Big Dutch export
8 Late stages, of sorts
9 W.W. II inits.
10 Course
11 More sharp
12 Georgian's neighbor
13 It's not measured in traditional years
14 1980 Pointer Sisters hit
22 Second youngest QB to win a Super Bowl
24 Ping and Pong are characters in it
26 Third of a Latin sextet
29 Show spunk
31 Not busy
34 Talk of swingers
36 Singer called the Texas Troubadour
37 No Mr. Macho
38 Cream additive
39 Mad-dogged
40 What's going on
43 It may follow a bridge
47 Grand alternative
49 Several departments, maybe
50 Far from bright
52 Dash follower?
54 Put on the back burner
56 One working on the cutting edge?
58 Tony's portrayer on "NYPD Blue"
60 ___ moth
64 Literature Nobelist Andric
65 What many an Indian is called

SATURDAY

ACROSS

1 Quick
4 Course yardstick
7 Standard pass
13 Hoity-toity
16 Unfrequented
17 Taking a grand tour, say
18 It's measured in radians
19 Buckthorn trees with medically useful bark
20 ___ Island, home for part of the Gateway National Recreation Area
21 Transistor electrodes
22 Stud
23 Postulate
24 Doesn't properly follow through
26 Not the common way
28 Things to pass in
33 Puffer's place
34 Flip
35 N.H.L.'ers, e.g.
38 Tops
39 Routs
44 Ran over
45 Volleys
47 Spam producer
48 Moving about
49 Go into banks, perhaps
50 1972 #1 hit with the lyric "I'm right up the road / I'll share your load"
51 Leaf sides
52 Person with a plan
53 Makes oneself appear smart
54 Actor Wass
55 Cape ___

by Robert H. Wolfe

DOWN

1 Caterpillar engager
2 Boater alternative
3 Need for a third degree?
4 Take illegally
5 Big fans
6 Beat poets?
7 Couple in a date
8 Signs
9 Privately
10 Does, as a Tennessee Williams play
11 Heirs, legally
12 Port on Massachusetts Bay
14 They bring tears to one's eyes
15 Big name in oil
24 Treaty violation, maybe
25 Place of debauchery
27 Media center?
28 William Gladstone, politically: Abbr.
29 Winning full house, for short
30 Shelled-out amount
31 Judge
32 Halloween costume
36 Natural
37 Potassium ___ (food mold inhibitor)
40 Cut back
41 Beauty spot
42 Pre-1962 British protectorate
43 Scribes
45 Mt. Agung locale
46 Demanding
47 Dwell

SATURDAY

ACROSS

1 Picnic side dish
11 Dosage abbr.
15 Defensive shell
16 Van ___ (Ohio county or its seat)
17 Difficult to eradicate
18 Ready to serve
19 Cutting-edge features
20 On pins and needles
22 "Momo" author Michael ___
23 It's often sweetened
24 A Pointer sister
27 On the way up
28 Springfield storekeeper on TV
29 ___ caramel
31 Sounding
32 Turn over
34 Blinds, essentially
36 Woodworking channel
37 ___ Kringle
39 MX-5, in the auto world
41 Pinup part
42 Country
44 Ponderosa choice
46 The Queen of Latin Pop
47 G.I. garb, for short
48 Make less threatening
49 Compound used to treat chiggers and scabies
53 ___ Sea (giant salt lake)
54 Jacqueline Onassis, professionally
56 It might be added with a twist

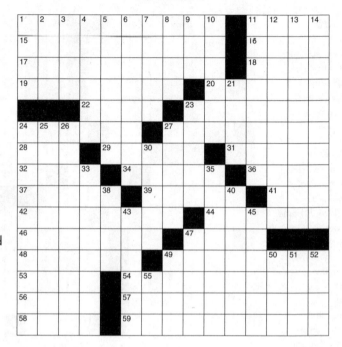

by James E. Buell

57 Surrendering sorts
58 Uses up
59 Requiring no preparation

DOWN

1 Fills out
2 State stat
3 Merganser relative
4 Hit list
5 It's detected by the Marsh test, in forensics
6 They can get caught in traps
7 Winged
8 Plaster base
9 Took a loss on
10 Gather
11 Ambiguous
12 Hill runner
13 Modern
14 Like some dads
21 Whom a bully may bully
23 "___ King this afternoon!": Emily Dickinson
24 Reverses course
25 Mozart's "La Clemenza di Tito," e.g.
26 Where visitors can barely relax?
27 Screened correspondence?
30 Jazz trumpeter Ziggy
33 Harris of "Seinfeld" and others
35 Approach
38 Remote hiding place?
40 Targeted
43 Shucked-to-order spot
45 Skipjack
47 High, in a way, with "up"
49 First name in gossip
50 Oklahoma native
51 Romance novelist Roberts
52 At first, once
55 Honour given to Joan Collins: Abbr.

SATURDAY

ACROSS

1 He wrote "I have the true feeling of myself only when I am unbearably unhappy"
11 N.L. East nine
15 Lloyd's of London locale
16 It gets notions
17 Short-lived constructions
18 Natives call it Mongibello
19 It's no marathon
20 It's unlikely to be realized
22 Hall of fame
23 Takers of Tenochtitlán
25 Formed
26 Literally, "baked"
29 Inclines
32 Isn't delicate with
33 Editor
34 TV cop with a pet cockatoo named Fred
35 Word after "attached"
36 A week's worth of groceries, perhaps
37 German town
38 Lot
39 One may be striking
41 Bank security aid, briefly
44 Follow priestly orders?
46 Municipality, in some financial names
47 Maker of running shoes

48 "Way Out West" co-star, 1937
51 Move merchandise
52 Cramped locale
53 Units in Physics 101
54 Really bug

DOWN

1 Top-___ golf balls
2 Like some potatoes
3 Better
4 Make out
5 Half-sister of Eva?
6 Figures from 1 to 24: Abbr.
7 Stationer's supply
8 Stealthy ones
9 Not drop
10 Confounded
11 Bum
12 Substantiates

13 Casserole option
14 Old kingdom name
21 Noah Wyle's "ER" role
23 It has a slightly heavier British counterpart
24 Entrance march into a bullfighting arena
25 Gets through quickly, in a way
27 "I'm history"
28 Somewhat
29 Code bits
30 ABBA's "___ the Music Speak"
31 Robust
32 ___ que (because, in Brest)
34 Makes the rounds?
36 Buckthorn variety

38 Olympus competitor
40 It may hold the thé
41 Around
42 Really bugged
43 "It's Too Late Now" literary autobiographer
44 Comedian Chappelle
45 During
46 One calling the moves for a round dance
49 Bell part
50 Twa into twa

by Brendan Emmett Quigley

SATURDAY

by Bob Klahn

ACROSS

1 Serious accident
10 Goal
15 Folk music scholar who helped popularize Woody Guthrie and Muddy Waters
16 Smashing
17 Dapple
18 "Jive at Five" composer/performer
19 Fall off
20 Very much for
22 Lukewarm reviews
23 American Airlines Ctr. team
24 Coasted at the Olympics?
25 Yanks
26 Dr.'s order?
27 Discombobulates
29 Took a course
30 City at the mouth of the Loire
32 "Take your pick"
34 Widely seen
36 Shade of black
37 Port alternatives
41 Waggish
45 Hacker
46 Treasured blankets
48 100 Bulgarian stotinki
49 Flapdoodle
50 Johnson who managed the 1986 championship Mets
51 Quiet types
52 Schooner's cargo
53 Hindu deities
54 Piano key, essentially
55 Complex unit
57 In one's spare time
59 Top-flight story
60 Intimate chats
61 Otterlike
62 Imbroglio

DOWN

1 Fossil remains of homo erectus discovered in 1891
2 Where Zelda Fitzgerald and Nat King Cole were born
3 Parade
4 Interlocks
5 Co-founder of the avant-garde Blue Four
6 Thick quaff
7 Words sung after "Hallelujah"
8 Flag
9 Critical analysis
10 0-198-61186-2, e.g.
11 1988 Meg Ryan thriller
12 "Popeye" cartoonist
13 Emperor beginning in 1989
14 "The Most Happy Fella" composer
21 Classic song that's the official anthem of the European Union
24 "A Study in Scarlet" inspector
27 Dahomey, since 1975
28 Drives off
31 Corn grower
33 Series finale
35 "Hubba hubba!"
37 Mexican rattlers
38 Southwestern salamander
39 Thaw
40 Grassland dotted with trees
42 Peridot, e.g.
43 Leaves the country
44 Major hurdle, metaphorically
47 Palace card
51 Quark-antiquark combo
53 Curtail
54 Shoot, slangily
56 Go out
58 It might turn up a lot

SATURDAY

by Will Nediger

ACROSS

1 Bantered
7 Early Hebrew king
15 Rise
16 Sponsor of a historic expedition
17 Sticks in the supermarket
18 Potential to get around
19 Food filtered from seawater
20 Some sorority women
21 Sliding door site
22 Sloughs
23 Principle
24 Ceramic muralist for the Unesco building in Paris
25 1960s sitcom role for Felix Silla
26 U-Haul alternative
27 Common catalyst
28 Increase
30 Energetic
32 Beset by problems
34 Nostrum
38 Spam locale
40 ___ Farms, Maryland-based food giant
41 Stressful things?
44 Some execs
46 Kelly Clarkson's record label
47 Constellation appellation
48 Adams of Sinn Fein
49 Potential con
50 Touch of frost
51 Mayan commodity
52 Exchanged notes?
53 Sara Sidle's player on "CSI"
55 Labor class?
56 Drive off
57 Henry Fielding title heroine
58 Beat
59 Matthew who founded a college in 1861

DOWN

1 Northern pike
2 "Die Fledermaus," for one
3 It might get under your skin
4 Cooled things?
5 Count, now
6 Uninteresting
7 Nobel-winning poet Juan Ramón ___
8 Rarefied
9 Capital on the Atlantic
10 Bands of geishas
11 With 43-Down, très witty person
12 Niece of Sir Toby Belch, in "Twelfth Night"
13 Sites for some swearers
14 Is forbidden to
20 Series finale, in Stafford
23 Laid-back
24 Debbie ___, triple gold-medal Olympic swimmer, 1968
26 Archaeologists' interest
27 Battle site of 1914, 1915 and 1917
29 Franco's first
31 Lightweight boxer?
33 Birdhouse, of a kind
35 Pair above the kidneys
36 Daughter of Pope Alexander VI
37 1984, e.g.
39 Reproduced, in a way
41 Asian region whose name means "five rivers"
42 Blue Jay opponent
43 See 11-Down
45 Century 21 alternative
48 Succeed in spades
49 Apples, e.g.
51 Means of support
52 Nursery cry
54 Nose-in-the-air model?
55 Head, for short

SATURDAY

ACROSS

1 Enclose
7 Plans out in detail
14 Unlikely beachgoers
16 Tyrant
17 Still, maybe
18 Goddess depicted holding a flute
19 Trisected
20 Real estate ad abbr.
21 "There ___ time . . ."
22 "A Heartbreaking Work of Staggering Genius" author
24 Heated competition?
25 Be sure of, with "on"
26 Bring in
27 Foaming at the mouth
31 Arrow poison
32 Heads
33 Blandished
34 Celsius who devised the Celsius scale
35 Most Marxian?
36 Bel ___
37 Plane-jumping G.I.
38 Auto loan nos.
39 Rant and rave
45 Needing a lift
46 Windjammer
47 Al-Anon member, maybe
48 Security personnel?
50 Heralds
51 If everything fails
52 Not moving

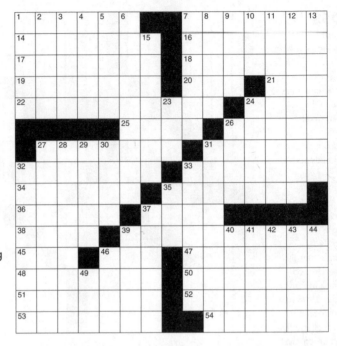

by Brendan Emmett Quigley

53 Picks again
54 Holders of conferences?

DOWN

1 Tasty
2 Actress Löwensohn of "Nadja," 1994
3 "Alias" airer
4 Ballerina-like
5 Naturalize
6 "I wouldn't have it any other way"
7 Gyroscope inventor
8 Associates closely
9 Refuse visitors
10 Burn up
11 Rules for allowing members of the opposite sex into dorms
12 Known to next to none
13 Like some swords
15 "Turn! Turn! Turn!" songwriter and others
23 Army of Hope member
24 Ancient capital on the Nile
26 Film maker
27 Historical Corsican family name
28 Soft support
29 Like English pronunciation in most of England
30 Sun-burned
31 Language of ancient Syria
32 Place to get paella
33 They can be carved out
35 Ringo's oldest son
37 Some cold ones
39 Kind of alphabet
40 Arabian capital
41 Legendary N.Y.C. club that launched punk rock
42 Woman from Chelsea, in the song "Cabaret"
43 Sam of "Wimbledon," 2004
44 Flying fish eaters
46 Spark
49 R.V. refuge org.

SATURDAY

by Harvey Estes

ACROSS

1 Product line
16 One whose pieces are slanted
17 Post office department
18 It's full of x's: Abbr.
19 Puts down
20 Slip
21 Pernicious pets
23 First name among diarists
25 Operating
26 Put down
30 Cabeza, across the Pyrenees
31 Sparkle
32 Mini-shutout on the court
33 Repair shop stock
37 Parmenides of ___
41 Some legal restrictions
42 Harsh calls
43 Sprays
44 They can be dulled
45 "___ lied!"
46 Burrow stash
50 There's a holy one every yr.
51 Variety show host inspired by the Grand Ole Opry
54 It might ward off a war
55 Flips

DOWN

1 Storage unit
2 Virginia Woolf's given birth name
3 Well-preserved one
4 Busy time in Saint-Tropez
5 1957 Jimmy Dorsey hit
6 Descendants of Ishmael
7 Coolidge Dam's river
8 Units of 100 ergs per gram
9 Part of a C.S.A. signature
10 Leather stickers
11 Annual opener
12 Relented
13 Stress, in a way
14 Takes to the other shore
15 Tax
22 Saskatoon-to-Winnipeg dir.
23 ___ stands
24 Old march organizers: Abbr.
26 Parlor piece
27 Turn outward
28 Raid targets
29 Rousing cheers
31 Bound
32 The Eagle and others
33 Relig. institution
34 Buddy
35 Catalogs
36 Many a senior
37 East ender
38 Track climax
39 Caller ID aid?
40 One removing doubt
42 Not pertinent to
44 Browne-colored dog?
46 Communiqué segue
47 "The Man Who Wasn't There" director, 2001
48 Without repetition
49 Some old theaters
51 Deodorant variety
52 Ruling party
53 Max. or min.

SATURDAY

ACROSS

1 "Sweet Liberty" director and star
5 Heroin, slangily
9 Air, in Augsburg
13 Free
15 Test versions
16 World War headgear
17 Prepare to take off?
18 Deserves a hand?
19 Less apt to trust
21 High in the Andes
22 Fiddles with
23 They may have private entries
26 September through April, to an oysterman
28 Superlatively severe
29 Snare
30 Tired-looking
31 Turner of records
32 Drew in
37 Operating expense?
41 Incentives
42 Least conventional
43 Possible result of infection
44 Very bright
45 Gushes, e.g.
46 Many cabins
50 Flat arrangement?
51 Viewers
53 Microwave feature
54 Told all
55 Honorees in l'Église catholique: Abbr.
56 Red-bearded god
57 Cold war grp.

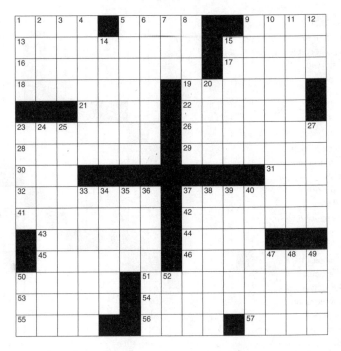

by Robert H. Wolfe

DOWN

1 Colgate brand
2 Cut off the spine
3 Terse bit of advice
4 Inside
5 Sugar and salt, often
6 Gardener's supply
7 Suffix with polymer
8 Near the right answer
9 Soft
10 Applesauce
11 Opposite of raw deals
12 Where Can. shares are bought and sold
14 "The Saint" creator ___ Charteris
15 "Pee-wee's Big Adventure" director
20 Michigan college or its town
23 William who rode with Paul Revere
24 "That doesn't seem feasible to me"
25 She said "Life is a banquet, and most poor suckers are starving to death!"
27 Like L-O-N-D-O-N
33 Levies
34 South Dakota county or its seat
35 N.B.A.'er Mario ___
36 Analyze
37 Resort port where Alfred Nobel died
38 Ivy, e.g.
39 Unaccented
40 High beams?
47 Scores quickly?
48 King of drama
49 Info put on some schedules: Abbr.
50 Flap and Fuzz of "Beetle Bailey": Abbr.
52 Cry of impatience

SATURDAY

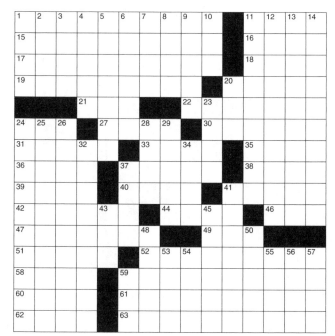

by Harvey Estes

ACROSS

1 Ivory Coast export
11 Literally, "king"
15 Neroli oil source
16 Blanchett of "The Aviator"
17 Acting, say
18 "Man of La Mancha" org.
19 Dynast
20 Primates, to humans
21 Bus driver's assignment: Abbr.
22 Featured performer in Berlioz's "Harold in Italy"
24 Instance, in Évreux
27 Good amts. to take in
30 Demonstration noise
31 Opposite of relaxed
33 Old Roman cry
35 Prayer pronoun
36 Instant
37 Doesn't do the job easily
38 Verbal flourish
39 Shadow
40 Dirt
41 They're put away in bars
42 Rub down
44 Bodily channel
46 This may bring in the big bucks
47 Divisions
49 Future shepherd's place: Abbr.
51 "Ariel" poet
52 1953 Eartha Kitt hit
58 Different
59 Road gripper
60 Goat's look
61 Celebrities
62 What dieters eat
63 Spots

DOWN

1 Fowl territory?
2 Little ___ . . .
3 Women's rights pioneer
4 "Rings ___ Fingers" (Henry Fonda film)
5 Go-between's business
6 Beat
7 Place in a Robert Redford movie
8 "Bond Smells ___" ("Diamonds Are Forever" soundtrack number)
9 Beersheba locale
10 Sheepish explanation lead-in
11 Composer of about 600 sonatas
12 Together
13 Gave evidence for
14 Serenity
20 "I could go for that!"
23 Does in
24 Was charming?
25 A wind chilled and killed her, in verse
26 Things that may wind down
28 Coon's age
29 Accounts of aliens, e.g.
32 Falls in drops
34 Stick together
37 Bank
41 Singer with the 1960 #1 album "G.I. Blues"
43 Cartoon cry
45 What's left behind
48 Practice run?
50 Corner cut, in Cambridge
53 Clean copy?
54 Models
55 Civil rights concern
56 "___ put it another way . . ."
57 Teutonic turndown
59 Some N.F.L. linemen

26

SATURDAY

ACROSS

1 Like the Marx Brothers in a 1935 film
11 Williams College athletes
15 It might include a built-in sharpener
16 Delivery after a delivery?
17 Drivers' surprises
18 Abbr. on old U.S. maps
19 Overcast sky, to some
20 See 52-Down
21 Pretentious one
23 Friend of Dr. Phil
25 Two-time Grammy winner Houston
27 He said "Champions aren't made in gyms"
28 French possessive
29 Pulitzer winner for "A Delicate Balance," 1967
31 He made a bust of Mahler
33 Grand
34 Component of some pools
35 It's supported by a cradle
38 Put
41 French possessive
42 Like many a campground
44 Some rules
46 "___ River"
47 One above a specialist: Abbr.
50 It may come out of a toy
51 Nickname in a 1970s crime drama series
53 Hall-of-Fame gridder Greasy
55 Immure
57 Sports fans' bonuses, briefly

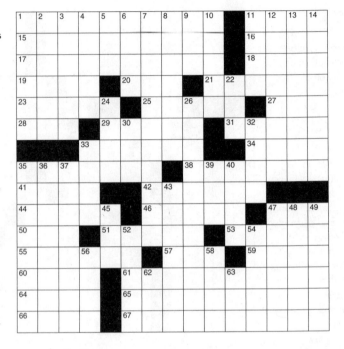

by Jim Page

59 Annual short-story awards since 1986
60 Major conclusion
61 Performers with dangerous acts
64 ___ end
65 Put under the table
66 Spoiled the surprise
67 When Mephistopheles appears in "Dr. Faustus"

DOWN

1 Sickroom chorus
2 ___ l'oeil
3 Old German coins
4 One carrying off carrion
5 Tithonus' abductor, in Greek myth
6 "Romeo Is Bleeding" co-star, 1993
7 Emergency response initiator
8 Some keys
9 Democrat Dellums
10 Turns over ice
11 Abbr. preceding a date
12 Daughters who became stars
13 Uncompromising
14 Like some wrists
22 Firth of Clyde river
24 Hamburger's home
26 Actuate
30 Shirt tag abbr.
32 Prayer start
33 Mine passage
35 Didn't straphang
36 Valentine figure
37 Like a Taser stun, usually
39 A train grp.

40 Brown alternative
43 1983 film about illegal immigrants
45 Cold war plan: Abbr.
47 One of the lives in Plutarch's "Lives"
48 Kearney's river
49 Security deposit payer
52 With 20-Across, writer who once lived with Gore Vidal
54 Gen. Ludendorff
56 Furnish
58 18th-century French marshal
62 Collier's work: Abbr.
63 Squiffed

SATURDAY

ACROSS

1 Sonnet ender
7 Boardwalk locale
15 Yoga instruction
16 Noble and chivalrous
17 Transitional figures
18 Afternooners, maybe
19 Ball girl
20 Riviera, once
21 Thanksgiving follower: Abbr.
22 Pueblo vessel
23 Villain
24 Nicaragua's second-largest city
25 After
26 2005 Isabel Allende novel
27 Something to sing
28 Plug in overnight, maybe
30 Lincoln Lab locale
31 Bowdlerizes, in a way
32 Debriefed group?
36 ___ pendens (pending lawsuit)
37 Like some guidance
38 Green spot
41 Event at which to ring necks?
42 Fitness advocacy grp.
43 PlayStation alternative
44 Sound studio job
45 Bulwer-Lytton's "Eugene ___"
46 Cowardly fellow
47 Monarchy ruled by the al-Thani family
48 Prefix with lineal
49 Icarus, e.g.
51 Junk, so to speak
52 Cover again
53 Measure
54 Support structures
55 Is unacceptable

DOWN

1 Littoral line
2 Booted one
3 Whups
4 Marvin Gaye's record label
5 Robert ___ Prewitt ("From Here to Eternity" soldier)
6 Real good-looker
7 Aid in drawing parallels?
8 Time Magazine's 1986 Woman of the Year
9 Like some gossip
10 Dundee of "Crocodile Dundee"
11 Sanctuary
12 What Zeus transformed Io into
13 Models sold from 1999 to 2004
14 Essential amino acid
20 They might scrape bows
23 Practices
24 Accept
26 3-D reference provider
27 Broadcast component
29 Screw
30 Dye-producing gastropod
32 Point of greatest despair
33 Open
34 Its fruit pulp is an ingredient in Worcestershire sauce
35 Rear-end, e.g.
37 Hair salon stock
38 Rural hauler
39 Exploitative type
40 Incursion
41 Take out of circulation
44 Swedish diplomat Wallenberg
45 First first name?
47 Alphabet run
48 Management issuance
50 Certain Coast Guard member: Abbr.
51 38-Down driver's cry

by Barry C. Silk

SATURDAY

by Patrick Berry

ACROSS

1 Became semirigid
7 Most likely to be hired
13 Liquor flavored with caraway seeds
15 Combat site of 1853–56
16 His tale follows the Friar's in "The Canterbury Tales"
18 Bow applications
19 Whence the word "futon"
20 Bothers
21 "A moment is a concentrated ___": Emerson
22 Carol starter
23 Playwright McNally
24 Canadian film awards
25 Litigation-prompting mineral
27 What businesses try to minimize
31 ___ Villa (English football club)
32 Two-seaters or four-seaters, e.g.?
34 Leader of the Connecticut Yankees in 1920s–'40s music
35 Bird named for its colorful breast and tail
42 Contacts go over them
43 Written work that explains one's actions
44 Prince ___ (frock coat)
45 Undoing
46 Life at a grocery store
47 Reading group
48 Keyed up
49 Holds high
50 Big jobs for a maid
51 Dry land

DOWN

1 Nozzle connected to a Bunsen burner
2 Consider comparable
3 One arranging things in large categories
4 "Blazing Saddles" villain Hedley ___
5 First name in 1970's women's tennis
6 Eat home cooking
7 Farmer's holdings
8 Least subtle
9 Heed
10 Release
11 Country houses?
12 Has a bit of
14 Precedent setter
17 California's Point ___
26 DNA sequence unit
27 Round numbers in England?
28 Peanuts and castor beans, e.g.
29 Cheapest traveling option
30 Roller coaster structures
32 1984 Maximilian Schell biopic
33 John Wayne had a little one
34 MTV owner
36 Like some notes on a music sheet
37 Record keeper
38 ___ Strait (water separating Australia and New Guinea)
39 Shining brightly
40 Water cannon target
41 Chuang-tzu, for one

SATURDAY

by Robert H. Wolfe

ACROSS

1 Brings down
6 1969 film starring Dick Van Dyke and Mickey Rooney
14 Of the north
15 Literally, "sheltered bay"
16 Brit who gets an award for showing?
18 Not too long ago
19 Half of an old comedy duo
20 You might drop glass into these
22 "In no way, shape or form," e.g.
27 Important Indian
31 A lot of a handyman's work
32 Mercenary
33 Meteorologist's body?
34 Chemical dumping, e.g.
36 Unappetizing bowlfuls
37 It's charged at a fountain
39 Yemen Gate locale
40 Gets by rudely
41 Products of glaciation
42 1954–77 alliance: Abbr.
45 Like some ancient Greek victors
51 Cataclysm
53 30-Down nullifier
54 Mate's reply
55 They know the score
56 They're bound to land

DOWN

1 Public assemblies
2 First asteroid orbited by a NASA spacecraft
3 When Quadragesima occurs
4 Slow-moving
5 They're not up
6 Regarding that matter
7 Bricklayer's burden
8 White coat?
9 Duo that had a hit with "Unforgettable"
10 Cooking vessel
11 Sierra Club's first president
12 "Casablanca" name
13 Album unit

14 Crude container?: Abbr.
17 Center of a debate
21 1974 film that was Jonathan Demme's directorial debut
22 Shattering grenades, for short
23 Bizet opera priestess
24 Airstrip area
25 Modern city where de Soto landed in 1539
26 His 1488 voyage opened the road to India
27 Wrap up
28 "America" singer in "West Side Story"
29 Wears down
30 Red light

32 Binders
35 Poetic breaks
38 Grooms
40 Investigator
41 Tipped
42 Ward awarded two Emmys
43 "House of Frankenstein" director ___ C. Kenton
44 Bends
46 "Hellzapoppin'" funnywoman
47 Hungarian city or its river
48 Page
49 Blue Bell alternative
50 Violet, maybe
51 Cap
52 Mekong Delta dweller

SATURDAY

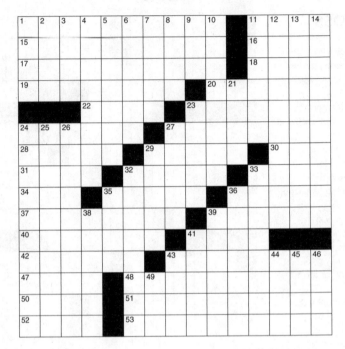

by Bob Klahn

ACROSS

1 Supporters of women's athletics
11 Gossip
15 Don't be cruel
16 Catch ___
17 Boardwalk buy
18 Leader in the Crimean War
19 Announcer who was the first to call DiMaggio "Joltin' Joe"
20 Hoaxes
22 It's a blast
23 Plot (with)
24 Ratify
27 Hits solidly
28 Greek island that was a source of fine white marble in ancient times
29 Meryl Streep's first film
30 Hotness
31 Mastermind
32 Steady worker
33 "Double Indemnity" writer, 1936
34 High no.?
35 Cone bearer
36 Babushkas
37 Landed
39 Disturb
40 Hittable
41 Whence the line "Whither thou goest, I will go"
42 Fast starter
43 1959 death row movie, with "The"
47 "What ___ for Love" ("A Chorus Line" song)
48 Number of people
50 Fall through the cracks?
51 Will Rogers's humorous self-description
52 Giant or D'back
53 Requests to compare and contrast, maybe

DOWN

1 Level
2 Crown
3 Amphitheater
4 Tie
5 They'll give you fits
6 Peace in the Middle East
7 "The Devil and Daniel Webster" writer
8 Eavesdropper?
9 Path across the sky
10 Put the pedal to the metal
11 Plug of half-smoked tobacco
12 Carefree
13 Face the people
14 Savvy
21 One out on a limb
23 Some commentary
24 Shade
25 1948 Ralph Richardson film, with "The"
26 Consort
27 Daiquiri resident
29 Sweetin who played Stephanie on "Full House"
32 Cabernet, say
33 Sweater choice
35 End of an epoch?
36 "It can't be!"
38 Hierarchy
39 Without bias
41 Jah worshiper
43 Remains
44 Goddess worshiped at the Temple of Philae
45 "South Pacific" girl
46 Fills the bill?
49 Directory listings: Abbr.

SATURDAY

by Trip Payne

ACROSS

1 Hardly poker-faced
6 Hamper contents
15 Nancy's friend, in the comics
16 It may be moderated
17 Hard to change
18 O.M.B. director under Carter
19 Word with heat or meat
20 Pays attention
21 16-team grp.
22 ___-wip
23 Back cover
24 Hirer of the stunt man in "The Stunt Man"
25 Dollar alternative
26 Skiing brothers of the 1984 Olympics
28 Excavation site
30 Course in African history
31 Go as far down as
32 Dialog box fill-ins
36 One may be hereditary
37 Give the benefit of the doubt
38 Upwardly mobile people
41 Tom Lehrer's anticensorship song
42 Yacht heading: Abbr.
43 Early 80's TV police comedy
44 Is touching
45 Separator of family names
46 Hot
49 Great-grandfather of David
50 Don't stop
51 Stop
52 From then on
53 In the main?
54 Many a conservative
55 Treasury

DOWN

1 Drought
2 Fizzled out
3 Tony winner for "Does a Tiger Wear a Necktie?"
4 Argued
5 It goes on and on
6 Help in constructing sites
7 They're made after a fight
8 A Manhattan restaurant is named for him
9 Angels' wishes
10 ___ parmigiana
11 They're obviously shocked
12 Progressing sequentially
13 Divertissement
14 Metric volume units
20 Hebrew tribe
22 Q-Tip, for example
26 Reason for a coup d'état
27 Many Pribilof Islanders
29 Ones making sports predictions
30 Connecticut resident
33 Frustrated cry
34 Screeners' targets
35 Make light of
38 Tool with a spiral
39 Swept off one's feet
40 Completely filled, say
41 Contact point?
44 Vanguard
47 Biblical verb
48 "Distant Correspondents" writer
49 Big loss
51 Campaign statement listing

SATURDAY

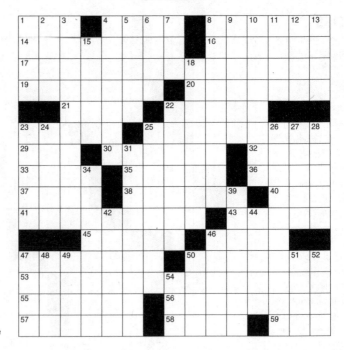

by Patrick Berry

ACROSS

1 Cheerleader's syllable
4 "Aunt" with a 1979 best seller
8 Former Dodgers owner Charlie
14 Windowless
16 Where the Chiefs play minor-league baseball
17 Achluophobic
19 Wet
20 Works over
21 Lancaster's "From Here to Eternity" co-star
22 Formulator of the incompleteness theorems
23 Material for a dry cleaner
25 Country club figure
29 Peaks on a graph
30 Winner of all four majors
32 Look
33 Put away
35 Tree with roundish leaves
36 D. H. Lawrence's "The Rainbow," e.g.
37 Cuckoo announcement
38 Two-part
40 Showed
41 Calculus calculations
43 1960's–70's vocalist known for his falsetto
45 Chieftains' groups
46 "___ Man" (1980s cult film)
47 Expo '74 site
50 New York river popular with kayakers
53 1988 film that precipitated the Buchwald v. Paramount lawsuit
55 Medium condition
56 Their work may involve banking
57 Touches (on)
58 Leftovers
59 Court sight

DOWN

1 Prajadhipok's kingdom
2 It's gathered by scouts
3 Unsuccessfully asks for a date
4 Where Tigrinya is an official language
5 Piece of pork?
6 Night light provider
7 Kennel sound
8 Medicine used to treat hypotension
9 Red meat sources
10 Like ghosts
11 Timeline divisions
12 It's worn on a road trip
13 Rival of Neiman's
15 Made better
18 Suit part
22 Biblical foursome
23 Futomaki or uramaki, e.g.
24 Long Island home of the Brookhaven National Laboratory
25 Clicker
26 Gibson garnish
27 À la king?
28 Gulf State resident
31 Pilots are found inside them
34 Demolition
39 Have a cow?
42 Bounce (off)
44 Not together
46 "Caddyshack" director
47 Where 46-Down got his start
48 Sweater?
49 Former Panamanian leader Torrijos
50 Goalie's feat
51 Planting unit
52 It goes on a break
54 Steering ___

SATURDAY

by Bob Peoples

ACROSS

1 Big belt
8 Some ladies' men
15 Minnesota resource
16 Patent
17 Team members near the infield
18 Looks after
19 Longtime NBC inits.
20 Rave V.I.P.
22 Comedian who appeared on the cover of Time, 8/15/1960
23 Match
25 It may pick you up
26 ___ esprit
27 Capital on the Gulf of Guinea
29 Former grp. of 15
31 Adjure
32 Yahoos
34 Get blitzed
36 Electrical converter
38 Expression of bewilderment
41 Backup singers in a 1960's R & B group
45 Keen
46 Minderbinder of "Catch-22"
48 Reserve
49 Nickname of B-western actor Robert Allen
50 Boots
52 Attraction at Chicago's Field Museum
53 Name for an Irish lass
55 One of five popes
57 Select
58 Made out
60 Court order
62 Annual White House event
63 Comparatively uncomplicated
64 Old "Your cup of inspiration" sloganeer
65 Grovel

DOWN

1 Site of a 1776 battle that gave New York City to the British
2 Major Atlantic Ocean feeder
3 Company picnic, maybe
4 Pop's kin
5 L'étoile du ___, Minnesota's motto
6 Religious denomination
7 Lumberjacks
8 "Keep your cool"
9 Judith ___, Tony winner for "Steaming"
10 42-Down ingredient
11 "The Wizard of ___" (short-lived Alex Trebek game show)
12 Old Buick
13 Busy, busy, busy
14 Bread with nuts and raisins
21 "Chill!"
24 Chicken-hearted
28 Sleep like ___
30 Center of power
31 Discarded
33 Like the Florida Straits, rarely
35 Self-proclaimed "singing journalist"
37 "Always Look on the Bright Side of Life" songwriter
38 Sentries
39 Extra
40 Necessary ingredients
42 Bar order
43 Punk, once
44 Authority on birds and bees?
47 How some books are sold
51 Roman general and dictator
54 Fuzz buster?
55 Popular magazine
56 Plane wing part
59 Indian state
61 Unburden

SATURDAY

ACROSS

1 Possible indicators of a change of heart?
12 Hang together, with "around"
15 "Dunno"
16 Pro
17 Tip-off
18 Easter bloom, in Évreux
19 TNT part
20 Things to stroke
21 Evidence of guilt, informally
23 Board
25 Computer security threat
27 Turns red, say
28 Japan's largest lake
30 Snap
31 "Moto Perpetuo" composer
35 "___ Autumn" (hit 1941 song)
36 Long-running TV show featuring match-makers
39 Hit the jackpot
40 He'd like you to put up with him
41 17-Across, perhaps
43 1990 Tony winner for "Gypsy"
44 Masterpieces
48 Passing notes?
50 Lure
51 With 47-Down, speaker's place
52 Golfer Aoki
55 Religious reformer Jan
56 Agcy. headquartered in Knoxville
57 First to see the sun, maybe
61 "I am worse than ___ I was": "King Lear"

by Henry Hook

62 Fondue ingredient
63 2000 title role for Richard Gere
64 Activity during which the blinds are never lowered

DOWN

1 Went (through)
2 Full of complexities
3 Something not often seen in France
4 One-named rapper with a self-titled sitcom
5 "Les Misérables" locale
6 Hitch
7 Snowthrower brand
8 Hamburger's one
9 Controversial 1980s plan: Abbr.

10 Some people take it to relax
11 Hardly snug
12 Mexican War battle site
13 Environmental woe
14 Lets up
22 Be short
24 "Dream Job" network
25 Going around and around
26 Onetime name atop N.Y.C.'s MetLife Building
28 Not a big chicken
29 Chip maker
32 Essen cry
33 Keeper for a rock collector
34 -ess overseas
36 Visit

37 What many saucepans hold
38 William ___ Center for the Arts, in Kansas
39 Kind of yarn
42 Mother or sister
45 Parroted
46 Lock holder?
47 See 51-Across
49 Clarification lead-in
50 Singer backed by the Aliis
52 "___ bird! . . ."
53 Mtg.
54 Sly
58 Shock's partner
59 Pack quantity, perhaps
60 Football Hall-of-Famer Hein

SATURDAY

by Mel Rosen

ACROSS

1 "The Mod Squad" role
5 "Being John Malkovich" director
15 Clock starter?
16 Show in parts
17 Port whose harbor is in the crater of an extinct volcano
18 Rates
19 Missed the point of
21 Flying wedge members?
22 Larghetto
23 "Say ___"
25 "Our Gang" dog
26 Long glove
30 Charity, often
31 Cuts out
32 Devon river
33 Those, to José
34 Those making firm decisions?
35 Aragón appetizer
36 Thonon-___-Bains, France
37 Stable arrivals
38 Host at church, say
39 Romantic
41 Like some points
42 "Crucifixion" artist
43 Suicidal
44 "Raising Dad" sitcom star
47 Naval escorts
49 Brew alternative
52 Low square
53 Garden transplants?
54 Highlander of old
55 BBC employee
56 Pieces of the past

DOWN

1 Put on
2 Unwilling
3 Style of pliers
4 Signifies
5 À la a stuffed shirt
6 Like some cleaning solutions
7 O.K., in a way: Abbr.
8 Little vixen
9 Abbr. in many dictionary definitions
10 Curél competitor
11 Situate
12 "Great shot!"
13 Puzzle pieces?
14 Sum, ___, fui
20 Affectedly dainty, in Derby
23 Stands by
24 Hogans
26 Kind of trip
27 Folivorous
28 Go through
29 Fly
30 Torpedo's place
31 Seeming
34 It can be seedy
35 Ngorongoro Crater locale
37 Roller without sides
38 Rugby position
40 Revokes, as a legacy, at law
41 Not so slanted
43 Mark over an unstressed syllable
44 Pen, e.g.
45 ___-mémoire (summarizing note)
46 Beleaguer, with "at"
47 Split
48 Large amounts
50 Not split
51 Site for Scheherazade

SATURDAY

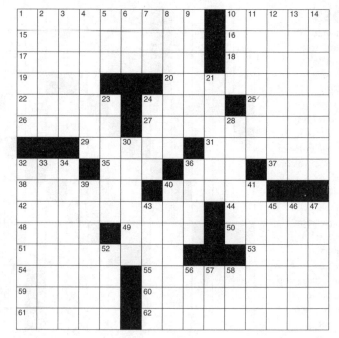

by Bob Klahn

ACROSS
1 Blockbuster
10 Inside job
15 "You'd better believe it!"
16 Hanging open
17 Base figure
18 Places for toupees
19 Victorian
20 Camp sight
22 Dirt
24 Thorny subject
25 Romance fiction award
26 Mocha setting
27 Neighbor of Draco
29 Mrs. Miller in "Ah, Wilderness!"
31 The Pleiades, e.g.
32 Noodlehead
35 Knock
36 Great time
37 Some E.R. cases
38 Dig
40 Thompson who played Fat Albert
42 Absorbent component of some cat litter
44 Thresholds
48 Rotten
49 #24 who played in 24 All-Star Games
50 Author Canin
51 His "J.B." won the 1959 Pulitzer Prize for Drama
53 Heart
54 Sticking point?
55 Odets hero Joe
59 Unhand
60 Smooth and white
61 Some nods
62 Warms up

DOWN
1 Displaying short-temperedness
2 County name in 17 states
3 Ratify
4 Well-groomed
5 It can turn over a lot
6 Head of lettuce?
7 Relieve
8 What there may be room for, barely
9 Fairy tale villain
10 Pops
11 Self-guided "tour"
12 Acquired with little or no effort
13 Having digital display?
14 Extra boots
21 Yuletide, e.g.
23 Some writers write this way
24 Remains to be seen?
28 Imperil
30 Makings of a hero, maybe
32 Knesset, literally
33 Noisy celebration
34 Goes after
36 They may shock you
39 Hamlet's cousin
40 Listening post?
41 Crank
43 Blowhard
45 Fan sound
46 Split
47 Derisive
52 "The Garden of ___" (Wilde poem)
56 Mr. Miller in "Ah, Wilderness!"
57 Workout target, for short
58 Stock figure

SATURDAY

by Michael Shteyman

ACROSS

1 Old afternoon TV staple, with "The"
6 Something light and soft?
14 Misrepresented
16 Prescription description part
17 Apprehensive
18 Joining-of-hands period
19 Number of the 2016 Olympics
20 Abbr. often before a name
22 Start of a critical call
23 Get worse
24 One of two extremes: Abbr.
25 Remains on the shoulder?
29 Retreat
33 Sore loser's cry
35 "Another Green World" composer
36 Island chains
37 It's held in an orbit
38 Inventor of a braking system for cars
39 The Rhineland Campaign was part of it: Abbr.
40 Tries to outfox
44 Curiously spelled 1960 Al Cohn tune
46 Somehow
47 One locked in a boat
48 Running things in a bar
49 Slime
51 "Now I get it"
52 Rake
56 Successful result in a DNA lab
58 Certain Ontarian
60 Three-time Emmy winner for "Nick News"
61 Drunken
62 Charges
63 Something struck from a book

DOWN

1 Big maker of small cars
2 Demographic group, briefly
3 Hoops Hall-of-Famer English
4 18-Across in France
5 Head shot?: Abbr.
6 Classic caution to a child
7 Start ___
8 Prefix with tourism
9 Where singles start out in love?
10 Lustrous
11 Mythical dweller across the Rainbow Bridge
12 Broad
13 Always, in verse
15 Try to profit from
21 Tiny waves
23 Calypso relative
24 Gooper's wife in "Cat on a Hot Tin Roof"
25 "The Old Swimmin' Hole" poet
26 Poem title start
27 Half-serious run?
28 Old Eur. money
30 Accepted
31 Hand and foot
32 "Munich" actor Ivgy
34 Spanish royalty
38 Have to return
40 Union organizers?
41 Always, in verse
42 They carry stigmas
43 Many men are registered with it: Abbr.
45 Having no charge
49 Molecular biology lab preparations
50 Some addresses
51 Unerringly, after "to"
52 Low in education
53 Frequent flier?
54 What comes to mind
55 Org. whose success is no accident?
56 Fabaceae family member
57 Breakers' equipment
59 Hardly a worthy competitor

SATURDAY

by Matthew Lees

ACROSS

1&9 Informally, what aleph-null is, in mathematics
15 Old salts
16 "Willow Song" source
17 Rivals of the Buckeyes
18 Knights, by nature
19 "Modern Gallantry" essayist
20 Prefix with gram
22 Turn in a game
23 Yarborough of Nascar
24 Shy
25 On ___ (equipotent)
26 Antigen identifier
28 Sp. name preceder
29 Fourth número primo
30 Set
32 Like aleph in the central black squares of this puzzle's grid
34 Truncation indication: Abbr.
36 Certain jazz soloist
37 Face to face
42 Gerrymander, say
47 They're expected
48 By
50 Devil
51 On
52 Canal banks
54 Check inside?: Abbr.
55 Gush
56 Ballade ender
57 Lord's body: Abbr.
58 Cyberhandle
60 Performers
62 Fought
63 Revolt
64 & 65 What aleph begins, in linguistics

DOWN

1 Web site frequenters?
2 Neither here nor there
3 Not so stout
4 Like the Merkava battle tank
5 Basket material
6 Apples for the teacher, maybe
7 Positions
8 Trammel
9 Superbly pitched
10 ___ War in Colorado, 1879
11 Swimmer with three appendages
12 Hit a Texas leaguer
13 Buoy
14 Shade similar to cherry wine
21 Some British lines
27 Bad looks
29 Private instruction?
31 Parts of some grids: Abbr.
33 Cordial surroundings?
35 Group of 13
37 Hurried
38 A love of kitsch, e.g.
39 Certain Bartlett's listing
40 Montezuma, for one
41 Bliss
43 Bathysphere's place
44 Put off paying, perhaps
45 Grow together
46 Strongly built
49 Unlikely to preach
52 Moisten
53 Show sudden interest
59 Elvis Presley's "___ Lost You"
61 Girl chaser?

SATURDAY

ACROSS

1 Politically unstable area
8 2005's "Walk the Line" and others
15 Derived by logic
16 Fit for the stage
17 Goes home for the night, say
18 "Dig in, everyone!"
19 Actress with the memoir "Call Me Crazy"
21 Producer of the megaflop "E.T."
22 Film about a blind man for which the lead won Best Actor
24 After much delay
26 Like some calendars
27 Navigational aid
28 Repairs a leak, possibly
29 Snap ___
32 Classic pencil- and-paper game
33 Kiosk item
34 Mouthful
35 Signal
36 Lacking in resonance
37 Coin with a two-headed eagle on the reverse
38 Savvy film/ TV character whose name, paradoxically, is Spanish for "idiot"
39 Bygone weapon
40 Some brass
44 Lose one's cool
45 Fiendish
48 Big farewell
50 1983 song that begins "Hate New York City"
51 Violinmaker Stradivari
52 Compared
53 Less natural
54 Brought to bear

DOWN

1 "Funny ___"
2 As yet undecided
3 Exchange words?
4 Brandy cocktails
5 Like a presidential suite, presumably
6 Help get settled
7 Color
8 With undisguised menace
9 Party supply
10 Council of Three Fires members
11 Flock's overseer
12 Rolled steel joist
13 Santa ___, Calif.
14 Arrive, as darkness
20 Exciting drive?
23 Auto racer Granatelli
24 Kind of adapter
25 Second person appearing in the Bible
28 Phrase in a police bulletin
29 Starting to mature
30 2004 title role for Anne Hathaway
31 Mountaineering goal
33 Car owner's annoyance
34 Swift traveler
36 Dessert topped with crumbled macaroons
37 ___ Colony (first English settlement in the New World)
38 Boss
39 Wordy
40 They're capped with caprock
41 "Aunts ___ Gentlemen" (P. G. Wodehouse's last complete novel)
42 Unelected officials
43 Former Lebanese president Lahoud
46 "Hard ___" (ship command)
47 "The Blue Dahlia" star
49 Cry of disgust

by Patrick Berry

SATURDAY

ACROSS
1 Specialty of some bakers
9 Fictional N.Y.P.D. cop
14 Absolve
16 "Good alone is good without ___": Shak.
17 It's not meant for a 3-Down
18 Corral
19 Wine holder
20 Smart, in a way
22 Facial pair
24 Shift
25 2001 album that debuted at #1
26 Doughy
28 Sixth in a pledge's recitation
29 Break
31 Chase scenes were once common here, informally
33 Part of a fault line?
36 Answer to "Good enough?"
37 Awesome, in slang
39 Very wide, in a way
40 Amtrak abbr.
42 Inquisitor's quarry
43 A long one may have legs
45 Author of "The Gremlins" and namesakes
46 Writer LeShan
49 Brain, heart, liver, etc.
51 Not rot
52 One subjected to disarmament?
55 Kind of dye
56 Expensive string

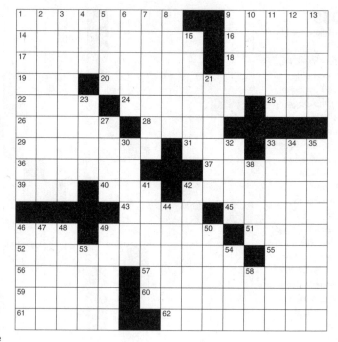

by David Quarfoot

57 Hiree after a move
59 Word before or after nothing
60 Wooded area surrounding a community
61 Dine, in Düsseldorf
62 Once

DOWN
1 "Oh well"
2 Choice
3 See 17-Across
4 "Nacho Libre" actress ___ de la Reguera
5 Jazzman Saunders
6 "___ you loud and clear"
7 Flip

8 Put in a ship's hold
9 Shot
10 "The ___ Love" (1987 hit)
11 Tylenol maker, for short
12 "Entrapment" director Jon
13 "Way of the sword" sport
15 Ornamental plume producers
21 It's big in Latin America
23 Convince
27 Zip
30 Hot
32 Enrich
33 Timeworn
34 Writer interred in the Panthéon

35 Longtime Indy 500 airer
38 Schnozzola
41 Completely clean
42 Some springs
44 Modern helmet add-on
46 Shake
47 Aspiring bands make them
48 1994 Noël Riley Fitch literary biography
49 Symbol of success
50 Astringent fruit
53 Olio magazine
54 Little ___
58 Typing letters?

SATURDAY

ACROSS

1 Hospitable host's invitation
10 Maid in "Die Fledermaus"
15 Notable return of 1969
16 Kick back
17 Modern flapper
18 Old "It's smart to be thrifty" sloganeer
19 Form 1099 amt.
20 Codswallop
22 "Snakes on a Plane" menace
23 Some bottled waters
27 Stuff sold in rolls
28 Kung ___ chicken
29 ___ cit. (footnote abbr.)
30 Part of an 800 collect call number
31 Japanese aborigine
32 Planners' paths
37 Intro to ancient history?
38 Numbers on the radio?
39 Supply center?
40 Blonde ___
41 M. equivalent
42 ___ volatile (pungent-smelling solution)
43 Black-and-white flash?
44 Pigged out
48 Writer LeShan
49 Comparable to a rose
51 ___ dye
52 City of Invention
54 George W. Bush, for one
58 Not made of brass
59 Like Argus
60 Louis Quatorze, for example
61 Pressed flowers, perhaps

by Byron Walden

DOWN

1 Pleasing to the palate
2 "Brusha, brusha, brusha" brand
3 Stuff of which some suits are made
4 ___-weekly (newspaper type)
5 Like some devils
6 Hawaiian juice brand that lent its name to a 1990s fad
7 Leavings
8 Line into N.Y.C.
9 Burlesque legend seen in "The Naked and the Dead"
10 Packing
11 Bona ___ (goddess also called Fauna)
12 Yosemite peak
13 Fails
14 Members of an old union
21 Entree from the oven
24 Self-titled 1991 female debut album
25 Playground yell
26 Postgame treatments for pitchers
30 French river that was the site of three W.W. I battles
31 Capella's constellation
32 Trade places
33 Something darn useful?
34 Ragtag force, say
35 Reading event?
36 Certain navel
43 Owner of The History Channel
44 Buffalo
45 Kind of surgery
46 Ultraviolet light filter
47 Home bartender's tool
50 Self-descriptive French name
53 See 57-Down
55 Power tested with Zener cards
56 French possessive
57 With 53-Down, ingredient in some soaps

42

SATURDAY

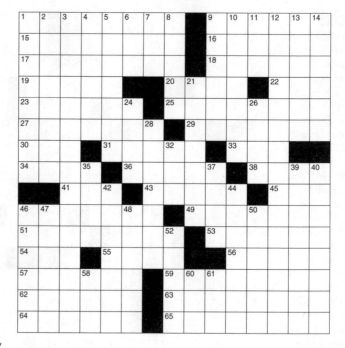

by David Quarfoot

ACROSS
1 Out of the woods
9 Peel provider
15 Pitched
16 "Immediately, boss!"
17 Bolts
18 Adenosine component
19 It may be found in an elevator
20 They're taken out in alleys
22 "___ hoppen?!"
23 Vaporize
25 Apocalyptic topic
27 Boost
29 Trendy
30 Musical syllable
31 As a friend, to François
33 Oaf, slangily
34 Capital of Manche, France
36 Some cap tossers
38 Nostalgic person's response
41 Saskatoon-to-Calgary dir.
43 Jam
45 Matter of debate in a sénat
46 Opposite of dolce
49 Delivery aid
51 "Go for it!"
53 Performer after whom a clone was named
54 Shape ender
55 MTV segment?
56 Crane's place
57 Had too much of, briefly
59 Go back further than
62 Turn (to)

63 Start of a rhyming taunt
64 Strict Sabbath observer of yore
65 Marketing mantra

DOWN
1 Fictional school whose motto is "Draco dormiens nunquam titillandus"
2 Bridge opening
3 Important person on the stand
4 Seigneur de Montaigne's output
5 Payment that won't change
6 Inexperienced
7 Old queen of Spain
8 Sporty Jaguar model
9 Full skirt with a tight waistband
10 1839 revolt site
11 Ruffian, to a Brit
12 Winter track
13 Directed a cry of contempt at
14 Not tense
21 Helping
24 Foo ___ (Chinese dish)
26 Radio talk host
28 Make uncomfortably hot
32 Yvette's evil
35 Bone head?
37 Old English poet
39 Totally lose it

40 Matching pair, informally
42 Opposite of peaceful
44 Family in a 1979 Oscar-winning film
46 First-ever speaker on C-Span, 3/19/79
47 Some fancy paperweights
48 ___ et quarante (card game)
50 ___ of civilization
52 Tolls
58 It might go for a buck
60 Never abroad
61 Take a toll on

SATURDAY

by David Quarfoot

ACROSS

1 Longhorns' rival, briefly
8 During
14 Leading evidence
16 Overnight success
17 "Way to go, bro!"
18 TV title role for Brandy
19 Film title role for Richard Gere
20 Agreement from the other half
22 Intimate
23 Brentford and Isleworth in the Thames, e.g.
25 Small finch
26 Anatomical term that's Latin for "hollow"
27 32-Down's place, briefly
29 Religious purview
30 Ursula's nemesis in "The Little Mermaid"
31 Hiding place, sometimes
33 Kahlúa's cousin
35 Wrestler once called the "Irresistible Force"
37 Comment when the shooting starts
40 Warren resident
44 Word with light or rock
45 Farming area: Abbr.
47 Sticker
48 Choler
49 Flexible weaving material
51 Daughter of Phoebe
52 Touchdown info
53 Working as a rep
55 River tower
56 Aged
58 "Impossible!"
60 1991 horror sequel
61 Rémoulade ingredient
62 Progressively smaller, in a way
63 Cursed

DOWN

1 Primes
2 Wifely
3 Move to and fro
4 Rag on
5 Something to bid on
6 14-year-old Grammy winner of 1997
7 Equilibria
8 City known in ancient times as Philadelphia
9 "Is it just ___ . . ."
10 Follower of McCarthy
11 Bad thing to sink into
12 "Me too"
13 "An American in Paris" song
15 Wrestler once called the "Immovable Object"
21 Follower of ducks, sheep or pigs
24 Start of a reprimand
26 Heady?
28 Anatomical hanger
30 Menotti boy
32 Dubya, once
34 Years ___
36 Russian fermented drink
37 Lake in Mist County, Minn.
38 Beau ideal
39 Connects (to)
41 Comment when you're almost done
42 Influence
43 Latter part of the Tertiary period
46 Web browser command
49 How many films are released
50 Like flip hairdos, say
53 Arthur lost to him at the 1972 U.S. Open
54 Prominent puppet show producer
57 Sioux Lookout setting: Abbr.
59 A nymph she's not

44

ACROSS
1 Words accompanying a flash
11 Dickens's pen?
15 Drifting time?
16 "Three Sisters" sister
17 "Huh?!"
18 Troubles
19 Mil. title
20 High roller?
21 Female donkey
23 Freshness
24 Composer Boccherini
25 Words to a boxer
28 Hand over
29 Use unlimited minutes, say
32 "__ Ordinary Man" ("My Fair Lady" song)
33 Without vigor
36 Relish
38 Custodian's charge
39 Literally, "god," in Sanskrit
40 Anti-apartheid org.
41 Wasn't true
42 Comparatively unadorned
43 Comes down
45 Big name in footwear
47 Antilles tribe
49 Worn smooth
50 Kind of case in gram.
53 Conclusion
54 Man on the street
57 Converse
58 Nobel Prizes, e.g.

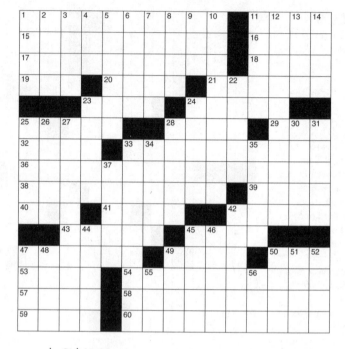

by Rich Norris

59 Fictional sailor
60 Geometric figures

DOWN
1 One may help support a nest egg
2 Screen
3 Not excluded from
4 Boarding place: Abbr.
5 Emergency discards
6 Impulses
7 Comes (from)
8 Capuchin monkey relative
9 Former name in tyranny
10 Court figures
11 Successful
12 It may be pulled
13 Eye

14 Wear
22 Nonsensical refrain
23 Loi maker
24 Like a Rockettes show
25 Standard deviation symbol
26 Explanation starter
27 Children's game for two
28 Preserved, in a way
30 "__ Supreme" (classic Coltrane jazz album)
31 Easily
33 Inventory __ (euphemism for shoplifting)
34 Finger __
35 Arab League member

37 "Drink to me only with thine eyes" dedicatee
42 Some stars
44 Up
45 Calendrier column
46 Squeeze
47 Follower of John
48 Drift
49 Carillon component
50 California's __ Valley
51 Forward
52 Old heavyweight champ Willard
55 TV control: Abbr.
56 Japan's __-Tokyo Museum

SATURDAY

ACROSS

1 They might be protected by an 8-Across
8 See 1-Across
15 Sites for small schools
16 Like rubble, often
17 Kind of grape
18 Where Marat was murdered
19 Associate
20 Haunted house worker's job
21 One may get pins and needles
22 Flowering plant with two seed leaves
24 "As I Lay Dying" father
25 Up
27 Editor Talese
28 "___ where it hurts!"
29 German chancellor after Kohl
31 Tabloid fodder
32 Villain
34 Villain
38 Ones in hip joints?
43 Curtain shades
44 Indicator of canonización
45 Trunk coverer
46 "Take heed ___ any man deceive you": Mark 13:5
47 Good
49 Mars: Prefix
50 It may be a bear to throw down
52 1984 movie with the tag line "It's 4 a.m., do you know where your car is?"
54 Google company
55 Varnish material
56 People described by Josephus

57 Classic R&B tune that inspired the "stroll" dance craze
58 Ice, e.g.
59 Appropriately named band with the 1984 hit "Drive"

DOWN

1 Some laryngitis sufferers
2 Marine, maybe
3 Member of the sedge family
4 Less together
5 Home of the Zagros Mountains
6 Like antlers
7 St. Louis Arch designer
8 Big name in guitars
9 "It's all ___"

10 First name in espionage
11 Biblical kingdom of the Hebrews
12 Slammed
13 1970–71 winner in Johnny Lightning
14 "Baseball Tonight" segment featuring the day's best defensive plays
23 Simón Bolívar's birthplace
26 Spanish uncle?
28 Projects
30 Hangout
31 Flying Cloud of autodom
33 Term paper?
34 Secured while rock climbing
35 Needlelike

36 "The King's Stilts" author, 1939
37 Changes
39 All over the place
40 Fleet of warplanes
41 Sugar daddy, e.g.
42 Jam band fans, stereotypically
44 Like the best advice
47 Arrowroot, e.g.
48 "Ugh!"
51 Something written in stone
53 ___ Noël

by Brendan Emmett Quigley

SATURDAY

by Victor Fleming

ACROSS

1 Interviewer in some mock interviews
9 Point in the wrong direction
15 Grad school administration
16 Eponym for an annual literary award since 1919
17 Attention-getter
18 Goal-oriented activity
19 Balmy
20 Actress who made her big-screen debut in "Julia," 1977
22 Inits. in a 1948 upset
23 It's often taken in night sch.
24 Like germs
25 Bubble
26 Souvenir shop staples
28 Rather, musically
29 Border
30 "Shake Loose My Skin" poet Sanchez
32 Losers
34 Able to draw
36 Captain's charge
38 Something to part with
40 ". . . lived in ___"
41 Envoy and others
43 Point in the right direction?
45 Look
46 Asian city heavily bombed during W.W. II
47 Alex Box Stadium sch.
48 Knock hard?
49 Ending words of inclusiveness
51 Millinery
52 Pungent cheese
54 Some cats
56 Enclosing rim in which a jewel is set
57 Longtime play-by-play announcer Chris
58 Works with one's hands
59 It may be planned before a move

DOWN

1 Clothing item with strings
2 Gets excited
3 Admiral Nelson victory
4 Expression of unhappiness
5 Natural trap
6 Cans
7 "Are you up for it?"
8 Scene of many demonstrations
9 Amble
10 Chain letters?
11 Tick
12 Earthquake Park setting
13 Quitter's cry
14 Allspice and clove, e.g.
21 Name on a historic B-29
25 QB Kosar
27 Easily attachable
28 Cousin of an agouti
29 Cancel
31 Resort site
33 Subway map array: Abbr.
35 How some trust
36 Cram
37 Boomer born in the 1960s
39 Pittsburgh giant
42 Car model beginning in 1970
44 Scrap
46 Tough posers
49 Like some cigars
50 Garland co-star of 1939
51 Nesters
53 ___ provençale
55 Pill, e.g.

SATURDAY

by Sherry O. Blackard

ACROSS

1 See people
8 Like Baylor University
15 Shows that one is in?
16 Either of two track stars
17 1970 B.B. King hit
19 Prepare for planting, perhaps
20 Legionella and listeria
21 Pro ___
22 English agriculturist and inventor
24 Wouldn't stop
25 Company acquired by Mattel in 1997
26 "___ directed"
28 Code on some N.Y.C.-bound luggage
29 High kingdom
30 It may be fit for a queen
32 To a greater extent
33 Claims
35 Faux family name in rock and roll
38 Peak east of Captain Cook
42 Co-star of Marcello in "La Dolce Vita"
43 "Mathis ___ Maler" (opera)
44 Put up with
45 Sunroof option
46 Actress Lords
48 Like a retired prof.
49 Billet-doux recipient
50 Catnip relative
52 Hi-tech organizer
53 "Believe you me"
56 Destroyed little by little
57 Galley of yore
58 Result of doing the twist?
59 1979 #1 song with the chorus line "Turn the other way"

DOWN

1 Novelty race vehicle
2 Staff-produced
3 Prepared for bad news, say
4 Worked (up)
5 Dept. of Labor arm
6 Less sinful
7 Went around and around
8 100 centesimos
9 Strange
10 Kisser
11 "Star Trek" series preceding "Voyager," for short
12 Duplicate specimen, in biology
13 Native New Yorkers
14 Voice lesson topic
18 Ways back
23 Rail
25 Like soybean leaves
27 Leg
29 Highest points
31 End of a race?
32 Spartans' sch.
34 Spirit transporters
35 Sound of a woodpecker pecking
36 Spiritedly
37 Handle
39 Aquatic sucker
40 Words under "E pluribus unum"
41 Pitching stats?
43 Utilized
46 "___ relax"
47 Chief god of early Hinduism
50 Upscale hotel chain
51 "The Wizard ___"
54 Autobahn hazard
55 Something to pick

SATURDAY

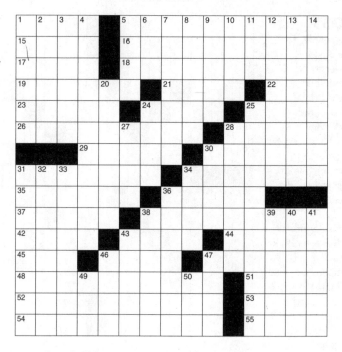

by Bob Klahn

ACROSS

1 Closing bars
5 Leaves for dinner
15 "The Green Hornet" trumpeter
16 Mixed drink?
17 Whereabouts
18 Roosevelt Island locale
19 Boxer on the cover of "Sgt. Pepper's Lonely Hearts Club Band"
21 Battle of Endor fighter
22 Submit
23 Brand of chips
24 Thin fastener
25 Anita Loos's autobiographical "A ___ Like I"
26 Lots
28 Musical notation pioneer
29 Blows
30 Hamper
31 Legs
34 Light housecoats
35 It's said to be everything
36 Third highest trump in card games
37 Saxophone great, familiarly
38 Common reply to a parent's demand
42 Plain sight
43 Inner ears
44 Ranger, e.g.
45 Alexander Pope's "Solitude," e.g.
46 Unlocked?
47 Hybrid women's clothing
48 Jackpot
51 Actress Petty of "A League of Their Own"
52 Park Avenue retailer?
53 Cross
54 Not the biggest thoroughfare in town
55 Flap

DOWN

1 Name shared by a Grace and a Muse
2 Putting on
3 Fast
4 Attitude
5 Sweet ___ of Avon (epithet for Shakespeare)
6 One in column A?
7 Washington posts
8 Main lane
9 Provincetown entree
10 Tilt
11 In
12 One making excuses
13 Black box
14 Decide by chance
20 Conservative
24 Dessert whose name means "peasant woman"
25 English composer of the opera "The Perfect Fool"
27 Kind of bean
28 Regular container?
30 Amateurish
31 Columbus discovery of 1493
32 Wiped
33 Alabama slammer ingredient
34 Toaster setting?
36 Author of the memoir "One Soldier's Story"
38 Thing that shrinks when inflated?
39 Cheap cigar, slangily
40 Monopoly's railroads, e.g.
41 "If music be the food of love, play on" speaker
43 Addition symbol
46 Sacks
47 G.E. Building muralist
49 Spring
50 Grand finale?

SATURDAY

ACROSS

1 Mathematical grouping
6 Is dishonest with
12 Climbers' goals
14 Illinois home of Rotary International
16 Friend you may never have met
17 Write seperately, say
18 Cinch
19 Altogether
20 Russian writer Andreyev famous for his horrific tales
21 Creepy crawler?
22 Some pizzas
23 Mason, at times
24 It's a sign
25 Chaplet relatives
26 "Le Mur" writer
28 Goya, for one
33 Connectors
35 Some vertical lines
37 Peaceful place
41 Row
42 Bull ___
43 Appellation for winter
44 Shade provider
45 Somewhat green
46 Note
47 Rejoinder to a doubter
48 Dark
49 It can be carved out
50 Things found by hounds
51 Orchestra section

by Robert H. Wolfe

DOWN

1 Auriga's brightest star
2 Full attention
3 Stimuli-perceiving brain parts
4 One who strikes out
5 Least joyful
6 Taps, in the British military
7 Unmoved
8 Wit
9 Knighted essayist
10 Quasimodo, notably
11 But
13 Winter Olympics equipment
14 Surface
15 Locales for trellises
25 Sentencing judge's prerogative
27 Points from which light emanates
29 Light hybrid vehicle of the 1910s
30 Trophies in a tournament, informally
31 Patient at a doctor's office
32 Lapped again
34 Freshwater fish of the perch family
36 Men of Manáos
37 Minute
38 Fix, as an old swimming pool
39 Baseball Hall-of-Famer Joe
40 Undesirable part of a record
41 Kind of barrier
44 Tax, in Tottenham

SATURDAY

ACROSS

1 Faux finish
8 Ancient fertility goddess
15 A position of prominence
16 Fundamental group
17 Pedigree, e.g.
18 Father's Day gift, perhaps
19 Prefix with center
20 Bowwows
22 Wait at the motor vehicle bureau, say
23 Ball material
25 Closer to perfection
26 Its motto is "Lux et veritas"
27 Capri, e.g.
29 Identify
30 Alter
31 Scarlatti's "Capriccio," e.g.
33 Composes
35 Kind of support
37 When doubled, a shore dinner order
38 1988 Burt Reynolds flop
42 Persian attraction
46 Time after retiring?
47 General Mills brand
49 Tundra or rain forest
50 1960's soul record label
51 Back parts of keels
53 Suffix with game
54 Flight board abbr.
55 Headdress wearer
57 Call
58 Home of the Moai statues
60 Certain Playgirl centerfold
62 Trapped

63 French politician ___ de Silhouette, from whom the word "silhouette" comes
64 Italian city, setting of a Walpole novel
65 Like some couples

DOWN

1 Martyred bishop of Paris
2 Wishful reply
3 Shackle
4 With 61-Down, 14th president's inits.
5 Informal denial
6 March
7 Struck
8 Where to work out, maybe
9 Less social
10 "___ bon"
11 Post-Manhattan Project org.
12 Issue
13 French poetic form
14 Cable program with team coverage?
21 Political suffix
24 Recurring economic proposal
26 Answer to "No, that's not!"
28 1980s TV quartet
30 Doctor's order
32 Maryland and Virginia are in it: Abbr.
34 Campaign grp.
36 Seikan Tunnel terminus
38 "Will & Grace" maid
39 Competitor
40 Like some bond prices
41 Debarking point
43 Intersection interdiction
44 Last song recorded by the Beatles
45 Puzzle
48 Annual competition since 1995
51 Surgical implant
52 A little, colloquially
55 Nabokov novel
56 Corey of "The Lost Boys"
59 Grp. concerned with defense
61 See 4-Down

by David Quarfoot

SATURDAY

ACROSS

1 Did some court work
11 Cow: Sp.
15 Set of routine duties
16 Argonaut who slew Castor
17 Locks up?
18 Things usually held while facing backward
19 Architectural projection
20 Ones with well-defined careers?
22 Farm sound
25 Players' tryouts
27 Fish also called a Jerusalem haddock
29 Play mates?
30 Alma-___, city where Trotsky was exiled
31 Walgreens rival
33 Separates
37 Not necessarily against
38 Hang out
39 Rock formation, to geologists
41 Contemporary correspondent
42 Saint-___ (France's West Point)
43 A following?
45 Formal introduction?
46 Couple in the news in 1945
50 Health reporter Blakey
51 Fly (by)
52 President between Farrell and Lonardi
54 1968 album with the song "John Looked Down"
55 Interested
60 One with special insight
61 Fails
62 "Look ___ . . ."
63 Carrots and mashed potatoes, e.g.

DOWN

1 What passes may lead to, quickly
2 Charge on a record
3 Crowd in old Rome?
4 Nevada county or its seat
5 Tannery workers
6 Monkey, so to speak
7 Stuck
8 "Royalty of the garden"
9 Twice 58-Down
10 Minute Maid Park's former sponsor
11 Dwarf plant of the eastern U.S.
12 Mr. Deeds player
13 Sign that something's missing
14 Clubs: Abbr.
21 Lago di Como locale
22 "Woman With a Pearl" painter
23 Foucault's "This Is Not ___"
24 Dispenser of gossip?
26 Image on Australia's coat of arms
28 Abstract sculptor whose work is seen at Lincoln Center
32 Consoles popular in the 80's
34 Like fashionable apparel
35 Word in several Dunkin' Donuts doughnut names
36 Its flag has two green stars
40 Low ___
41 Iran-contra figure
44 Filched
46 Swimming
47 Lithium, on the periodic table
48 Waste at the polls
49 Lifetime winner of the most Grammys (31)
53 Intelligence
56 Island staple
57 Quote from Homer
58 Amount past due?
59 Accepts

by Myles Callum

ACROSS

1 Cross, maybe
6 Met expectations?
11 Refuge
20 Nitrogen compound
21 TV exec Arledge
22 Last czarina of Russia
23 "Absolutely, ambassador"
25 Colonies, e.g.
26 Frigid
27 Southern group address
28 Alliance dissolved in 1977
29 "Wonderful!"
30 Pulitzer Prize subj.
32 Continental capital
34 Starter: Abbr.
36 Island with a Hindu majority
39 Like some unpopular leaders
45 Computer pioneer Lovelace and others
48 The Huskies of the N.C.A.A.
50 Fraternity letters
51 Captivate
52 Antivenins, e.g.
53 Award-winning TV host
56 Charles Lindbergh, once
58 Buzzer
59 Blue-pencil
60 Advance
62 Academy head
63 Follower of mars
64 Modern greeting
66 Narrow the gap with

67 Marine mammal
70 Advantageousness
71 Fair fare
72 Friends
73 Went downhill
74 "___ ramparts!"
75 St.-Tropez's Place des ___
76 Bingo call
77 Cuneiform discovery site
79 Cartesian conclusion
82 "It's dark in here!"
84 x
86 Ad time
87 Main international airport of Japan
91 Width measure
92 Holy text
93 Raison d'___
94 1+1=2, e.g.
97 Great American Ball Park team
98 Death on the Nile cause, perhaps
100 "Brave New World" drug
101 Usher in
103 ___-Boy
105 Keep an ___ the ground
109 Some Wall St. deals
112 Daughter of Zeus
116 Claim
118 Weighty issue?
120 Scoots over
121 Prudential competitor
122 Female demon
123 Nickname for Tasmania
124 Waste
125 City on the Rhone

DOWN

1 "Apocalypto" subject
2 Like some profs.
3 Wink in tiddlywinks, e.g.
4 "Take your pick"
5 Sainted pope of 682
6 Airport sign abbr.
7 Classic theater name
8 Seat of Allen County, Kan.
9 Shaker leader
10 Shut off
11 Dirge
12 Natural balm
13 Relief provider, for short
14 Out
15 Capital once known as Thang Long ("Ascending Dragon")
16 Cuckoo bird
17 Streaming content
18 Composer Dohnányi
19 Ambassador or Statesman of old autodom
24 Campus 100 miles NW of L.A.
31 Hip
33 Oysters ___ season
35 Molotov cocktail component
36 Onion, for one
37 Teen trouble
38 Treasure-trove
40 Not built up
41 Tiny time unit: Abbr.
42 Capacitance measure

43 Richard of old westerns and action films
44 Pentagon fig.
46 Playground retort
47 It's a wrap
49 Most gutsy
54 ___ Circus (where St. Peter was crucified)
55 Enter
57 Fictional knight named for a bird of prey
60 Carriage
61 Fabulous monster
63 Property recipients
65 Do, re, mi
66 "I've ___ Strings" (Pinocchio song)
67 Like tears
68 Bring out
69 Rare ex-prisoner
70 Classic Jaguar
71 Some horns
73 Brooking no dissent
74 Lead-in to bow or hike
76 Show pride, in a way
78 Memory: Prefix
79 About
80 Just barely
81 Much of Colo.
83 "Mad TV" rival, for short
85 Marin and Sonoma's region
88 "I'll get this"
89 Chinese "way"
90 Two bags of groceries, say
95 Talk on and on, Down Under
96 Get wind of

SUNDAY

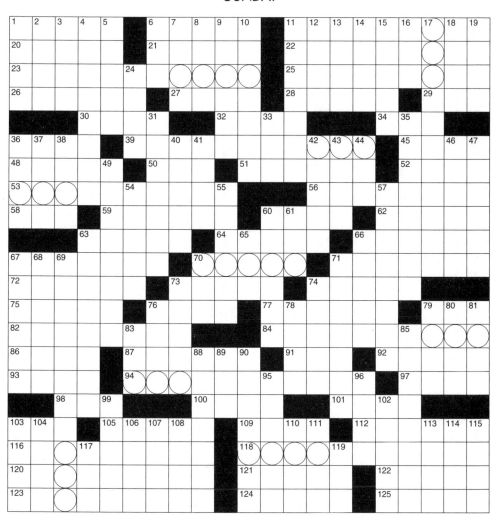

by Ashish Vengsarkar

53

AD REPS

ACROSS

1 Failures
7 Strolled
13 Mob action
20 Foothold facilitator
21 Annual October event, with "the"
22 "That really touched me"
23 Scene of some disgraceful one-nighters?
25 Traffic caution
26 Longtime Syrian president
27 Singer Redbone
28 Business honcho Perelman, who was once the richest man in America
29 Bad testimony
30 Headline about a philanthropist's settled loan?
37 Several periods
40 Bribe
41 Vacationer's destination
42 Rudy's coach in "Rudy"
43 Take off (on)
45 Wife of Saturn
47 Like a piece of cake
49 "That'll do, thanks"
53 "I'll say it again ___ I'm outta here"?
58 A
59 Slows
60 Slow
61 Largest island in the Cyclades
62 It may blow when it's hot
63 Prefix with angular
65 Pour
67 Made privy to
69 Darning some smelly socks?
75 Early French settler in the Maritimes
76 "Oxford Blues" star, 1984
77 Fitness centers
78 Meticulousness
79 "Julius Caesar" role
83 When repeated, a South Seas getaway
85 Tattered Tom's creator
88 D.C. setting
89 Item on a busboy's to-do list?
92 Donne, for one
94 Spent
95 Behind
96 Bygone time
97 Notebook maker
99 Can't stand
102 Diving bird
104 Grp. with some crack staff
105 Retrieves a phone message again?
111 Had something
112 Kicks
113 Ill-gotten gains
114 Old Russian ruler known as "The Moneybag"
118 Big cheese?
121 Drive Dali back?
125 Occupied, as a saddle
126 Irish P.M. Ahern
127 Calm
128 Running out of gas
129 Vital ratings period
130 Password preceder

DOWN

1 Bologna bread, once
2 First-rate
3 Perks (up)
4 Skater Hughes
5 Moving experience?
6 It makes waves
7 Bloodless
8 Recounted account
9 "The Professor: A Tale" novelist
10 Turned on
11 Clown's foot spec, maybe
12 Cable alternative
13 Wisconsin college town
14 Egyptian god of the universe
15 Mid-millennium year
16 Curse
17 Walled city near Madrid
18 Contents of lamps, maybe
19 Just beat
24 Played pat-a-cake
28 Blue
31 Secure
32 ___ mgr.
33 Actor Atkinson, player of Mr. Bean
34 "The Faerie Queene" character
35 Faerie land
36 One of TV's Ewings
37 Work units
38 Go wild
39 Opening-night celebration
44 Md. town near Baltimore
46 Reject
48 Fairy tale character
50 "O.K. by me"
51 TV journalist David
52 Minute
54 PC character system
55 Slate, e.g.
56 Put ___ on (go for at auction)
57 ___ directed
62 "It's about time!"
64 Bit of evidence
66 Frequent English football score
68 Late name in rap
69 Toy on a track
70 Online shoppers might use it
71 Unsuitable
72 Gen. ___ E. Lee
73 Old draft category
74 ___ Buena, Calif.
80 Came home dusty?
81 "Put it here," basically
82 Prefix with nitrile
84 Farm plant also called lucerne
86 To be over there?
87 Mother of Hades
89 Country name
90 Place at the start
91 Pin holder

SUNDAY

by Joe DiPietro

93 .001 inch
98 "Ri-i-i-i-ight!"
100 City connected to the Sunshine Skyway Br.
101 Nickname of baseball's Leo Durocher

103 Hibachi chef's pride
105 1969 Hoffman role
106 Novelist Canin
107 Senior Tour golfer Calvin
108 Bright

109 Someone ___ problem
110 Dodge
115 Purim month
116 Denier's comment
117 Hot
119 Queen ___

120 Across the street from: Abbr.
121 N.F.L. ball carriers
122 "That's gross!"
123 School opening?
124 The Fighting Tigers, for short

ACROSS

1 Quakers or Shakers
5 Old film magnate Zukor
11 Bill collector?
15 Low-___
19 1940's–50's actress Raines
20 State bordered by the Colorado River
21 "It is my suggestion . . ."
22 Baseball star born in Santo Domingo
23 The marijuana dealer tried to . . .
25 Confidentially
27 Wasted
28 The veterinarian tried to . . .
30 Goes off
34 Title for a 50-Across
35 Clinton or Dole: Abbr.
36 Crosstown rival of the Bruins
39 Store outside a city?
41 "When I was young . . ."
44 What markers may represent
48 Actress Vardalos
49 Bette Midler and others
50 All-wise one
52 Bird feeder fill
53 Canasta plays
56 Budapest-born conductor
58 Flattens
60 Core of a PC
61 Radiant
62 Almost too much
64 Awestruck
66 Bottom line figure
69 The arsonist tried to . . .
71 Shades of red

73 Srs. may take it
74 Shakespearean term of address
75 The demolitions expert tried to . . .
79 Fuel
82 Use over, as tea leaves
83 Sonata finales
84 Tragic figure in Greek myth
85 Ending with rest or fest
86 Wheel on a spur
88 Slip by
91 All-purpose connector
92 Baklava ingredients
94 RCA competitor
96 Give a lift
98 It may get into deep water
99 Old-fashioned adventure
101 Food for thought?
102 Forward
104 Urban gridwork: Abbr.
105 42-Down users, for short
107 "Now I get it"
109 Baseball Hall-of-Famer Fox
111 The artist tried to . . .
117 Keyboard commands
121 National park in Colorado
122 The hair stylist tried to . . .
126 Angle (off)
127 Patient wife of Sir Geraint
128 Big bookseller
129 Somalia-born supermodel
130 Louver feature
131 Somewhat, to Salieri

132 Counters
133 Miss

DOWN

1 1999 war combatant
2 Ben-Gurion arrival
3 Sister in myth
4 Refinement
5 Bowl over
6 Cry made with a head-slap
7 What I will always be?
8 Prune
9 T.A.'s superior
10 Is averse to
11 Related to
12 "___ It Time" (1977 hit)
13 Plaster base
14 Instruments played by 3-Down
15 Denture parts
16 Tremendously
17 50–0, e.g.
18 In use
24 Verb origin of suis and sont
26 Scratched (out)
29 Taker of a bow?
31 Electric flux symbols
32 Modern subscription service
33 Zigzag
36 Frighten
37 War tactic
38 The telemarketer tried to . . .
40 One of the ones waiting in "Waiting for Godot"
42 Manuscript marks
43 Offshoot of punk rock
45 The rodeo rider tried to . . .

46 Crow's home
47 Gives an electric jolt
51 Supplement
54 Place marker
55 More stylish
57 Go where one's not welcome
59 Title girl in a 1979 #1 hit
63 Start of a full house declaration, maybe
65 Luke Skywalker's father
67 Paired up
68 "No dice"
70 Part of H.R.H.
72 Big name in women's tennis
75 Raise, with "up"
76 Song-and-dance special
77 "Unbelievable!"
78 Alternative education institute since the 1960's
80 W.W. II menace
81 Salon jobs
87 Ton of money
89 Broad
90 List ender
93 Popular late-night host
95 Home of the superhighways H1, H2 and H3
97 Actresses Fulton and Brennan
100 Ron Howard flick of 1999
103 "The Mod Squad" role
106 Wolf's prey
108 "And the ___ goes to . . ."
110 Web biz
111 Auto lic. bureaus
112 Part of a Hollywood archive

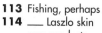

by Michael Ashley

113 Fishing, perhaps
114 ___ Laszlo skin care products
115 It helps prevent runs: Abbr.
116 Philosopher David
118 First name in newspaper humor

119 Vitamin bottle info, for short
120 Personal ID's
123 Keyboard key
124 China's Lao-___
125 In

ACROSS

1 ___ once
6 Blood-related
11 Spot on a horse
17 Not as nice
19 Oscar winner who made his film debut in "Me, Natalie," 1969
20 One who works on walls
21 Chant
22 Patch type
23 Go from worse to bad?
24 Female competitor in springboard competition?
26 Personal points of view
28 Pouchlike part
29 "House of Incest" author
30 Smidgen
31 Breathing space?
32 Cooped (up)
33 Decree
34 Where the smoke rises in a sty's chimney?
37 Sounds of impact
39 Cardboard pkg.
40 Suit to ___
41 Wal-Mart rival
42 Normandy city
43 One of the Borgias
45 Film role played by both Vincent Price and Bill Cosby
47 They have quarters downtown
50 Newspaper no.
52 Without carrying charges?
55 Be-bopper
56 Start of the second quarter
59 It fits in a lock
61 On a high
62 Notable #4 with a stick
63 Lionize
64 Cashew family member
66 Contents of a diamond bag
67 Theater org.
68 Cross promotion?
69 Fellini's "La ___"
70 Part of T.G.I.F.
71 Not quite right
72 Solo in space
73 Where Brahmans build their houses?
76 Hard to believe
78 Get moving
80 Addition symbol
82 Imp
86 Barbering area
87 Produce plays, say
89 Grate
91 Corrosive chemical, to a chemist
92 Protractor measurements
94 A choice between cinnabar and galena?
96 Rush
97 One and only
98 Fraternal letters
99 School since 1440
100 Puerto Rico hrs.
101 Mexican Mrs.
102 Baltimore's Enoch ___ Free Library
104 Command to a gardener?
108 Maximilian, for one
110 Handle an F-15, e.g.
112 It may zip out
113 Chefs, at times
114 Gave birth on a farm
115 Sound setup
116 Underhanded, to put it nicely
117 President born in Charles City, Va.
118 It may be rolled up in a bun

DOWN

1 In the thick of
2 Early Russian Communist
3 Modern-day inhabitants of old Livonia
4 Apply chrism
5 Home of Ft. Donelson Natl. Battlefield
6 Author Ellison
7 Green subj.
8 Go for the gold
9 She rescued Odysseus
10 Topographic map feature
11 British title
12 Computer programs, briefly
13 In accordance with
14 What you'll find at a prison library?
15 Mediterranean region
16 Puts up
18 Make an impression
19 Devout acts
20 Toll road
25 Heavyweight champ Riddick
27 Lover of Aphrodite
31 Appointment book
32 Bargaining factor
33 TV overseer: Abbr.
35 Last word of Missouri's motto
36 Alarm
37 Show in theaters
38 Roughly measured (off)
40 Seed coat
44 91-Across, e.g.
46 Wear away
47 Oil worker
48 What Shakespeare called "the little O"
49 Leave the straight and narrow
51 Student's selection
53 Kay Thompson character
54 Firmly secured
56 Kind of star
57 Song of joy
58 Miler's mistake?
60 Latin 101 word
64 Union members
65 Chalk or marble
67 Needs a doctor
69 Land's end?
71 Uproar
74 Word of honor
75 Leaves home?
77 Weapons collections
79 ___ bonding
81 Stepped lively
83 Cheese type
84 Some solvents
85 Letters after a barrister's name

SUNDAY

by Richard Silvestri

87 Shed tears
88 Reading to the
unruly
90 Lined up
92 Stocks and
such
93 Everyday
95 One who's lying

96 One of the original
Not Ready for
Prime Time Players
98 Components of
some codes
102 Veep's boss
103 Calhoun of TV's
"The Texan"

104 Mental
power
105 Overhang
106 "Norma Rae"
director
107 Vanity cases?
109 Greek vowel
111 "Oy ___!"

When this puzzle is completed, the circled letters, read in order from left to right (column by column), will reveal the name of a Mystery Person.

ACROSS

1 Oliver Twist, e.g.
5 Little fight
10 Squawker
14 Advanced
18 Some chorus voices
19 Run ___ of
20 Father-and-son name in football coaching
21 Modeler's need
22 As a toddler visiting a farm, Mystery Person heard a pig squeal and . . .
26 Dorothy's transport to Oz
27 Aardwolf features
28 Puncture
29 "Comin' ___ the Rye"
31 Blunderbuss
32 Francis, e.g.
33 After a single hearing of a sacred piece in the Sistine Chapel, Mystery Person . . .
44 Continental money
45 One of Alcott's "Little Men"
46 Privy to
47 Concept embodying yin and yang
48 Founded: Abbr.
49 Jawbreaker?
51 Less loco
53 Mythical creature
55 Mystery Person once composed a piano piece that, to be performed correctly, required the . . .
59 One pole: Abbr.
60 Hematite component
61 Song from on high?
62 Med. specialty
63 Use for support
65 Massenet opera
66 Jewish sect
70 Back
71 Trowel wielder
72 Uncommon
73 Singer with a palindromic name
74 Mystery Person would sometimes compose symphonies . . .
80 Assailed
81 Revere
82 Well
83 Cars once advertised as "The Gold Standard of Value"
84 Loosen up, maybe
85 Org. with an acad. near Colo. Spr.
86 ___-mo
87 Country north of Tonga
88 Scholars believe that "A Musical Joke" by Mystery Person was . . .
95 Tribe with a state named after it
96 Part of l'année
97 Carrier whose name means "skyward"
98 G-rated
101 Whine-making?
105 Throw
110 Mystery Person once wrote a waltz in which the choice of measures played was determined . . .
113 Suffix with switch
114 12 on a cube
115 "Whole ___ Love" (1969 hit)
116 Gusto
117 Buzzed
118 Gregor Mendel research subject
119 Northernmost county of Massachusetts
120 Cuts off

DOWN

1 "Hold it!"
2 Fashion executive Gucci
3 Path of Caesar
4 Spender of markkas, once
5 Greeted informally
6 Pains
7 Vous, familiarly
8 January 27, 1756 (Mystery Person's birthdate), e.g.
9 Chicago district
10 Bloke
11 Deceit
12 "___ the heavy day!": "Othello"
13 Catch
14 Celebratory toast
15 Gusto
16 Buster?
17 Family
20 Working ___
23 "Soap" family
24 Part of Bush's "Axis of Evil"
25 ___-eyed
30 Favored
32 He outpolled H.H.H. in '68
33 Tots
34 Brown shade
35 Sandinista head
36 List heading
37 Swear words
38 Finished cleaning
39 Youngest Oscar winner in history
40 Poetic time of day
41 1931 Medicine Nobelist Warburg
42 Some stingers
43 Days of ___
49 1960's TV series set at Fort Courage
50 Exuberant casino cry
51 Ice treat
52 Simple arithmetic
53 U.S.-born grandchild of Japanese immigrants
54 Nay sayer
56 Act antsy
57 Reply to a captain
58 So very much
64 Simba's mate, in "The Lion King"
65 Furlough
66 Campus building
67 Long green
68 Away from the elements
69 Israeli intelligence group
71 Letter salutation
72 Five-carbon sugar
74 "Hold your horses!"
75 Locks
76 Furloughed
77 Use a surgical beam
78 "Road" picture destination
79 ___-American
85 One-eighty
86 Doctor's signboard
87 Canonized fifth-century pope
89 Edible clam
90 Minneapolis-based magazine
91 Old Dodges
92 Game stopper
93 Missouri feeder

SUNDAY

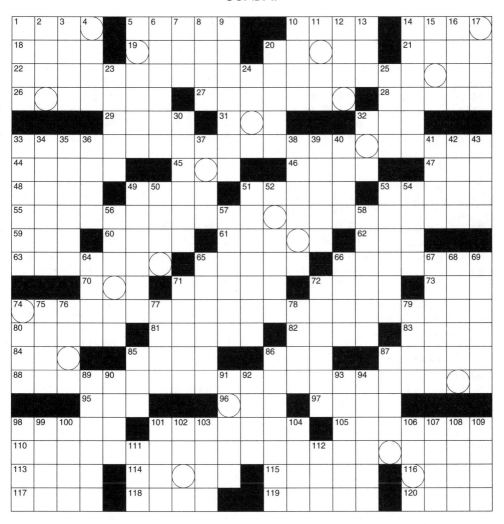

by George Barany and Michael Shteyman

94 Swab target
98 "Good buddy"
99 Neighbor of
   Draco
100 ___ jacket
101 Fashion
102 "Eugene
   Onegin" girl
103 Pub quaffs

104 Gunks
106 Chisellike tool
107 It means nothing
   to the French
108 Golden State
   sch.
109 Understands
111 Agt.
112 Basketball stat.

ACROSS

1 Printing array
6 Eats
10 Not very bright
14 Eighty-six
18 Like tinned fish
19 Pointer's pronoun
20 Sommelier's prefix
21 Fixes holes, say
22 Important part of mayo
23 Site for stretchers
25 U-shaped river bend
26 Raise money using heavenly messengers?
29 "Romanian Rhapsodies" composer
30 Something may be taken in it
31 TNT alternative
32 ___-Seltzer
35 Defense grp. formed in Bogotá
36 Farm workers
40 Like a phobic longshoreman?
45 Suffix with ranch
46 Mid-seventh century date
47 Tip, in a way
48 Appetizer or entree
49 Geiger with a counter
50 Here, in Juárez
51 Cross inscription
52 Close encounter
54 Tax check
55 Portrait of an explorer with his timepiece?
58 One expressing the same thoughts

59 ___ Clemente
60 Kind of pass
61 Agcy. spawned by the Manhattan Project
62 Brewpub staple
63 F.D.R. program
64 Erasers?
66 Force a physician and a "Star Trek" officer into a plane?
71 "Stand and Deliver" star, 1987
72 Hydra, for one
73 Dash
74 Can. money
75 Sangre de Cristo Mountains resort
76 "It's Impossible" singer
77 Middle: Prefix
78 "Rocks"
79 Onetime Jeep mfr.
80 Result of wires down in a blizzard?
85 Prepare for firing
87 Cock and bull
88 Restrain
89 Québec's Côte-St.-___
90 Works together
93 Not fooled by
98 Brews in an elm instead of an oak?
102 The Wall Street Journal visual
104 Draft, basically
105 "Them" author
106 European capital, in song
107 ___ B'rith
108 Alternative to Breyers
109 Surgical tube

110 Blown away
111 Short pans
112 Secretary, for one
113 Wiesbaden's state

DOWN

1 Archives unit
2 Bagel flavor
3 Time being
4 Seconds on a watch
5 Toy racer
6 It's found on a lid
7 "Whoops!"
8 House gofers
9 Begin
10 Akin to Ken?
11 Check the total
12 Looped handles
13 Cap'n's underling
14 Accountant's concern
15 Planets, to poets
16 ___-Globe (common paperweight)
17 Jacksonville-to-Tampa dir.
21 Makes out
24 One of diamonds?
27 Guadalajara greeting
28 Deep ravine
33 Take illegally
34 Sew on sequins, say
36 Fancy-schmancy
37 Herd containment device?
38 1944 Pulitzer-winning journalist
39 Cosa ___
40 Ridicule of a foreign speaker?

41 It might be only a scratch
42 "The Wizard ___"
43 Cabinet dept.
44 Poker chip, e.g.
46 1989 Peace Prize recipient
49 "Say what?"
51 "The fix ___"
52 One may replace an oath
53 Fabled fliers
54 Super-duper
56 "Concord Sonata" composer
57 Encrusted
58 Sommer of "The Prize," 1963
59 Like clay pigeons
62 Buttonhole
65 Calendar pages: Abbr.
66 N.Y.C. cultural center
67 Like crazy
68 ___-à-porter (ready-to-wear)
69 Havens
70 Bank regulating org.
72 Work with feet
76 Pain in the neck
77 1960's TV show set on a farm
80 Lacking tact
81 Thingy
82 Author/ screenwriter Ben
83 Chopped down
84 Valley Girl exclamation
86 Chose the window instead of the aisle?
90 Giving a line to
91 Book club name
92 Nobel, for one

SUNDAY

by Rich Norris

94 Condition
95 Some Deco works
96 Cold temps
97 270° from norte
98 Stripped
99 Indian-born actor in "A Tiger Walks," 1964
100 They're caught at the shore
101 City on the Irtysh River
102 Univ. stat
103 Damp and chilly

CENTRAL INTELLIGENCE

The eight theme answers in this puzzle are clues to common words. When the grid has been filled, guess these missing words and enter them on the numbered dashes shown. Then transfer each letter from a dash to its correspondingly numbered square in the middle of the grid. Every letter in the middle will be used twice in the missing words. When you're done, the 25 squares, in order, will reveal a bit of advice about getting ahead.

ACROSS

1 Father of Magnus the Good
5 "Uh-huh"
8 Pressure: Prefix
12 "There ___ goes . . ."
15 Mrs., in Madrid
18 Auto with a trident logo
20 Far from home, perhaps
22 "If only ___ listened . . ."
23 17-20-24-12-8-9-13
25 Latin 101 word
26 Suffix with violin
27 Radio advice-giver
28 "Outta here"
29 Quarrel
30 Corp. bigwig
31 5% of a C-note
32 Like many adherents to 55-Down
34 17-9-19-10-2-12-22-7
39 Loonies
40 Smells
41 Charlemagne's realm: Abbr.
42 English exclamation
43 Foot soldiers: Abbr.
44 Classic gas brand
45 Level
46 Baby kisser, maybe, in brief
47 Hard times
51 Fraction of a min.
53 Parisian article
54 "___ Baby" ("Hair" song)
55 Suffix of approximation
58 Seize
60 Like many sports interviews
62 Place for Us and Them
64 How bananas are bought
65 Breaking news
66 Mighty boss's opposite
67 River at Ghent
68 Actor Guinness
69 "Brat Farrar" mystery writer
70 Turning point?
72 Place on a TV?
74 Woman in a personal ad: Abbr.
77 Hang
79 Road ___
83 Good times
84 Code in which many Web pages are written: Abbr.
85 Suffix with Capri
86 Bit of Gothic architecture
87 Bite-the-bullet type
89 1-15-6-11-5-22
92 Followers of philosopher René
94 Make like
95 Youngster
96 Common conjunctions
97 Joker, e.g.
98 Roils
100 Lawyer: Abbr.
103 Original "King Kong" studio
104 25-14-2-19-7
107 Hosp. readout
108 Ethiopian river
109 Discharge into the air
110 Crown maker: Abbr.
111 Mormons: Abbr.
112 Restaurateur Toots
113 Like some ears
114 Leisure

DOWN

1 Popular hotel chain
2 Vientiane's land
3 Secy.
4 Whimsical
5 Peter who wrote "Puff the Magic Dragon"
6 Elec., e.g.
7 Garment worn like an apron
8 Ludlum protagonist
9 Reebok rival
10 Lawyer's thing
11 Something that gets copied
12 Fishing nets
13 ___ cow
14 Compass point
15 24-8-20-16-11
16 Observation
17 Prettifies
19 Places for clowns
21 Hip's opposite
24 Arrow's place
29 It started about 2$\frac{1}{2}$ million years ago
30 Storage medium
32 Japanese soup
33 It may leave its mark
34 The "vey" of "oy vey!"
35 They often have photos
36 Rebuffs
37 Red squirrel named for the sound it makes
38 Upholstery problem
45 4-23-14-10-3-18-25
47 How many proposals are delivered
48 15-21-13-1-18-6
49 British tar
50 Burpee product
52 Slow-cooked meal
53 Start of Superman's catchphrase
55 See 32-Across
56 Reach the top of
57 4-23-16-21-5-3
59 Vortex
61 "___ 'clock scholar"
63 New members
71 Weave
73 Some time ago
74 Subs
75 One rationale for the 2003 invasion of Iraq: Abbr.
76 "Alice" waitress
77 Baked entree
78 Kind of cable for a computer
80 Stomach muscles, for short
81 Day-___
82 Poetic time of day
84 Car known for its storage space
86 Staples of annual reports
87 One way to run
88 Bloody drunk

SUNDAY

by Eric Berlin

89 Break
90 "Our ___ . . ."
91 Connect, in a way
93 Say "tsk" to
98 Historic Normandy town
99 California's ___ Valley
100 Three oceans touch it
101 Ring wins, briefly
102 Actress Daly
104 Two-bagger: Abbr.
105 Biomed. group
106 Lao-___

ACROSS

1 Staff
5 Test group?
10 La Scala cheer
15 Germ jelly
19 "I smell ___!"
20 Financial mogul Carl
21 Indian bread
22 Plain and simple
23 Nostalgic person's utterance
24 Why the convent's head couldn't find information on the nun?
27 Basilica of San Francesco site
29 "Er-r . . ."
30 First step in addicts' treatment
31 Kind of school
32 Merged coastal access?
36 Gives more than a licking?
38 Social sort
39 Wall protector
40 Victory: Ger.
42 Staple of Italian cuisine
44 Unilever?
47 Mexican Mrs.
49 Reason for school cancellation
50 "Ouch!"
51 Canadian Club and others
52 Henhouse sounds
54 Iceland is part of it: Abbr.
57 Pops
60 Accepts oppression no longer
63 Reason to lube a tube?

69 Certain canine
71 Tape, for short
72 Surrender
73 Artist's board nearby?
76 Circular
77 Cast
78 Word said with a tip o' the hat
80 Stomach and intestine, e.g.
81 View from the Gulf of Catania
85 Speaker of the line "Help me, Obi-Wan Kenobi; you're my only hope"
87 Spanish flower
90 French connections?
91 Cabaret singer in the style of an old pope?
97 Square things
98 "Cut it out!"
99 "___ take arms against a sea of troubles": "Hamlet"
100 Knock over
103 Second-stringer
104 Top knot?
107 Mil. address
108 Washersful
112 Accelerate, for short
113 Lesser hit locations
114 Rubber mania?
119 Stakes
120 Moscato d'___ (Italian wine)
121 Lion's home, to Hercules
122 Dander
123 "Waiting for the Robert ___"

124 Sound before "Your fly's open"
125 Dagwood and Blondie's dog
126 ___ Foods, Fortune 500 company
127 Cat with tufted ears

DOWN

1 Winter melon
2 Up
3 Bothers
4 Standard of living?
5 They're easy to park
6 "Baudolino" author
7 Time out?
8 Fuchsia, e.g.
9 Belief of many Africans
10 Cold comment
11 Felt sorry about
12 Area with a curved wall
13 Flak jacket, e.g.
14 Like some exercises
15 Cinemax competitor, for short
16 Class of planes?
17 One in handcuffs
18 Funny Foxx
25 "___ vincit amor"
26 Have a place in the world
28 Big Apple park
33 It takes the cake
34 Quark-plus-antiquark particle
35 Counting-out starter
37 See the sights
41 Kind of room
42 Unfair treatment
43 Surgeons' sites, briefly

44 Philip Seymour Hoffman title role
45 Substitute
46 Pays, as a bill
47 "Bye"
48 Make merry
52 Princeton Review or Kaplan study
53 Exertion aversion
55 Modern recording option
56 It's addictive
58 ". . . so long ___ both shall live"
59 Crouch
61 Carry
62 Enter quietly
64 "So Big" author Ferber
65 In chains
66 Acclaim
67 Smart guys?
68 Etta of old comics
70 "___ heart" ("Be kind")
74 Power to control
75 Put in stitches
79 Tool along
81 Ingredient in a flip
82 Poach
83 Bases from which profits are figured
84 Golden or teen follower
86 Isn't naturally
88 Novi Sad resident
89 High-speed roadway
92 Seed-to-be
93 Get well fast
94 Time of operation
95 "Bon ___!"
96 Propagates
100 In many places
101 50 to two

by Manny Nosowsky

102 Setting for many Thomas Hardy novels
105 Part of EGBDF
106 Defamation
107 "Do I need to draw you ___?"
109 Well off the coast

110 Half: Prefix
111 "___ Gotta Have It"
115 Do nothing
116 "Way to go!"
117 Bradbury's "___ for Rocket"
118 Prefix with morphic

60 IT'S NEXT TO NOTHING

ACROSS

1 Small turnover
7 Careless
15 Gut feeling?
20 Preener's partner
21 Color similar to turquoise
22 Shades
23 "Now!"
25 Make into law
26 Stephen of "Breakfast on Pluto"
27 Thought some more about
28 Gas company known for its toy trucks
30 Gas company known for its tiger slogan
31 Tiny ___
32 Ceremonial burner
33 Gob
34 Crescent point
36 "A Passage to India" woman
38 Bawdy
40 One way to chop peppers
42 For one
45 Certain turtle
48 One with a thin skin?
50 "I'm not impressed"
53 Jacket style
54 "Make ___ away"
55 Vice
56 Cry of distress
60 What the connected may have
62 The D.A. probably took it once
63 Dear ones
65 Graph component
66 Pension recipient
68 Afternoon hour in Italy
69 Puts on a coat
71 Bother
72 Cartoon collectible
75 Worked up
77 It may be met or filled
78 2002 Olympics venue
80 Musical opening
82 Gran Canaria, for one
83 Support
85 Blood designation, for short
86 Old sports org. featuring the Minnesota Kicks
87 Florida Rep. ___ Hastings
89 Theseus abandoned her
91 Fugard's "A Lesson From ___"
93 Not just lean
96 Shelters
97 "Yeah, right"
99 Angelo's instrument
100 Trac II alternatives
104 Off-white
105 It has nine figures: Abbr.
107 Markets of yore
111 Greeting of yore
112 Carl Sagan's subj.
114 Popular insulator
116 Dyemaking material
117 Raiders' org.
118 Old war story
120 Debt cause
123 Describes
124 "Just a little bite?"
125 Crumbly Italian cheese
126 Symbol of strength
127 Certain math sign
128 Staggered

DOWN

1 Ancient military hub
2 Work recounting Dido's suicide
3 Butterfly, e.g.
4 An omega stands for it
5 Specialty of Russian painter Aivazovsky
6 A joint that's hopping?
7 Short cuts
8 Leaves something behind
9 Loser
10 ___ Station
11 Under the name of, as a co.
12 Part of many stars' names
13 A-one, or one living in 1-A, perhaps
14 Attention getters
15 Had a beef?
16 Declined
17 Instantly
18 P.I.'s
19 Concerning
24 Poetic time of day
29 Genetics, e.g.: Abbr.
33 Use keys
35 Afternoon hour in Italy
37 Dish out the beans?
39 Punishes, in a way
40 Healthful dessert
41 Eastern discipline
43 Alliance created in 1948: Abbr.
44 Not take risks
46 Ikhnaton, for one
47 Automaker Maserati
49 "Hardly"
50 Swig
51 Actor Novello
52 "Be a little more patient"
57 & 58 Common cake ingredient
59 Fire starter?
61 Nothing that plays a prominent role in this puzzle
64 Resting place
67 Ad salesman, informally
70 "___ was saying . . ."
71 March word
73 Knotted up
74 Ticket choice
76 Character on "Frasier"
77 Quite odd
79 Not just poke fun at
80 Santa in California
81 Cartel city
84 "___ Day" (1993 rap hit)
88 Dash
90 Just partly
92 It's 94-Down for south
94 See 92-Down
95 The Arrow constellation
98 Coke's partner
101 Michelin offering

SUNDAY

by Joe DiPietro

102 Get payback for
103 Neptune, e.g.
105 Display
106 Vaults
108 Football Hall-of-Famer Merlin
109 Splitting image?
110 Something lent or bent, in a phrase
112 Hurts
113 Opening
115 Object of worship
116 Room to swing ___
119 Cable alternative
121 Letters within the theme entries that are, literally, next to nothing
122 Quit working

61 WRITING LESSON

ACROSS

1 Constitution
8 "___ 70's Show"
12 Operating
17 "How dare they?!"
18 Darn it
19 Uranium-exporting country
20 Infinitives . . . it's ___
23 Word we share
24 Daily Planet worker
25 Reach
26 Beverage served with le dessert
27 More, in music
29 Big fish, to a fisherman
31 Paleontologist's discovery
32 Frat party detritus
34 The passive voice ___
38 Agcy. once involved with fallout shelters
40 Carrier with HQ in Tokyo
41 Gift on "The Bachelor"
42 N.F.L. linemen: Abbr.
43 Ambiguity ___
49 Trip planning org.
51 Pub order, maybe
52 Rhetorical questions . . . ___
57 Fantastic
58 Author's desire
59 Pope after John X
60 Org. that rates members of Cong.
61 C-worthy
64 Cold capital
66 Latin foot
67 Meshlike
70 ___ Life ("Porgy and Bess" character)
74 1997 title role for Demi Moore
77 Subject-verb agreement ___
79 One in the fast lane?
81 Deface
82 Contractions ___
84 Show whose theme song is "Who Are You"
86 Shortstop Chacon of the 1962 Mets
88 Malodourous room?
89 84-Across airer
90 Prepositions are not good ___
97 Sad poets
98 Creator of "All in the Family"
99 Mule alternative
103 Outworn
104 Scratch (out)
105 Not much
106 Daydreaming, say
108 Word said with a salute
109 Exaggeration is among the ___
114 Put back at zero
115 Ticked
116 Toughened
117 Macho types
118 Proceed slowly
119 Reporter's purchase

DOWN

1 Vacuuming, e.g.
2 Setter
3 Perspectives
4 Comeback
5 Adviser of Capt. Picard on "Star Trek: T.N.G."
6 When to call, in some ads
7 M.L.K. Jr., e.g.
8 Seat of power
9 Inexpensive place to stay
10 Brand in a can
11 Bus. card info
12 Ahead
13 Bistro, informally
14 "I don't like it"
15 Overlook, as someone's weaknesses
16 Fine furs
17 Steadfast
20 Bowl-shaped pan
21 They may be stroked
22 Receipt listings
28 Mt. Rushmore State sch.
30 Apparel company Evan-___
31 Round end?
32 Part of a talk show staff
33 Work for a museum
35 Spanish eyes
36 Restaurant waiting areas
37 Lecture badly
38 In pieces
39 Abu Dhabi, e.g.
43 Creature in a Tennessee Williams title
44 Cellular stuff
45 Elusive swimmers
46 Member of the flock
47 Doo-wop syllable
48 Piece of property
50 Communication for the deaf: Abbr.
53 Night school subj.
54 Not hoof it, perhaps
55 Planes
56 Lowest state?
58 Tree trauma
62 Jardin zoológico attraction
63 Trainers treat them
65 Meanie
68 Comic's asset
69 Singer Sumac
71 "The Facts of Life" actress
72 Spike TV, formerly
73 Cousin ___ of "The Addams Family"
75 Collection agcy.
76 Heifetz heard at Carnegie Hall
78 Media handouts
79 Big suits
80 "Don't have ___!"
83 Pgh. Pirate, e.g.
84 Nabs
85 Tiny start
87 Wings hit "___ In"
90 Formula One driver Fabi
91 Lost on purpose
92 What a picador pokes
93 Got warm
94 Bad boyfriends
95 "Perhaps"

by Randolph Ross

96 Do some fancy footwork
100 Counterfeited
101 Spotted
102 Hi-___
105 What a soldier shouldn't be
106 "___ Angel" (Mae West movie)
107 Force
110 Baton Rouge sch.
111 Medium ability?
112 Whip
113 ___ king

ACROSS

1 Country that won its first Olympic medal in 2004
8 1959 Ricky Nelson hit
15 Summons
20 Nay sayers
21 Tennis star Zvereva
22 Essence
23 Shady accountant's April 15 work?
25 Allied (with)
26 Saxophonist Al
27 Racer Al
28 Director of "Chicago" and "Dancin'"
30 Hula hoop
31 Connects with
34 Chinese "way"
36 Smash hits
38 G.R.E. takers
39 Caroler's reward?
44 Kind of D.A.
45 Rolodex no.
46 Pad site
47 Handy-andies
49 Unsmiling
51 Slip in a pot
53 1940's–50's All-Star Johnny
55 Pilot announcements, for short
57 "Little Shop of Horrors" dentist
58 Persistent photographers?
61 Sorority letters
63 Main entrances?
65 Wisecracker
66 Analyze
68 Turkey part
69 Mischief makers
73 Deep Throat, e.g.
74 Owls
76 Vandal
77 Comparatively small
79 Late 80's sitcom
80 Unfolding view for a hapless hang glider?
84 Summer cooler
85 Summer coolers
87 Art containing 4-Down
88 Elvis or Madonna
89 Honeyed drink
90 Tens, e.g.
92 Cry of eagerness
94 Et ___ (following)
95 Asunción assent
97 "Faucet drips ahead"?
101 Nutrition info, for short
104 Graffitist's addition to a face
106 Org. that drafts guards
107 School zone requirement
109 Goals in 106-Across, quickly
110 "Cool!"
113 Runner
116 Served past
117 Dull
119 Roller coaster inventor?
123 Top guns
124 Waist reducer, perhaps
125 Current contraption
126 Comic Lewis
127 Sits atop
128 Fancy parties

DOWN

1 Puts out
2 "La Loge" artist
3 Feels irritated
4 Kids' TV staples
5 Like some sleep, for short
6 ". . . ___ he drove out of sight"
7 Not dull
8 "Need You Tonight" group, 1987
9 Weight allowance
10 Catch off-guard
11 Ontario, par exemple
12 Request
13 Dutch filmmaker ___ van Gogh
14 Packs away
15 Old Toyota
16 Jackie's "O"
17 Concern for Rev. Falwell?
18 Gulf State V.I.P.'s
19 Tormentor
24 Soon
29 Sports venue seen from the Grand Central Parkway
32 Twosome
33 King's org.
35 Hairy Halloween costume
37 Fountain order
40 30's migrant
41 M.D.'s who may cure snoring
42 "Got it"
43 Like city land, usually
45 Soldier's helmet, slangily
48 Instruction unit
49 Nutritious nosh
50 Where the ice skater fell?
51 "Evita" narrator
52 English pianist who was made a dame
54 Works of Michelangelo
56 Follow
57 Hold 'em variation
58 Mild cigar
59 Part of the 1992 Olympic Dream Team
60 Knolls
62 Metric measure
64 ". . . and I mean it!"
67 1968 hit with the lyric "I like the way you walk, I like the way you talk"
70 Dr. ___
71 Shoos
72 W.W. II site
75 Projecting part at the foot of a wall
78 Dark time in poetry
81 City south of the Salt River
82 Stylish gown
83 Yearn
86 Get to work on Time?
89 29-Down team
91 One way to turn
93 Rural valleys
94 Liverpool-to-Plymouth dir.
95 Military V.I.P.
96 Halogen salt
98 Comic Don
99 Staff leader
100 Main lines
101 Say poetry, say

SUNDAY

by Ashish Madhukar Vengsarkar

102 Political pundit Myers
103 Puff ___ (Old World menaces)
105 Other side
108 Kitchen implement
111 Way off
112 Yarn

114 Chocolaty treat
115 No-no on office computers
118 Salt
120 Plenty steamed, with "up"
121 Wellness grp.
122 Recording giant

ACROSS

1 Professional bouncers' org.
5 "Chicago" star, 2002
9 Ne plus ultra
13 Significance
19 Omelette ingredient
20 Lena of "Havana"
21 Gymnast's worry
22 Charlotte ___, Virgin Islands
23 Rabbit cliques?
26 "Phèdre" playwright
27 Caffeine-free drink
28 Foreign title of respect
29 Poker prize
30 Elect
31 "The Godfather" actor
33 Word before "dear" or "sir"
35 Parenting author Eda
37 Training with building strips?
40 Ex followers
44 Desktop feature
46 "Scram!"
47 Prairies
48 ___-kiri
49 Old troupe member
52 Dr.'s order?
53 Autobiographer of "Speak, Memory," 1951
55 Did lunch, say
56 Extreme admirer of a Poe poem?
60 "Oh, really?"
61 Way to address a sweetheart
63 Saturn model
64 Saturn model
65 More fitting
66 Closet feature
69 Spacecraft that began orbiting Saturn in 2004
71 "This time ___ me"
74 Basis of illegal discrimination
75 Disperse, with "out"
76 Driving a nail obliquely
80 1953 film or the last word spoken in it
81 Pics featured at Dollywood?
85 "." follower
86 Certain NASA craft
88 According to
89 Pharmaceutical plant
91 1947 romantic comedy "The Egg ___"
92 Times up
95 National League city: Abbr.
96 Rug source
97 Imbroglio
98 Fees for removing dead animals?
102 Not caring anymore
104 Site for 125-Across, with "the"
105 Sleep: Prefix
106 Money may be held in this
109 Prefix with system
111 Speed
113 He was cast into the lion's den by Nebuchadnezzar
117 Bowls
118 Permit from the Nuclear Regulatory Commission?
121 Very much
122 Within: Prefix
123 Gunfight time, maybe
124 Concessions
125 Performances at 104-Across
126 Saxophone, e.g.
127 Bygone fliers
128 Graceful fliers

DOWN

1 Blows away
2 Tide type
3 Vice president under Jefferson
4 Just over 6% of U.S. immigrants nowadays
5 Attacked
6 Trickster
7 Shore indentations
8 Make secret
9 "___ was saying . . ."
10 Walking sound
11 Olympus competitor
12 Brian who managed the Beatles
13 Italian noblewoman
14 Creighton University site
15 Cry of joy in Georgia?
16 Bush and Kerry, once
17 Small square
18 Adolescent
24 Conseil d'___
25 Class
32 Israeli desert
34 Author Rushdie
36 Wall fixtures
37 Filleted
38 West ___ virus
39 Ones sharing a crest
41 Siberian people
42 Weaken
43 Relish
44 Prayer leader
45 Washington or Madison
50 Apprentice
51 "Bloody"
52 One way to have gone
54 Close
57 Warmer and sunnier
58 Several czars
59 Part of the E.U.: Abbr.
62 Commotion at an English school?
67 Tupac, for one
68 Turkish title
69 Marriage site in a Veronese painting
70 "Sock ___ me!"
71 Submission, literally
72 Feudal aristocrat
73 Bygone Las Vegas hotel
75 ___ Prison, setting for the 1979 film "Jericho Mile"
77 Ones who take the cake?
78 "A Doll's House" wife
79 Fed
82 Comical Jacques
83 "Hell ___ no fury . . ."
84 Southwestern crocks
87 Harness tracks
90 Like some waltzes
93 Intelligence officer, at times
94 Classy French theater
95 Behavior
99 ___ Corp., former name for Royal Crown Cola
100 "The Thinker" and "The Kiss," e.g.

SUNDAY

by Daniel C. Bryant

101 Auto financing co.
103 "There!"
106 Old station name
107 Period in English literature
108 Kind of package
110 Bone: Prefix
112 Slaughter in Cooperstown
114 "___ out?"
115 ___ Zone
116 Minus
119 It has roots
120 Builder's purchase

ACROSS

1 Item on a chain
7 Deep water
14 Microwaveable lunch sandwich
18 3½ million square mile expanse
19 Lapse
20 Antarctica's Prince ___ Coast
21 Diethyl ether, to butanol
22 Medium, maybe
23 Bone: Prefix
24 Whizzes (by)
25 "Go!"
26 Prepare, as leftovers
28 Authorize
30 Renaissance family name
31 Playground retort
32 ___ given
34 1998 British Petroleum acquisition
36 It has frozen assets
42 Constellation next to Telescopium
43 1969 N.H.L. M.V.P., familiarly
47 Tree with pods
48 Undo, as binder rings
51 Hua's predecessor as Chinese premier
52 Many
54 Starting
55 Recliner feature
57 Brand X
59 Hit, in Variety slang
61 Not far from
62 Bit of editing
64 Big name in construction
66 One making calls
67 Powerful handheld electronic devices
70 Game played on a 49-Down
72 Avalanche victim's salvation
73 Spectra maker
74 Radiate
75 Popular candy since the 1780's
77 Like King Gyanendra
79 "Quién ___?"
81 "Aha!"
85 Place to see a camel
87 Scandal
89 Must
90 Spore producer
91 Aunt Chloe's husband, in literature
94 Ethelbert who composed "Mighty Lak' a Rose"
95 Classic brand whose symbol is a tiger
96 "___ bad"
97 Kitchen fixture
99 "Understand?"
101 O's predecessors
102 Simple itinerary destination
106 Interstate sign
109 Old 280Z's and 280ZX's
115 Covered
116 Temperatures
118 Capital that's the home of Lenin Park
119 Distant
120 Lecture
122 Blasted, with "at"
123 See 103-Down
124 Exposed to oxygen
125 Object in le ciel
126 Subtle thieves
127 Big fish, say
128 Lint collector?

DOWN

1 Miniature
2 Had a base in baseball
3 "What ___ !"
4 1960's singer Terrell
5 Procter & Gamble brand
6 Laugh sound
7 Vintner's prefix
8 Turn out
9 Some Art Deco works
10 Tokyo airport
11 Road atlas part
12 Port. is part of it
13 Language that favors "sedans" to "saloons"
14 To-do
15 Half of a 1930's vaudeville duo
16 Byes
17 Presidential prerogative
25 Mojave Desert vista
27 Green: Prefix
29 Family pooch
33 Actress Karina who played Scheherazade
35 City SSW of Moscow
36 Heroin, slangily
37 Anemic-looking
38 Coll. major
39 Judges
40 Longtime Lone Ranger player
41 Old section in Algiers
43 Prophet who led Jews back to Jerusalem
44 L.P.G.A. star ___ Turner
45 Campaign need
46 Like some expenses
49 Image this puzzle grid is supposed to suggest
50 Mistaken
53 Quick timeout
56 Prefix with centric
58 Early second-century year
60 Lacking sparkle
63 Cpls.' superiors
65 Morlocks' prey in "The Time Machine"
67 Handy-dandy tool
68 Shares
69 Tricks
71 Farm cries
72 Complimentary closing
74 Roth who directed the 2005 horror flick "Hostel"
76 Silas ___, emissary of the Continental Congress to France
78 River to the Ligurian Sea
80 Half of a noted 1955 merger: Abbr.
82 River that flows by the Hermitage
83 Suffix with neur-
84 Overstudious sort
86 Rope expert's favorite radio station?
88 Poet who wrote "To err is human . . ."
92 Do
93 Smart set?
98 Org. for Va., but not Md.
99 Sporty Pontiac
100 Kicker's aid
102 "Fingersmith"
103 With 123-Across, pleading, perhaps

by Michael Shteyman

104 Lazybones
105 Lymphatic system parts
107 Like quaking aspen leaves
108 Stop
110 Angle denoter, in math
111 Permanent site?

112 Pitch-black
113 Seasonal music
114 Start of 67-Across or end of 72-Across, literally
117 Some roulette bets
121 Low mark
122 Rural affirmative

ACROSS

1 Military academy freshman
6 Cowbell sound
11 Fingerboard ridge
15 Weaken
18 "___ Gets Drafted" (1942 Disney cartoon)
20 Much-climbed Alpine peak
21 Actor Jared
22 Hamas rival grp.
23 California, compared to Kansas?
25 Kiss
27 Call's companion
28 ___ Ark
29 ___ polloi
30 Jeweler's unit
31 Tweak
33 Silk undies, compared to cotton undies?
37 White-collar worker?
39 Dance to 1920's–40's jazz
40 Big time
41 "We've been ___!"
42 1990's sitcom based on the British series "One Foot in the Grave"
45 Having seniority
47 Claim valuables
51 Strong suit
52 A waistcoat worn in summer, compared to one worn in winter?
54 In addition
56 Subject in religion class
58 Hero of Tom Clancy novels
59 Jai alai basket
60 Some H.S. math
61 Clinton cabinet member Hazel

63 Dolly of Dollywood
64 Naval base?
65 A one-milligram tablet, compared to a five-milligram tablet?
70 Employee of M
71 Chevrolet sedan
73 Land created by C. S. Lewis
74 "QB VII" novelist
75 Froth
76 Small indentation
80 Go ___ length
81 Formal vote
82 Potatoes and cucumbers, compared to apples and eggplants?
85 Rows on a calendar page
87 Actor Omar of TV's "House"
88 Hang it up
89 1996 Olympic gymnast Strug
90 Spoon-___
93 ___-pitch
94 Tribe of the Amistad slaves
96 Intense, as a gaze
98 Dog show winners, compared to dog show also-rans?
105 Africa's largest country
106 Benefit
107 Wise actions
108 Get the better of
110 Novelist Jaffe
111 Measureless
113 SpongeBob SquarePants's pants, compared to Humpty Dumpty's?
116 Dead heat
117 Stylist's creation
118 Cliff's edge
119 Pass on

120 Airport checkpoint needs
121 Palindromic girl's name
122 Napster downloads
123 Some Southwest scenery

DOWN

1 Pseudonym of musician Peter Schickele
2 Gossipy Parsons
3 Passed
4 Televangelist paroled in 1993
5 Priest in 1 Samuel
6 French film award
7 How ballerinas dance
8 Tennis star with a shaved head
9 Human cannonball's destination
10 Test for M.A. seekers
11 Elevator stop
12 Is an integral part of
13 "You know the rest" abbr.
14 Bird on a Kellogg's Froot Loops box
15 Slash on a scorepad
16 Here comes the bride
17 They're "born, not made," according to an old saying
19 TV room
24 Pistol, slangily
26 Scientist's formulation
29 Prime
32 Puerto ___
34 Winter blanket
35 Do-nothing
36 Fixed course

38 Spanish city where Seneca was born
43 Pricey vodka, for short
44 Produce
46 H, in Hellas
47 Goes on a spending spree
48 Fix up
49 Where kroons are spent
50 Doesn't take a hit
51 Low-aimed headlights
52 Bollywood film costume
53 Camcorder brand
54 Fabricate
55 Crankcase device
57 One sitting on the porch
60 Pyramus's lover, in myth
62 Hunger
63 Actors or athletes
66 "Darn!"
67 Tennis club teacher
68 Stupefied
69 Protective covering
72 Hawaiian band?
76 Fate
77 Natl. Adopt-a-Dog Mo.
78 Hampers
79 "M*A*S*H" setting
83 ___ Stanley Gardner
84 Colonial ___ (insurance firm)
86 Litter contents
89 Banshee sound
90 Zoot suit hats
91 Hyundai model
92 Rulers who inherit their power
93 Flint is a form of it
95 Toxic compound found in cigarette smoke

SUNDAY

by Patrick Berry

97 "When Paris
sneezes, ____
catches cold"
98 Leafless plants
99 Like planetary
orbits
100 Attorney's
workload

101 Kipling novel
about an
orphan boy
102 Musical syllables
103 Vichyssoise
vegetables
104 California's
Big ____

109 Abbr. on a
boiler's gauge
112 Yardbird
113 Air rifle ammo
114 It's sought by
conquistadores
115 "That's
curious . . ."

ACROSS

1 Mistress of the spirit world?
8 Was an Orly arrival?
14 "The Old Man and the Sea" catch
20 Handles differently?
21 Historic Honolulu palace
22 Beethoven symphony
23 Writer Fleming as a two-year-old?
25 Ibsen's "Hedda ___"
26 Ring count
27 Sweet 16 org.
28 Yevtushenko poem
29 Shark pools?
30 J.F.K. advisory
32 Playground retort
34 Scrubbed
35 Puzzling
36 Scotland?
41 Sprinkling
42 Talk like a baby
43 "Winnie-the-Pooh" baby
44 Estrous
46 Picture on a $5,000 bill
50 Country with a pentagonal flag
54 View
57 Onetime capital of India
58 One lacking bucks?
61 Austin of TV's "Knots Landing"
62 Actress Meyers
63 Game sometimes called "bucking the tiger"
64 French entree
65 Unwelcome twist
67 Far from loaded
69 Burdensome bird
73 Prepares for a Masters?
74 Lose track?
76 It may need a big jacket
77 Cartoonist Addams
79 Wasted
80 Frost lines
81 Bar owner's job on "The Simpsons"?
85 Prefix with -gon
86 Catalan is its official language
88 Fast ___ Felson, real-life hustler portrayed in "The Hustler"
89 Mister
91 Release
93 With 107-Down, Westerner with an oxymoronic-sounding name buried on Boot Hill
95 Forever and a day
96 Doctor's bag?
98 Guillotine?
103 Heads overseas?
106 Mine transport
108 Flambé
109 Take the course
110 ___ Tzu (dog)
111 Well-armed predator?
114 You can be in it and out of it at the same time
116 Indo-Iranian language
119 John Glenn, e.g.
120 Warning on court testimony?
122 "Star Trek: T.N.G." engineer
123 It was named for the infant Jesus
124 Playroom threat
125 One of the Gallo brothers
126 Actress who starred in two Hitchcock films
127 Emergency situation

DOWN

1 Bach bit
2 Listed
3 The Muses, e.g.
4 40, 60, 75 or 100, commonly
5 Chat room initialism
6 Stocking stuffers
7 Treasure
8 Oregon's state tree
9 Desolate
10 Provoke
11 Part of the Illinois/Indiana border
12 Arriving home after curfew
13 "When Schweine fly!"
14 Prefix with millions
15 ___-American
16 Early bird
17 Comedian Tomlin as a bowler?
18 The Pleistocene Epoch, familiarly
19 Shoe specification
24 Door sign
28 Ape's home
31 "One never knows, ___?": Fats Waller
33 Robe fastener
36 Jolly sounds
37 Alley Oop's girlfriend
38 Grendel and Beowulf
39 W. C. Fields affirmative
40 Special request at a shoe store
42 9/11 Commission subj.
45 Nolan Ryan, for most of the 80's
46 The folks
47 Mutually approve
48 Course for a Maytag repairman?
49 Mrs. James Joyce
51 Foreshadow
52 Marc Antony's love
53 Jared of "Panic Room"
55 Opening
56 Sheriff's badge in the Old West
59 Nick name?
60 Hustler's hangout?
63 Just so you know
66 Some film ratings
68 Devoted friend of Greek legend
70 Shade of white
71 In the heart of
72 The Beatles' "___ Leaving Home"
75 Old global positioning system
78 Destination in the movie "Dumb and Dumber"
82 Bearcats
83 Coolidge Dam river
84 Rodents, playfully
85 Judo ranking
87 Baseball scorecard letters
90 Certain buck
92 Distinction, slangily
94 Tenuous
96 Second fiddle
97 Bow pro
99 Cartoonist Hollander
100 Pulverized
101 Moss Hart's "Act One," e.g.
102 Biased writing?

SUNDAY

by Bob Klahn

103 Kvetch
104 There's simply no end to it
105 Ozone layer, for one
107 See 93-Across
110 Clobbered
112 Launch sites . . . or crash sites
113 Complex part?
115 Tyler who wrote "Breathing Lessons"
117 Storage space
118 Didn't break
120 Mumbled assent
121 Chaney Sr. or Jr.

ACROSS

1 Cab Calloway catchphrase
7 Another time
14 Deep-sea diver's worry
22 Tiger cat
23 Not your normal imports
24 After-tax investment choices
25 Elevators . . .
27 Deferential
28 Bar in court
29 Sounds at doctors' checkups
30 Reduced by
32 Owner of the History Channel
33 Dumb bunny
35 Diet centers . . .
40 N.Y.U., e.g.
43 Harbor tower
44 ___ test, given to newborn babies
45 Plains tribe
46 Anvils . . .
49 Mice and men, e.g.
54 Pop singer Lavigne
55 Media of exchange
57 Stable baby
59 Cut for a column
60 Settle, for one
61 ___ example
63 Short dash
65 Bride, in Bari
66 Caterpillars . . .
70 Guillotines . . .
72 Paris-to-Lyon dir.
73 Study grant named for a senator
74 Outburst from Homer
76 Ottoman governor
77 Overdoes it
78 Very cool, in 50's slang, with "the"
79 Patio grills . . .

81 Two caliphs
82 Like Sartre's "No Exit"
85 Part of the W. Coast
86 Peace, to Pedro
87 Spanish snack
88 Dernier ___
91 Pace cars . . .
94 Nails . . .
97 Brewery fixtures
98 Make like crazy
100 Department that is home to the Parc Astérix amusement park
101 ___ speak
102 Hilarity
103 Embargoes
104 "Ecce homo" utterer
107 Computer acronym
108 Chews out
110 Real estate developers . . .
113 Minotaur's home
116 Utah lilies
117 NASA vehicle
118 Saint, in Portuguese
119 Cattle . . .
124 "La classe de ___" (Degas work)
126 Make disappear
127 Folk tales
128 Singer Anderson of Jethro Tull
129 Ford competitor, although not in autos
133 Hitchcock specialty
136 Freight trains . . .
141 Boarding school crowd
142 First name in popcorn
143 Typical downtown sign
144 Rasta's messiah
145 African pests
146 Runners' aids

DOWN

1 Julia ___, first woman elected to the American Academy of Arts and Letters
2 Cold treats
3 Ding
4 John of pop
5 Place to wear a gown
6 Polo Grounds slugger
7 Longtime Vermont senator
8 ___ of Evil
9 Dress (up)
10 Biblical verb ending
11 Slowing, in music: Abbr.
12 Visual
13 Barbers brush them
14 "To your health!"
15 Burgle
16 Monet's "Vétheuil en ___"
17 Alternative to reflexology
18 Rough rug fiber
19 Heavens: Prefix
20 Shoemakers' strips
21 Opera singer Simon ___
26 A to Z, e.g.
31 ___-mo
34 Center
35 Self-serving slant
36 Lambs: Latin
37 Conducts
38 Cheer at Gillette Stadium
39 It may be raised at a party
40 Equilibrium
41 Inquisition targets
42 "Dulce et decorum est pro patria mori" writer
44 Make up (for)
47 Friends and neighbors

48 Menotti opera character
50 Prints
51 Pass
52 Stocking material
53 Collar inserts
56 Tanning lotion letters
57 Seafood entree
58 "Members ___"
61 Carol starter
62 Highway department supply
64 Nixon friend Bebe
65 Dr. Seuss's green eggs and ham offerer
67 Times to remember
68 Nutrition author Davis
69 Palme ___ (Cannes award)
71 "S.O.S.!"
75 With it, once
78 Fisher-Price's owner
79 Goes on strike, informally
80 Unlikely pageant winner
81 Penlight batteries
82 Science
83 Author Zora ___ Hurston
84 Son of Henry and father of Henry II
85 Scott of "Ocean's Eleven," 2001
87 Last president of South Vietnam
88 Orangish yellow
89 Acne cream ingredient
90 Enthusiastic assent
92 Violent, perhaps
93 Poodle's cry
95 Hauls around
96 Canadian pump name
99 Bruce of old films
103 Prepared to streak
105 Italy's ___ di Garda
106 State categorically

SUNDAY

by Paula Gamache

107 Frequent subject of government approval
109 Hauls around
111 Dallas suburb
112 Mil. commander
114 "Thy Neighbor's Wife" author
115 Rock's Brian

116 Says with a raised hand
119 Godfather's utterances
120 Habituate
121 Photographer Adams
122 Soho serving
123 Grain disease
124 French face cards

125 Counting word
128 Asleep, say
130 Mount SW of Messina
131 ___ Belt
132 CPR pros
134 Serbian city, birthplace of Constantine the Great

135 Six, in Siena
137 "___ had it!"
138 Minor carp
139 Noisy rollers
140 250th anniversary of the incorporation of Los Angeles

ACROSS

1 Berates
8 Customary manner of doing things
13 Orbital extremes
20 City near Fort Roberdeau
21 Smooths
22 Live it up
23 Tornado abhorrence?
25 Nice 'n Easy maker
26 "___ Isn't So" (Hall & Oates hit)
27 Merry-go-round music
28 Change, chemically
29 Where a prince might work at a hospital?
37 Sounds of understanding
40 These, in Madrid
41 Thicket
42 Mekong River land
43 Never
45 Swabs
47 Foreign, to an American, briefly
48 Lesson from Jack Nicklaus?
51 Cargo on the ill-fated Edmund Fitzgerald
53 Close
54 Nike competitor
55 Fakes it
56 Plunder
57 Road warnings
59 Met highlights
60 Homily about gymnastics?
66 Dye-yielding shrubs
67 Oozes
68 Ballet move
70 Forsaker of the faith
74 "___ here"
75 "Peter Pan" dog
76 Users of barbells, e.g.
77 Losers on "The Apprentice"?
82 Coin words
83 Brings in
84 Wore
85 Onslaught of cold weather
86 Kind of princess
88 K. T. of country music
90 Cockney residence
91 Place for unhappy diners?
96 Schools for engrs.
97 Greek theaters
98 Represent
102 Recent reputed spy organization scandal
105 Red Cross sales strategy?
109 Like a size 8 blouse vis-à-vis a size 10
110 "It's déjà vu all over again" speaker
111 Capitol feature
112 Anarchists, sometimes
113 Fresh
114 Extreme joy

DOWN

1 Dosage units
2 Inter ___
3 Tiny, informally
4 This makes sense
5 Boston area, with "the"
6 Response: Abbr.
7 Make lace
8 Goes up against
9 Grammy winner Lou
10 Disciple's query
11 Cariou of Broadway
12 Dropped stuff
13 Entry
14 Camelot sight
15 Spinachlike plant
16 Solo
17 Where Lux. is
18 Inner: Prefix
19 French seasoning
24 Spicy stew
28 Tears
30 Fungal spore sacs
31 Numbered rds.
32 Mark Harmon action drama
33 Ninny
34 Babbled
35 Noggin
36 Tough turns
37 Uneasiness
38 Uproars
39 "The beloved physician"
44 More frequently, old-style
45 One of five
46 Makes a mess of
47 "Untrue!"
49 King of music
50 Pizza places
51 Maya Angelou's "And Still ___"
52 Opens up a hole in
55 Self-congratulated
57 Deep-sea fishing aid
58 Some O.K.'s, for short
59 "What ___!" (famed Bette Davis line)
61 Defeated, in a way
62 Boards
63 Cousin of radial
64 Close by
65 Two-seater
69 ___ basque (dance step)
70 Elite
71 Feather, zoologically
72 Gift ___
73 Traffic control
77 Actress Garr
78 They can be caught at the beach
79 Vacation destination
80 Political slant
81 Spies' info
83 Relieves (of)
86 Nourish
87 Dessert, in Dover
88 Sometime in the future
89 Native South African village
92 Related on a mother's side
93 Maker of Zima and Killian's Irish Red
94 Locker room emanations

Sunday

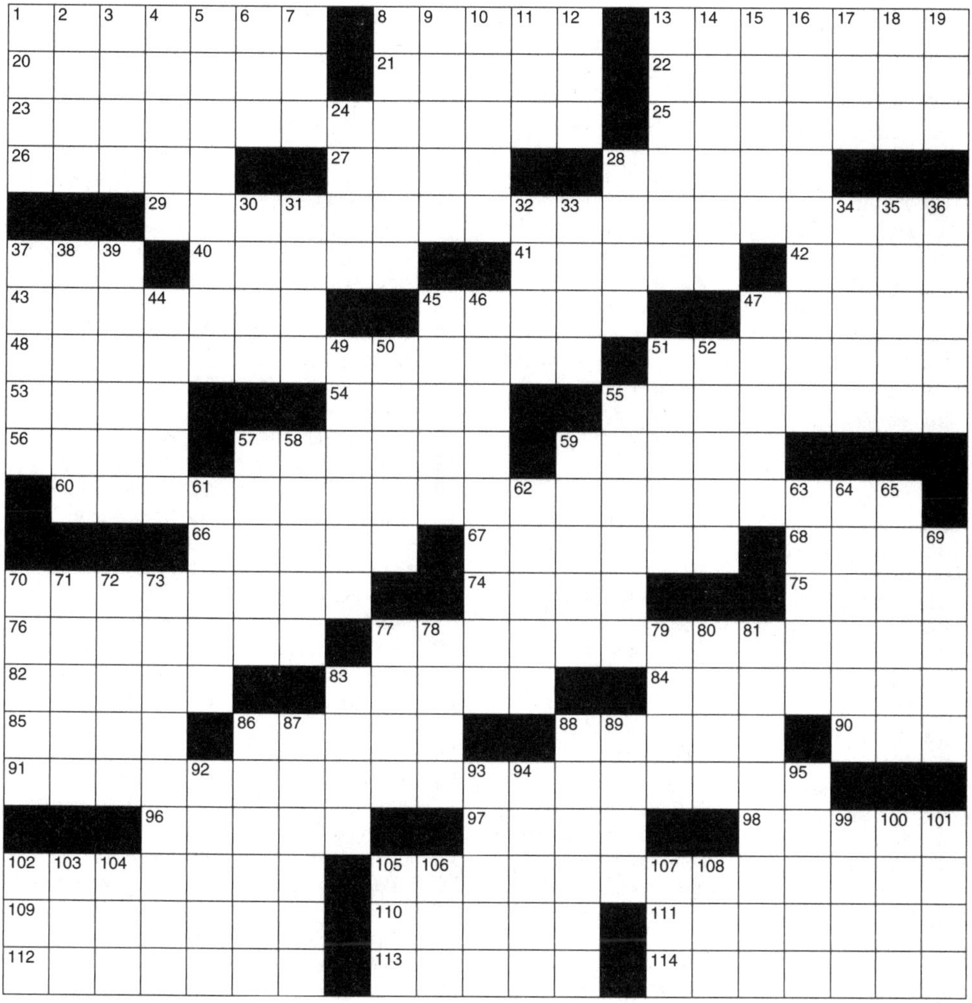

by Mike Torch

95 Recon, perhaps
99 Kind of steak
100 Added conditions
101 "Don't go!"
102 Municipal facility: Abbr.
103 The "Rocky" film with Mr. T
104 In the past
105 Kids' ammo
106 Grazing area
107 Anger
108 Assn.

ACROSS

1 Picks up
6 Sea lettuce, e.g.
10 Wide open
15 15-Down rival, once
19 Taxing time
20 Attends
21 They're towed away
22 See 98-Across
23 Footwear eaten by an animal?
26 Tumults
27 Page
28 Instant
29 General ___ chicken
31 Old-time welcome
32 Clue that helped convict a movie snack thief?
38 Wretched
39 Get all lovey-dovey
40 Police car maneuver, slangily
41 Cell, e.g.
42 Like the ans. to this clue
43 One in a six-pack
44 N.Y.S.E. and Nasdaq, e.g.
46 Like some fishing hooks
48 Stubborn person getting on another's nerves?
53 Black
54 ___ weight
55 Built
56 Weed
59 Went after
61 Shot up
62 Rub the wrong way
63 Home to some Mongolian nomads
64 Thug whose books aren't selling?
68 Dust Bowl refugee
69 Mitsubishi competitor
70 Vandals
71 Famed Georgia football coach Vince
72 Sparkle
73 Tuna salad ingredient
74 River isles
75 Thick
76 Nicholson negotiating with Stiller and Affleck?
81 Less than explanatory parental explanation
84 Bowls over
85 H.S. class
86 Call from a meadow
87 Cousin of a cobra
88 It must be in the genes
89 B. A. Baracas portrayer on TV
90 Starting to get blue?
92 Supreme rulers blow up a major hardware store?
98 With 22-Across, movie hero of 1977
99 Hot
100 Mortar mixer
101 Acute
102 Twin sister of Ares
104 Cousins of a disheveled wading bird?
111 Going ___
112 Spots on a graph
113 One of the Waughs
114 Priest's urging
115 "Only Time" singer
116 Annual parade honoree, for short
117 Point
118 Sound at the front of East Hampton

DOWN

1 Buddy of the Clintons, e.g.
2 Apple had one in 1980: Abbr.
3 Funky do
4 Called
5 Due for a drop-off?
6 "Like that matters"
7 Actor Cariou
8 Bugs
9 Leftovers at a barbecue
10 Hedge fund whiz, for short
11 "Whaddaya know"
12 What two palms up may indicate
13 Hoop star's entourage
14 Prevent
15 Traditional Olympics powerhouse
16 Sugary quaff
17 Eastern European
18 Like some provocatively colored lips
24 Pencil holder
25 System start-up?
30 William Styron title heroine
32 Kind of support
33 "This should get you started . . ."
34 Unelite, in London
35 Eccentric
36 Singer/radio host John
37 "___ Lap" (1983 film)
38 Did nothing
43 They don't provide outlets
44 Stuck
45 Be acquainted with Vanna?
46 Diplomat Boutros Boutros-___
47 Tear-jerkers often have one
49 Try
50 Biblical shepherd
51 Shepherd's concern
52 Radiates
56 It has six holes
57 Peter and the Wolf's "duck"
58 Like some sums
59 Horse sound
60 Long walk
61 Andrea Doria's domain
62 Wash out
63 Write (for)
65 Columnist Mike
66 ___ Chris Steak House (restaurant chain)
67 Saturn and Mercury, for two
73 House keepers
74 Negative campaign feature
75 Water, perhaps
76 Be in harmony
77 Billionth: Prefix
78 Intruder's deterrent, maybe
79 Chaps
80 Starr of song
81 "Count me in"
82 Arid
83 Extra
88 Dusty floor cleaner
89 Breakfast cereal
90 Ungodlike

by Joe DiPietro

91 Must pay
93 Station house figures
94 Jump for joy
95 Ship over there?
96 Show agreement with
97 Pint-sized, downsized
103 Irish ___
105 Elhi org.
106 Mil. transport
107 Knockout of knockouts
108 ___-Tiki
109 Beethoven's "Minuet ___"
110 Once

ACROSS

1 "Exodus" hero
4 Film director Petri
8 "Pow!"
12 Chicago's ___ Aquarium
17 Novel by Toni Morrison
19 Coquette
20 View from Mauna Kea
21 Frighten away
22 Winning it is a sweet victory
25 Many an archaeological site
26 Lock, stock and barrel
27 Overdoes it
28 Eats at home
29 Goes over again
31 River in Irkutsk
32 Meddle
33 Big name in ice cream
34 Cheapskate
36 Latin case
40 Lo-___
41 TV show since 1/6/75
43 Treasury
45 Imported wheels
48 D.C. bigwig
49 "À votre ___!"
50 Signature piece?
51 Emulated a cat burglar
53 West Indies isle
55 Deflected
59 Gradually decline
61 Car wash sight
62 Stern who saved Carnegie Hall
64 Whopper
65 Music producer Brian

66 Add light, or not (and do this 13 more times to solve this puzzle)
69 Ocean State sch.
70 Put down, on the street
71 Gushes forth: Var.
72 Owns
73 Criminal
75 Not in the middle
77 Something's brewing here
80 Accompanies to the airport
81 Film buff's cable choice
82 Nut tree
84 Never, to Mozart
86 Followers: Suffix
87 Sweeping
90 Concealable weapon
93 Prefix with friendly
94 1960's TV western
95 Lowermost ship deck
96 Abbr. in a personal ad
99 Like some student housing
102 Subject of a May tribute
104 License
106 Bad state to be in
107 Security holder
110 Bacteriologist's study
111 Sound of a willow in the wind
112 End-of-meal serving
114 More beloved
115 Make up for
116 Needlepoint shop purchase

117 One of two bath towels
118 Popular mixer maker
119 Commuter map points: Abbr.
120 Some 20th-century art
121 Aug. clock setting

DOWN

1 Have big plans (to)
2 Like an imploded soufflé
3 "Well, here goes . . ."
4 Personifies
5 Lucy of "Ally McBeal"
6 Regarding, to counsel
7 Deafening silence, e.g.
8 "Bummer!"
9 Word just before a snap
10 Orders at McSorley's
11 Skylight?
12 Barely enough
13 More strapping
14 Elimination
15 Judge
16 Quality of cooking
18 Spiky plant
21 Resoluteness
23 Hospital danger
24 ___ choy (Chinese vegetable)
28 Intentional loss, in boxing
30 Trapshooting
35 Where gringos live
37 "___ cost to you"
38 King in 1922 news
39 Follower of Paul?

41 Use a towel
42 Show Me State river
43 Pieces of cake
44 How Elvis albums are rereleased
45 Followed, as advice
46 Pertaining to element 92
47 Boot out
50 Statue of Liberty attraction
52 "I'm not making this up!"
54 Skeptics' remarks
55 Corpulent
56 Dodges
57 Most hopeless
58 Little-used clubs
60 How many magazine articles are written
62 "As ___ saying . . ."
63 "Yes sir!," south of the border
67 Land on the other side of the Atl.
68 Figures in Iranian history
74 "No, mein Herr"
76 Badger
77 Shepherd
78 Commerce department staffers
79 "The Da Vinci Code," e.g.
82 High jump need
83 Collie's charge
85 "I" trouble
87 "Portrait of a Musician" artist, familiarly
88 Earns over time
89 Loudly enjoys, as a joke

SUNDAY

by Elizabeth C. Gorski

90 Freshness
91 Hit one out of the park
92 Raised
94 Siren
96 Reacted to a heartthrob
97 Works of artist Max
98 Least restricted
100 Oxford measure
101 Needing more sun
103 Hurrah for El Farruco
105 N.Y. Philharmonic, e.g.
107 Trump
108 Voyaging
109 Singer James
112 Gets into
113 Place for a meeting: Abbr.

ACROSS

1 Long narrative poem
7 Outlaw Kelly
10 Uses a ring, maybe
17 Camp Pendleton group
19 Summer treats
21 Brand of sports drink
22 Long time that just flies by?
24 An Easter egg hunt may have one
25 Long bones
26 Nickname of a boxer who converted to Islam?
28 Board member: Abbr.
29 3 for 2 and 4: Abbr.
30 A camera may be set on this
31 Matter to the jury
32 Mao's grp.
33 Wing, say
36 Supermarket checkout action
39 It gets in the groove
42 Bee product?
47 Befalls
50 Enjoys a hammock
51 Slip into
52 Whom bouncers might bounce
53 Law firm aide, for short
54 Not just approximately
55 Conventioneers' place
57 Duo that might review films based on arcade games?
62 In a workable manner
67 Most fibrous
68 Like some siblings
69 Water color
70 Ticks off
71 What King Arthur's men would like to have seen more of along the way?
73 Offensive basketball position
75 Where a haircut may end
76 Claim of a sort
77 ___ for the long haul
81 Don't chug
82 Stage after pupation
84 Monte ___
86 "Therefore, I have proven the existence of jalapeños!"?
90 With 40-Down, a 1975 horror novel
91 Some crockery
92 Director's second try
96 1940's spy grp.
97 Sound made with outstretched neck
99 Rings of islands
101 O.A.S. member: Abbr.
102 Sitarist Shankar
104 Grizzlies who give great interviews?
108 Movie with a posse
110 Photographer's setting
112 Possible response to "My boss is leaving and I hate his replacement"?
114 Fitting into a joint
115 Phrase usually before a colon
116 1972 U.S. Open champion
117 Stew
118 Cartoonist Avery
119 Got behind, with "for"

DOWN

1 Printer's unit
2 Pope of 1963–78
3 Rubber gaskets
4 Printer's unit
5 Speed-skating gold medalist Karin
6 Common Market letters
7 Angina treatment, for short
8 O.A.S. member: Abbr.
9 "Citizen Ruth" actress, 1996
10 Senators' wear
11 "Trainspotting" star Bremner
12 Short-finned ___
13 Uncommon delivery
14 It's used with some frequency
15 Singer Brickell
16 Where scenes are seen
18 Title with a number, perhaps
20 Heroine of TV's "Alias," for short
21 Cut back
23 Kook
27 Brunch buffet items
30 Father-and-daughter fighters
32 Small brain size
34 Places for fish
35 Forest sticker
36 Part of a heartbeat
37 Cool ___
38 Stubborn one
39 Where God sent Jonah
40 See 90-Across
41 Officer with a half-inch stripe: Abbr.
43 Stepped
44 Substantiate
45 Outhouse issue
46 Simple bunk
47 Part of "The Alphabet Song"
48 Italian-born explorer of the New World
49 Blintz relative
54 Destructive stuff
55 Grass and such
56 Disbeliever's cry
58 Sub
59 Hockey stat
60 Mag. staff
61 Grabs some chow?
63 Put a stop to
64 King Louis XII's birthplace
65 "Network" director, 1976
66 Kind of question
69 Sault ___ Marie
71 Letter before resh
72 Each
74 Trader ___
77 Test results, sometimes
78 United Feature Synd. partner
79 Warm assent
80 Joan Collins's villain on "Batman"
82 U.N. agcy.
83 With, in Wiesbaden
84 Non-dean's list grades
85 Reading and the like: Abbr.
87 Chanted sounds
88 Device with a scroll wheel
89 Con junction
93 Surpass in gluttony
94 Ominous-sounding phrase
95 Put down roots?
97 Reims's department
98 Universal donor blood type, for short

SUNDAY

by Trip Payne

99 Skintight material
100 Tomfool finish
102 Hindu avatar
103 Fat as ___
104 Classroom handout
105 E.P.A. pollution meas.
106 Batter's ploy
107 The Auld Sod
108 "In that range"
109 About
111 Plane heading?
113 Onetime Mideast union: Abbr.

ACROSS

1 White-collar position
7 Big guy
11 "Did you ___?!"
15 Moo goo gai pan pan
18 Sonata movements
19 Not the most reliable set of wheels
20 -
22 Little-known
24 It surrounds the Isle of Man
25 "New Look" pioneer
26 Eastern way
27 Half-German/half-Indian film hero
29 Cymbal in a drum kit
30 -
34 3-D figures
35 "I hope to see London once ___ I die": "Henry IV, Part 2"
36 Cognizance
37 Carnegie's cronies
39 Comment made after jumping in a pool, maybe
42 State strongly
44 Faultfinders
47 Throaty sound
49 Eye sockets
52 Certain ID check
53 Cross shape
54 Obstructor of congress?
57 -
59 ___ Sunday, the fourth Sunday in Lent
60 Farm pitcher
61 "The Time Machine" race
62 Agatha and Dahlia, in P. G. Wodehouse books
63 What this puzzle's circled spaces represent
69 Subject of a Michelangelo sculpture
72 Westminster area
73 L. L. Bean competitor
77 Made fun of, in a way
78 Ring duo
81 -
82 Hairstyling need
83 2000 Elton John/Tim Rice musical
84 Fluoroscope inventor
86 Traditional Christmas Eve meal in Germany
87 Drink served in a tall glass
89 Hoof handlers
92 Rtes.
93 -
97 Startled cry
98 Reuters competitor
100 Refresher
102 Casino fixture
108 Hunter slain by Artemis
109 Gillette brand
110 "What ___ care?"
111 Five or ten, say
112 Unsuccessful, as a mission
114 -
118 Bear in mind
119 Appropriate
120 Blubberless marine mammals
121 Leftmost digital watch no.
122 Recycle bin fillers
123 Tap sites
124 Boon to Scottish tourism

DOWN

1 Fuddy-duddy
2 1998 De Niro thriller
3 Under a false name, briefly
4 -
5 G
6 Sleeping sickness carriers
7 Sports ___
8 Cereal grass
9 Schindler's business partner in "Schindler's List"
10 Sonatas, e.g.
11 Like some mushrooms
12 Florida's ___ Beach
13 "Hostel" director ___ Roth
14 1950 film that retells the same events four times
15 -
16 Mountain nymph
17 "Beauty is truth, truth beauty" writer
19 Potsherds
21 Passed (away)
23 "What nonsense!"
28 Intersected
31 Grp. involved in "the Troubles"
32 Flavor lender
33 Ludicrous
34 M.I.T.'s ___ School of Management
38 Ending with defer or refer
39 "Goldberg Variations" composer
40 Daughter of Uranus
41 Count
43 Super-duper
45 Big ___
46 Appeals to
48 Out of sorts
50 -
51 The place of one's fodder?
52 Does a run
55 Snakes with vestigial limbs
56 Escort's offering
58 Lettuce type
59 Country
62 "Son of ___!"
64 It serves many courses: Abbr.
65 Juicer
66 Former Hong Kong leader Tung ___ Hwa
67 Lacking sense
68 One of the Bobbsey Twins
69 Star followers
70 Group that includes the U.A.E.
71 Picks
74 Girder with flanges
75 It may come with a gift
76 -
78 Render unavailable
79 First of all
80 Molière comedy, with "The"
81 Became an item

SUNDAY

by Patrick Berry

83 -
85 Brother of Ham and Japheth
88 Honored alumni, usually
90 -
91 Rest cure destination
94 Bugs that live in trees
95 Actress Merkel
96 Ancient Turkish dynasty founder
99 Mini-maps
100 Whistle wearer
101 Garden spot
103 Shabby treatment
104 Soirees
105 Pillbox quantities
106 ___ ware (Japanese porcelain)
107 Clipped
109 Hot room, colloquially
113 Gilbert & Sullivan princess
115 Carry with effort
116 Collection agcy.?
117 Took in

ACROSS

1 Codger
5 Mischief maker of myth
9 1945 news, in headlines
14 "Amerika" author
19 Part of the Dept. of Labor
20 Option for heads
21 Indian queen
22 It begins "Sing, goddess, the wrath of Peleus' son . . ."
23 Seasonal salutation
25 "Jeopardy!" phrase
27 Start of quote
29 Column of boxes on a questionnaire
30 Failing grades
31 Shipboard cries
32 Nursery cry
35 Column of boxes on a questionnaire
38 Of a heart chamber
42 New at the beach, maybe
43 Part 2 of quote
49 Very wide spec.
50 Command to a dog
51 -like
52 Geometry figure?
53 Of a certain hydrocarbon group
54 Crew alternative
57 Bombay-born dancer Juliet
59 Lao-tzu follower
62 "The Return of the Jedi" girl
64 Latin 101 verb
65 Montgomery of jazz
68 Part 3 of quote
73 Originally
74 Carry
75 Drug drop, maybe
76 Goolagong of tennis
77 Sight for sore eyes?
79 Capital of Meurthe-et-Moselle, France
82 Trials
83 Like some cats
86 ___ minimum
88 Langston Hughes poem
90 ___ the finish
91 Part 4 of quote
96 Zero
97 Shark, e.g.
98 Postpaid encl.
99 Suffix with lact-
100 Cup holder
102 Alternative to gov or edu
104 Related maternally
108 End of quote
115 Time to grow rice
117 Pictorial
119 Kind of acid
120 Dock site
121 Tongue site
122 Slick
123 Actress Graff
124 Goes a mile a minute
125 Cache contents
126 Fill

DOWN

1 Shipping option, for short
2 Words on a medicine bottle
3 Opposite of hog
4 Closet contents of a 21-Across
5 Trysts
6 Admits, with "up"
7 Acquaintances
8 Very impressed
9 Ray, Klee and Millais
10 Thai money
11 "That's ___ haven't heard!"
12 Willfully tightening the screws, say
13 Calcutta native
14 Wellington natives
15 Architect William van ___
16 Computer protection
17 Chiang ___-shek
18 Pop-ups, e.g.
24 Pad user
26 Slippery
28 Miles away
33 Jai ___
34 Drove
36 1999 Ron Howard comedy
37 Nine inches
39 Robert, for one
40 Police dept. employee
41 Guru habitat
42 Purple shade
43 Colorful wrap
44 Fictional donkey
45 Oliver's love in "As You Like It"
46 "___ the Needle" (1981 movie)
47 Like some acoustic music
48 Composer Mahler
49 Stationery brand
55 Something to pop
56 Nobel-winning economist Lawrence
58 Medical suffix
60 Rodney Dangerfield's "I don't get no respect," e.g.
61 Like the arrangement of gems in some bracelets
63 "The Shelters of Stone" heroine
65 A Ryder
66 The Supreme Court, e.g.
67 View for Shakespeare?
69 Eur. land
70 Undo
71 One of the Gandhis
72 "Holy cow!"
77 Grabber's cry
78 People: Prefix
80 Cig. purchases
81 Film character who says "Do, or do not. There is no 'try' "
83 Fifth-century year
84 2003 A.L. M.V.P., to fans
85 Go-getter
87 1977 double-platinum Steely Dan album
89 Checks out

by Ashish Vengsarkar

92 Exclamation at the end of a trip
93 Résumé parts
94 ___ Mix
95 Actress Zellweger
100 Utah's ___ Canyon
101 Literary inits.
103 Bright circle?
105 Bushes rarely seen nowadays
106 Leg part
107 Glorify
109 "Come ___!"
110 Fall off
111 Madonna's "La ___ Bonita"
112 No bystander
113 Physicist with an element named after him
114 ___ Penh
115 Diamond stat.
116 MSN competitor
118 Burn cause

ACROSS

1 Voyaging
5 Hitchhiker
10 Percentage
15 Somewhat
19 Writes quickly
21 Plaque, e.g.
22 Volcanic formation
23 Show a Woody Allen feature?
25 Heart
26 Mangy mutt
27 Medical research org.
28 Not a substitute
29 Thomas Paine, for one
30 Magazine supply
32 Certain spawner
34 Quick trip
35 Bryologists' study
36 What ageists do?
41 Sad
44 One side in a debate
45 Kung ___ chicken
48 Off the mark
49 Razzes
53 Ties up
55 3.26 light-years
57 Abandon the Centennial State?
59 Sound from a hot tub
60 Yellow flag
61 Env. science
62 Night school subj.
65 Not-so-Big Apple?
72 Lead-in for long
73 Abbr. on an envelope
75 Words of concession
76 Airline abbr.
78 Cut an awful demo?

84 Sot's state
88 Saw
89 Feel extreme discouragement
91 Sports page news
92 Show featuring many alumni of L.A.'s Groundlings comedy troupe
93 Mineral residue
95 Made multiple
97 Drink at a Kyoto reunion?
101 Certain Arab
104 Each
105 Book before Phil.
106 Make a mad dash
110 On the range, say
111 Summertime quaffs
114 Like about half the world's pop.
116 God, in Roma
117 Insipid
118 What a hypnotist might do for help?
121 Construction financed by a hedge fund?
122 Eastern European
123 Happens
124 Tavern selections
125 To the point
126 Köln or Nürnberg
127 Like a spent campfire

DOWN

1 Org. for pound watchers?
2 Flu fighter
3 Vast, in verse
4 Descriptive wd.
5 Most spicy
6 Wrapped up
7 Monk's title
8 Greek vowels

9 Best Musical of 1996
10 Experts, slangily
11 Babe or fox
12 Alternative to a dish
13 Big laugh
14 West end?
15 Public ___
16 Czar in a Mussorgsky opera
17 Busy
18 Transcripts
20 Capitol Hill abbr.
24 Biblical verb
29 Crunchy chip
31 The Pearl of the Black Sea
33 Like ears
35 Traveler's stop
37 It runs down the leg
38 Peter Fonda title role
39 Actor Beatty and others
40 Completely
41 Baby's resting spot
42 G.P.'s grp.
43 45-Down in Russian
45 43-Down in English
46 Fire
47 "___ Mio"
50 One-pointers
51 First name in courtroom drama
52 Stay up nights
54 Charlemagne's realm: Abbr.
56 A.L. or N.L. Central city
58 Ejaculate
62 Tombstone brothers

63 Place for an outboard motor
64 Maj.'s superior
66 Just a bite
67 Suffix with form
68 Mary in the White House
69 Longtime Ferrara family name
70 Places for forks: Abbr.
71 Where something may be brewing
74 Mo. with topaz as its birthstone
77 Precisionist
79 Automaker's bane
80 Donald Duck, e.g.
81 Stove or washer: Abbr.
82 How you may know something
83 All-American name
85 La ___, Bolivia
86 Ben Jonson wrote one to himself
87 Like Twizzlers, usually
90 Hospital hook up
94 Unknown element
96 Emily Dickinson's home
97 Bidding card game
98 Cultural entertainment
99 Spin
100 Candid
101 Kind of queen
102 Acoustic
103 Cup, maybe
107 Best and Ferber
108 Common aspiration
109 Grier of the gridiron

SUNDAY

by Timothy Powell

111 Memo starter
112 Makes a move
113 Politician's goal
115 Star athlete, briefly
118 Outer: Prefix
119 Reggae relative
120 In the manner of

ACROSS

1 Wide-eyed
6 "Help wanted"
9 Bass productions
13 Big name in cards
18 Kind of spray
19 Investment
   mgr.'s subject
20 Exasperated cry
   in a 1950's sitcom
21 "Wake up!"
22 Gold gathering
   dust?
25 Shish-kebab need
26 Tested in a
   fitting room
27 Lower oneself
28 It has wings
   but doesn't fly
29 On Soc. Sec.
30 Deportment
   on the Discovery?
32 One having a
   ball at the circus?
35 "Don't make
   such ___!"
37 Prefix with
   phobia
38 Hi-___
39 Rear ends,
   slangily
41 One slightly
   higher in a tree
44 Very, very
   soft, in music
46 Supersized
   marathon?
50 Attacked, in a
   way
54 Summer cooler
55 Not agin
56 Target
57 Hit musical with
   the song "Razzle
   Dazzle"
59 Kind of badge

61 Mix
62 Spread dirt
63 What Edmund
   Hillary had?
68 Advertising
   "spokesman"
   since 1916
71 Oscar ___ Hoya
72 Strepitous
76 Model
77 1945 Robert
   Mitchum war film
79 Datebook abbr.
81 Old home loan
   org.
82 Shorthand taker
83 "Let's try
   e-tailing!"?
87 Dress (up)
89 Snoopy
90 Lets go
91 Trouble
94 Place for a stream
96 Like some buggy
   drivers
98 Sudoku and others
99 Pre-trial
   blunder?
104 "Concentration"
   pronoun
106 Struck out
107 Turn red, maybe
108 She may be
   off her rocker
112 Outdid in
113 Neigh?
115 Diner
116 Really digging
117 It may be inflated
118 Bait
119 Comics canine
120 Role for 45-Down
   in "Angels in
   America"
121 Spotted
122 Some hook shapes

DOWN

1 Acad.
2 Product that comes
   as a cream or wax
3 City ESE of Turin
4 Ignominious end
5 Pass over
6 Ink
7 Venus or Mars
8 Allies in the
   Gulf war
9 "___ lost!"
10 Dramatist
   Pirandello who
   wrote "Six
   Characters in
   Search of an
   Author"
11 Low-budget
   prefix
12 Dict. listing
13 Ruthless attitude
14 Thalassographer's
   study
15 Tankard material
16 State capital
   since 1889
17 Pressure
21 Only key Irving
   Berlin composed in
23 What a lover of
   kitsch has
24 Marked down
28 HBO competitor
30 Deliberate
31 Turkey club?
32 Split
33 ___ Cologne
34 Li'l Broadway role
   for Peter Palmer
36 Longtime baseball
   union head
   Donald ___
40 Strong out
   of the gate
41 Hershey bar

42 Diminutive suffix
43 Little louse
45 See 120-Across
47 ___ fide
   (in bad faith)
48 Sundial hour
49 Ones getting base
   pay?: Abbr.
51 High fiber?
52 Sensitive subject,
   to some
53 Strauss's "___ und
   Verklärung"
58 Philosopher
   Chu ___
60 Words from a
   backpedaler
61 12-time baseball
   All-Star, 1934–45
62 Fed. property
   overseer
64 Game with a
   seven-card draw
65 Trevor who
   directed "Cats"
66 Low hand
67 First Hebrew letter:
   Var.
68 AWOL chasers
69 Backstabber
70 Opposite of
   post-
73 Red leader?
74 Drew back
75 Eastwood's
   "Rawhide" role
77 It was "really
   lookin' fine" in a
   1964 pop hit
78 "___ for Innocent"
   (Sue Grafton
   novel)
79 Dos follower
80 In the sky, maybe
84 "Dedicated to the
   ___ Love"

SUNDAY

by Patrick Blindauer

85 Russian poet ___ Mandelstam
86 Transgressions
88 High spirits
91 Building blocks
92 Put down
93 Sleep inducer
95 Part of a U.K. business name
96 On the calm side
97 Playful creatures
100 Playful creature
101 Home of the Black Bears
102 Last inning, usually
103 Secretly watch
105 Refuse
108 Wax
109 Turns down
110 Brood
111 Army members?
113 Quick shot?
114 Org. for drivers

ACROSS

1 Where to stick a pick
5 Stay-at-home dad
10 Volunteer's words
14 Spanish eyes
18 Seller of Kenmore appliances
20 Belly button type
21 Well-known
22 Chianti or Orvieto
23 Horoscope Writer
25 Hostlers
27 ___ kwon do
28 "Two eggs over easy," e.g.
29 Look
30 Illegal lighting?
31 Hardly a hipster
33 Puzzle Editor
37 Rainbow component
38 Fifth word of the Gettysburg Address
39 Bakery offering
40 The son on "Sanford and Son"
42 Foreign Affairs Editor
46 "Jurassic Park" terror, for short
48 Soldiers of Saruman, in Tolkien
49 Connecticut collegian
50 Go over again, in a way
52 Like a prima ballerina
54 Nickname for Dartmouth
58 Peak in Thessaly
61 Pince-___
62 Washington city on Puget Sound
63 "Handyman's Corner" Columnist
67 Survivor
68 Sicilian seaport
69 Debonair
73 Obituary Writer
75 Start eating
76 Clear (of)
77 Survive
78 Dogs that rarely bark
79 Lettuce
81 Sparkle
85 A as in Amiens
86 Coin in Cancún
87 Nero's love
90 Book Reviewer
94 Some are blessed
96 Opposite of kick
98 One way to go
99 It may be run up
100 Travel Editor
102 Fruit with a pit
106 Like the stone that slew Goliath
108 It's just over a foot
109 Cockpit need
111 Isaac Asimov mystery "Murder at the ___"
112 Lost one?
114 Weather Page Editor
117 Shamu, for one
118 Bounder
119 News in sports
120 Traditional Sunday fare
121 Oom-___ (tuba sounds)
122 Something that's struck
123 Alternative to stamp
124 Cinematic beekeeper

DOWN

1 Send an invitation for
2 Untamed
3 Like the crown of the Statue of Liberty
4 Places for M.D.'s and R.N.'s
5 Antiquated
6 Any of TV's Clampetts
7 Turkey's highest point
8 Quaker State, e.g.
9 Tillis who sang "I Ain't Never"
10 Viewable
11 Party professional
12 Maytag acquisition of 2001
13 Colo. neighbor
14 [continued on the other side]
15 High School Sports Reporter
16 Perfume quantity
17 14-liners
19 Butt of jokes
24 Element whose name comes from Greek for "inactive"
26 Holy man
29 Non-PC?
32 Away's partner
34 "Good shot!"
35 Present time in France?
36 A year before the Battle of Hastings
39 Fats Domino's "I've ___ Around"
41 Velvety cotton fabric
42 Physicist with a unit named after him
43 Ticking
44 Star in Orion
45 ___ à manger (ready to eat, in France)
47 Morales of "N.Y.P.D. Blue"
51 "M" star
53 Hire
55 Area between posts
56 Change, as part of a computer program
57 Accusatory phrase
59 British actress Sylvia
60 "No seats left"
63 Pantry stock
64 Put on cloud nine
65 Race
66 Spanish cubist Juan
68 Org. whose members' lies are discussed on TV
70 Twain's ___ Joe
71 "Goosebumps" author R. L.
72 Canadian lout
74 Light
75 See
76 Gardening Columnist
78 The N.B.A.'s Elvin Hayes, to fans
79 First Irish P.M.
80 Ski wear
82 Hurl everywhere
83 Number's target?
84 Person living along a large stream, informally
86 Litter site
88 Lover of Eurydice, in myth
89 Gold watch recipient, maybe
91 Animal with a flexible snout
92 Turmoil
93 King, in Portugal

SUNDAY

by Maxwell H. D. Johnson Jr.

95 Air Force noncom: Abbr.
97 Shell game
101 Schoolyard retort
102 Chicago's ___ Planetarium
103 Lock site
104 Scale-busting

105 Discrimination
107 Peeples and Vardalos
110 White House worker
113 Dadaist Jean
114 NCR product
115 Ante-
116 Slip in a pot

ACROSS

1 Trumps
6 Frame part
10 Thrill
14 Slaves
19 Ring around the collar?
20 Copycat
21 Tones
22 Like some monuments at night
23 Dear old dad the comedic foil always told me to ___
26 Châteauneuf-du-Pape locale
27 This may shock you
28 Scottish turndowns
29 German crowd?
30 Whine
31 Tower, often
34 The first place
35 "Quit dreaming"
36 Peace, in Russia
37 Common connections
39 Period
41 Supermarket chain with the slogan "Hometown Proud"
42 Dear old dad the umpire always told me to ___
47 Termite clearer?
49 Oxlike antelope
50 Windflowers
52 [That punch hurt!]
53 Brooklyn-born rapper
54 The Seven Dwarfs, by profession
56 Tropical ornamental
61 Blaster
62 Hatha and others
63 Hick
64 Horse/donkey cross
65 Extend, as a line
67 Clinch, with "up"
68 In
70 Traffic director
71 W.W. II aircraft
74 One making a pit stop, maybe
76 New Test. book
77 Hollywood setting
79 Like some sects
80 Bygone polit. cause
81 The Maurice Podoloff Trophy is awarded to its M.V.P.
82 "Green Acres" co-star
84 Tony winner Uta
86 Learn about through books
90 Dear old dad the builder always told me to ___
92 Commuting options
93 Impala, e.g.
95 Booster grp.?
96 Fairness-in-hiring abbr.
97 Marine bioluminescence
99 Stay in line
101 Honeyed pastry
105 This clue has two of them (for short)
106 Eats
107 Big name in faucets
109 Wallace who wrote "Ben-Hur"
110 Habituate
111 Dear old dad the sharpshooter always taught me to ___
115 They're easy to catch
116 Support, with "up"
117 Jackie Robinson's alma mater
118 An emirate
119 Panda hangouts
120 Itches
121 Turn off
122 Economize

DOWN

1 More lowdown
2 Woman's name that sounds like two consecutive French letters
3 Sell outside the stadium
4 Great deal
5 Regular: Abbr.
6 Modern name for old Cipango
7 Place for icons
8 Queens subject?
9 "It's a cold one!"
10 Bilbo's home
11 City NW of Crater Lake
12 Old pop
13 Reason to reset the clocks: Abbr.
14 Dear old dad the cosmetic surgeon always told me to ___
15 Wealthy biblical land
16 "Fantastic!"
17 Extraction
18 Out of this world
24 Pacify
25 Supplements
30 Pie chart part
32 A sultanate
33 Dear old dad the C.E.O. always told me to ___
34 Coated Dutch exports
35 Geometry suffix
37 Problem in bed
38 Braves, but not Indians, briefly
40 Out
42 Prime
43 South American cowboy
44 Hunting times, for kids
45 Three Gorges Dam site
46 Fund, as a museum
48 From south of the Mediterranean
51 Cry at the sight of 107-Down
55 Marker
57 Spider-Man foe
58 Busy
59 Lip curler
60 Aid for the blind
63 Thumbs-up
66 ___ behold
67 "'Tis a pity"
69 Island chain
72 Alexander's wife in "Uncle Vanya"
73 Gun on the street?
74 Keeler and Dee
75 Hello or goodbye
78 Wowed ones
79 Procter & Gamble soap
83 Of yore
85 Baseless?
86 1967 #1 hit whose title is spelled out in the lyric
87 Noted Roosevelt
88 Generally
89 Words of praise
91 Was serious, with "it"
94 PC protection brand
98 ___-lance
100 Removes from the schedule
101 Joy of daytime TV
102 Out
103 One with a strict diet
104 At all
106 People's 1999 Sexiest Man Alive

by Ben and Mark Tausig

107 See 51-Down
108 Look like a creep
111 Person with intelligence
112 Yukon or Xterra
113 60's grp.
114 Word repeated before a hike

ACROSS

1 Day-___
4 Hat trick trio
9 Envelope opener
14 Racket
17 Race
18 Greenwich Village resident of a hit 1980's sitcom
19 Low clouds
20 Ponte Vecchio's river
21 Enzyme suffix
22 Pastel shade
23 Jeweled pieces
24 Hand holder
25 "The Sound of Music" role
28 Channel bought by TV Guide in 1999
30 Many new corp. hires
31 Flock member
32 Stout relatives
33 Comparison shoppers
34 Capital of Pas-de-Calais
36 Lab vessel
37 Prefight ritual
38 Fixing up a house in Britain
42 See 7-Down
43 "No problems here"
44 Wear
46 Not the most maneuverable ship
49 Endorse
53 Series of shocks?
54 Come across as
55 Epoch 50 million years ago
58 Month after Shevat
59 Toothpaste tube abbr.
60 They're out of reach
61 National flower of Mexico
62 Home of golf's Blue Monster
64 Asian country in which English is an official language
68 Puts (away)
69 Clothed
71 Too smooth
72 2002 champion at 62-Across
74 Da-dah, da-dah, da-dah, poetically speaking
75 Cocktail with 108-Down
76 Cold spot
77 ___ were
78 Overthrows first, e.g.
79 "Love is my ___ . . .": Shak.
80 Lose badly
82 Lei Day greetings
84 Become active
87 Ones with guns put away
92 Shut (up)
93 Heroic verse
94 Bouncing off the walls
95 Noisy censure
96 In the past
97 Fox dialect
100 Dealer in futures?
101 Chemical "twin"
102 Former western English county
105 Prep exam, for short
106 Capital city captured by Mussolini's forces in 1939
109 Heads-up
110 Edible South American tuber
111 Mark of a ruler
112 Toughens
113 Item often stored upside-down
114 Pro ___
115 "Ixnay"
116 Set, as a price
117 Lady love?
118 Help-wanteds, e.g.

DOWN

1 What this clue ain't got?
2 Former Buick
3 Kind of pitch
4 Inaugural ball, e.g.
5 It may be stuck in a bar
6 Sanction
7 With 42-Across, an NPR host
8 Part that's broken off
9 Leaflet appendage
10 Tourist hazards
11 ___ candy (pop music)
12 ___ loss
13 Like some highly collectible paper money
14 Quick deposit receiver
15 Successively
16 Jottings
19 Year-round camp
20 Don of "Cocoon"
26 Golfer ___ Aoki
27 Monsoonal
29 Truck stop stoppers
33 Tree in a Christmas song
35 Reagan program inits.
36 It has two jaws
37 Maine radio station whose call letters spell a pronoun
39 Rachel's baby on "Friends"
40 Phoned-in info
41 Tropical porch
44 Like land not drained
45 Baja bread
47 One that makes one
48 Wild things
49 Noted German spa
50 Hebrew title for God
51 Arizona football V.I.P.
52 Reuben ingredient
54 Musical exercise
56 Intl. assn. created in 1948
57 Make sore
60 Like a tightrope walker
63 Herd hangout
65 Breakfast place
66 Fix, as a golf green
67 Root of diplomacy
70 "Laugh-in" host
73 Yds. rushing, e.g.
76 Golf course feature
77 Melmac alien et al.
81 No-goodnik
82 Up to, in poetry
83 ___ orch.
85 Friendliness

SUNDAY

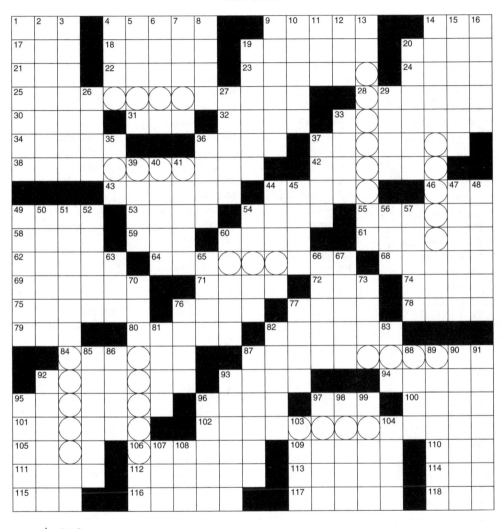

by Jim Page

SOUND CONNECTIONS

ACROSS

1 Some radio dispatches, for short
5 Album feature
10 ___ Popular
15 Small handful
19 "George of the Jungle" elephant
20 Historic symbol whose shape can be found hidden in this completed puzzle
22 ___'acte
23 Southern side?
24 Made better
25 French noodle product?
26 Shot by a doctor
28 1776–1876: Abbr.
29 Guitarlike Japanese instruments
31 Better set
32 Hypodermics
34 Alexander Hamilton's place, informally
35 It's filled with bills
36 Allegro ___ (music direction)
38 Grps.
40 Prefix with dermis
41 Lateral lead-in
42 Takes power away from
46 Henpeck
47 Bard's nightfall
48 Shavings
51 TV canine
52 Old washing machine feature
56 34th U.S. pres.
57 Opposite of blow up

59 "I beg to differ!"
61 Neat
63 Stage elevator
64 Bighearted one
65 Out
66 Ones making amphibious landings?
68 They go all out at beauty shops
69 Center of Florida?
72 Coulter who wrote "Godless: The Church of Liberalism"
73 Mention
77 Kind of I.R.A.
78 Broadcasts
81 Big bird
82 U.S. atty. gen. in 1962
83 In a Weird Al Yankovic song, he "looks like a Muppet, but he's wrinkled and green"
84 Get-up-and-go
85 Certain fungus
86 Book before James: Abbr.
87 "Cool" amount
88 Saturate, in dialect
89 "Sweet as apple cider" girl
90 Cheesehead
91 Ballantine, e.g.
92 First group of invitees
95 "Consider it done!"
98 More fit
100 Moving away from the sides
102 German auto pioneer Gottlieb
103 Carpentry supplies

104 Like Saturn
105 Skin cleanser component
106 In the middle of
107 Not dis
110 Whirler
112 Comedy shtick
113 Twisty turn
116 Within reach
121 Savory French appetizers
125 "Tell me about it"
126 Much-photographed White House area
127 Accent
128 Misses the wake-up call

DOWN

1 Like many T's and P's
2 Emergency calling plan
3 Image that appears with the 20-Across on an old half dollar
4 Go over the limit?
5 Groups that run
6 Olympic officials
7 Still snoring
8 Actor Gibson
9 Like a Rolls-Royce
10 Talking Heads co-founder David
11 Legal org.
12 Pulls in
13 Baseballers' wear
14 Graybeards
15 Houdini's real name
16 Longtime setting for 20-Across
17 Things needed around dictators
18 High reputes

21 Ornament that may be worn with sandals
27 Org. with operations
30 Pulls
32 Original ___
33 Hang
37 Mozart's birthplace: Abbr.
39 From Phila. to Miami
43 Hard stuff
44 Repeated phrase in Martin Luther King Jr.'s "I Have a Dream" speech
45 Like a juggernaut
48 Elapse
49 Polished off
50 Fraudulent contestant
53 Welcome, as the new year
54 Green: Prefix
55 Check over
58 Hat, slangily
59 Top-secret grp.
60 Sounds of woe
62 It often gets glossed over
66 Airport area
67 Previously recorded
70 Dish prepared in a skillet
71 Rutabagas, e.g.
74 Starr and others
75 Japanese noodle product
76 Temple with curved roofs
78 Put forward
79 Muslim leader

SUNDAY

by Elizabeth C. Gorski

80 Call
93 Series
94 Rocks
96 June honorees
97 Author Deighton
98 Direct contact
99 Routine
101 Domestic Old World birds
103 Creme-filled chocolate treats
107 Talking point?
108 I.R.A. part: Abbr.
109 "There's gold in them ___ hills!"
111 Oil producer
112 Afrikaner
113 Earth, to Mahler
114 Flight segment
115 Payroll dept. ID's
117 Follower of Benedict?
118 Pastoral cry
119 P.O. box item
120 Comics shriek
121 Granada gold
122 Natl. Novel Writing mo.
123 British verb ending
124 It may follow you

KNEECAPS

ACROSS

1 Makes sticky
7 Old Spanish gold
14 Plato dubbed her "the tenth Muse"
20 Turkey's highest peak
21 Buddy
22 Served the drinks
23 It means "strained" in drink names
24 Author of "The Fall of the Horse of Usher"?
26 Mad cap?
28 Dudgeon
29 "Dinner and a Movie" airer
30 Prefix with friendly
31 Caring grp.
32 Coal byproduct
33 Hard slog
35 Arthur and others
36 It may be legally beaten
37 Accomplish flawlessly
39 Essential part
40 American representative to France during the Revolutionary War
41 Love hate?
46 Iron man?
49 If things go well
50 Cry with a pompom
51 What golf pencils lack
54 Brand of craft knives
55 Cubes
59 Unable to make "Ocean's Thirteen," maybe?
62 Actress Olin
63 Break down
64 Professionals' earnings
65 From scratch
68 Exotic means of suicide
69 Brewed beverages
71 Organ that can perform martial arts moves?
78 Writing set?
81 Alprazolam, more familiarly
82 Femme fatale, often
83 Progressive ___
84 Quick-change artists?
86 1983 Nicholas Gage book
87 Ex-wife's refrain?
93 Products with earbuds
94 2004 spinoff show
95 Lip-puckering
96 Long ride?
99 Recording device
100 Blue
101 All for
104 "___ dien," motto of the Prince of Wales
105 Specialist M.D.
106 Reason to retire
107 Monstrous bird of myth
108 How a diaper is removed?
111 Cry to a lunch sandwich before it's eaten?
115 Set off
116 Arctic natives
117 "Eureka!"
118 "Is this a ___ which I see before me": Macbeth
119 Salary after deductions
120 Sequoias and Siennas
121 Whiles away

DOWN

1 Angel
2 Beethoven's Third
3 Hurry on horseback
4 River through Kazakhstan
5 Jotted down
6 Alien
7 Three-sided blade
8 Mubarak's predecessor
9 Company with the motto "A Business of Caring"
10 Old carrier name
11 Have the gumption
12 ___ roll
13 Roman Helios
14 Catalyst
15 Top-notch
16 Spot early on?
17 Able to change shape
18 Unwanted plant in farmyards
19 Spacecraft orbiting Mars
25 Mislead and then some
27 Hook worm
33 Pan coating
34 Off-color
35 Hebrew for "house of God"
38 Wahine accessory
39 Very, to Verdi
40 Horror movie figure, informally
41 British bludgeon
42 Year that Spenser's "The Faerie Queene" was published
43 Set of rings?
44 Food item that can be soft or hard
45 Historic Swiss canton
46 Prepare to give what you received?
47 Brooks Robinson, for 23 years
48 Secure tightly, with "down"
52 Lament
53 Chooses to leave
55 Units of force
56 Late wake-up call?
57 Seemingly not there
58 Ancient manuscripts
60 Black layer found in Morbier cheese
61 Put dishes away
66 Stretch (out)
67 Pull ahead yet further
70 Small suit
72 Left
73 Actress Bates
74 Ending with sever or suffer
75 ___ avis
76 It'll turn you around
77 In a proper manner
79 Shaw's "___ and the Man"
80 Research center
84 On-the-water front
85 Wildean quality
87 Drug taken mostly by kids
88 Inferior imitator
89 Pack up and go
90 Deplane dramatically
91 Common street name
92 Nero Wolfe's obsession
96 Not harmful
97 Together
98 They're rounded up in a roundup
100 Punk
101 Utah County seat

SUNDAY

by Patrick Berry

102 Big name in reference books
103 ___ vincit amor
107 Nino who composed the music for "The Godfather"
108 Scold severely
109 Feedbag's fill

110 "Splendor in the Grass" writer
112 Currency of Laos
113 It may come straight from the horse's mouth
114 "Now the truth comes out!"

ACROSS

1 Pelvic
6 P.M. times
10 Fast feline
14 They don't do Windows, as a rule
19 Sheryl Crow's "All I ___ Do"
20 Goggle
21 City south of Moscow
22 Lollygag
23 EVIL BRAT IN THERE
26 Muchachas: Abbr.
27 Part of the refrain before "hey hey hey" in a 1969 #1 song
28 ___ League
29 Absorbed
30 CANNY OLDER AUTHOR
34 Notches, usually
38 Honk
39 Frown
40 School for King's Scholars
41 Not manual
42 Signs
44 Passers, briefly
47 TO APPEAR ON ELBA, NON?
52 Diminutive suffix
53 Nevada county
54 Sharper
55 P.O. items
56 1940's–50's All-Star Johnny
57 Old cars with 389 engines
58 Secretary of state before Shultz
59 Diet doctor

61 EAGER TO USE LYRICAL MOLD
68 Benedict XV's successor
69 Vault
70 Narc tail?
71 Playfully roguish
72 Jason ___, longtime Denver Bronco
73 Touch
76 Recipe instruction
79 Sci-fi drug
80 SEEN ALIVE? SORRY, PAL!
84 Co. founded by Perot
85 Old-fashioned contraction
86 Good buddy
87 Abbey area
88 Like some Fr. nouns
89 God whose wife had hair of finely spun gold
90 Storyteller's challenge
93 EVER THE CRISP HERO
98 Taos sight
99 Picnic hamperer
100 "Clever thinking"
105 Esther of "Good Times"
106 I VALUE NICER ROLE
109 Affaire
110 Some wings
111 B'way showing
112 Part of a platform
113 Carryalls
114 Dying words?
115 It's usually slanted
116 Pete ___, 1970's–80's General Motors chief

DOWN

1 "Bingo!"
2 Source of basalt
3 ___ uproar
4 Tolstoy heroine
5 Short break
6 Operatives
7 Al ___ (Mideast group)
8 Philosopher Mo-___
9 Sun. talk
10 Herculean literary character?
11 Concentrated, in a way
12 Peach ___
13 Cask contents
14 "I give up"
15 St. Stephen, in the Bible
16 Soviet cooperative
17 One doing heavy lifting
18 Meth.
24 Hopper
25 Nocturnal animal: Var.
29 Start of a refusal
31 Part of an instrument measuring fluid pressure
32 Kind of blade
33 Pirates and Cards
34 Kind of diagram in logic
35 Dog command
36 Word before and after "against"
37 "Wheel of Fortune" buy
41 Industrious one
42 Some nerve
43 Pulitzer-winning critic Jefferson

44 Dennis of "The Alamo"
45 Hip-hop jewelry, in short
46 Pick up
48 Glove material
49 Potentially dangerous strain
50 Boot
51 Winged
56 Their tips turn up
57 Wax rhapsodic
58 Short flight
59 Race of Norse gods
60 Group of three
61 Rush
62 Was on
63 Goos
64 Texas hold 'em announcement
65 Catalytic converter?
66 Temple tender
67 Flight maneuver
72 Boot
73 Pergola
74 Baseball Hall-of-Famer Bobby
75 Dad's namesake: Abbr.
76 "Kubla Khan" river
77 First name in 50's TV
78 Salon supplies
80 Amazon.com and others
81 Stop from running, maybe
82 One-seeded fruit, botanically
83 Parked oneself
88 1959 #1 hit by the Fleetwoods

SUNDAY

by Ashish Vengsarkar

89 Craving
90 Start a drive
91 Like Ford's logo
92 Garment size
93 1980's–90's New York governor
94 Spartan serf
95 Toothbrush handle?
96 1945 Physics Nobelist Wolfgang ___
97 Madrid month
98 Something to fall on
101 Composer Charles
102 Force
103 Clown shoe width
104 Culture
106 August person
107 "Wait Wait . . . Don't Tell Me!" network
108 Bus. driver?

ACROSS

1 Corp. honcho
5 Some Filipinos
10 Starter's need
13 TV alien
17 Storyteller of Samos
19 Virtuous sort
20 Duration of many a TV show
23 Wine that causes incoherent talk?
25 Vietnamese city painted in soothing colors?
26 Pseudopod formers
27 Capital on the Mississippi
29 "Missed it!"
30 Literary governess
32 Girl's name that's a Texas county seat
33 Second word of many limericks
34 What a dummy!
37 French priest born in early July?
41 Worry, it's said
45 Calif. hub
46 Not quite right?
48 Mint hardware
49 Fillet
51 Poppy derivative
53 W.W. II-era enlistee
55 They're trident-shaped
57 Dries, in a way
58 Popular British society magazine
59 Steamed
61 Authorize
63 Life of ___
64 Monologist of note
65 Start of Montana's motto
66 Source of iron
67 Defeats regularly, in sports lingo
69 Cracker spread that's a little sparse on top?
74 Shook down
75 Game with matchsticks
76 Yearbook sect.
77 Brownie, e.g.
78 ___' Pea
80 Dasher, to Dancer
83 Gave in
84 Haberdashery item
87 Put out
88 It melts in your mouth
90 Journal add-on?
91 Attire
92 Bungled, with "up"
94 Common order, with "the"
96 Bit of sports news
98 Foreign exchange option
99 Kind of engr.
100 Discontinued investigative series?
103 Chanson de ___
105 Some choristers
107 Spot in a Manilow tune
108 Ad headline
110 Centers of squares, maybe
113 Brute
116 Deli offering
120 Expert in ornamental fabrics?
122 Rate at which a personnel manager works?
124 Orchard starter
125 Cream
126 "Not my problem!"
127 1940's first lady
128 Rehabilitated, in a way
129 Boxer-turned-actor
130 Ring

DOWN

1 Jumper, briefly
2 Enlarge, in a way
3 Salinger dedicatee
4 Lamenting one
5 Common Internet letters
6 Bireme gear
7 Sidesplitter
8 With no guarantees
9 Was of use to
10 Make it big
11 ___ corda (music marking)
12 Trojan War sage
13 Like pure gold
14 Dept. of Labor div.
15 Romp
16 Place for a pad
18 After-school arrangements
21 Punished, in a way, in the Bible
22 Fair-hiring org.
24 U.S. ally since '48
28 Green
31 Old five-franc coin
34 Place on the schedule
35 Auto parts giant
36 Trick shot that knocks the balls off a French pool table?
38 Freely
39 Drew nigh
40 Old "public diplomacy" org.
42 Enthusiastic cheering section at a bullfight?
43 Unbroken
44 Just back from vacation, say
47 They do the thinking
50 River whose delta is Cape Tortosa
52 [sigh]
54 "Please?"
56 St. Andrews golf club member
60 Pacific kingdom
62 Like a cardinal
67 Promptly
68 Peace Nobelist called a "messenger to mankind"
70 Concerning
71 "Had enough?"
72 Lively tempo
73 Catkin bearers
74 Kind of blast
76 J. M. Barrie pirate
79 Flute, e.g.
81 Sweet after-dinner drinks
82 Additionally
83 "You've got to be kidding!"
85 Lend support to
86 ___ Coty, predecessor of Charles de Gaulle
89 Simple, pretty songs
93 Grandparents, often

by Fred Piscop

95 No longer good
97 He hoped to succeed H.S.T.
101 Authorized to travel
102 Actress Anderson
104 Fishing gear with fine mesh wire
106 Garage job
109 Enzyme suffix
110 Simple headstone
111 Put on record, but not actually on a record
112 Intensifies, with "up"
114 Clarifying phrase
115 Rink leap
117 Sleek, for short
118 Jazzman Saunders
119 Tranquil scene
121 Suffix with front
123 Apology starter

ACROSS

1 Carousel contents
5 Life may be spent here
11 Ones whose work isn't picking up
16 Flightless birds
21 Nabisco brand
22 Against
23 Country/rock singer Steve
24 "Anybody home?"
25 Start of a comment by 3- and 126-Down
28 Oil holder, maybe
29 Wig wearer
30 "It's ___ to the finish"
31 Overhead bin, e.g.
33 Dearie
34 Kia model
36 Yellow or gray
37 Popped
38 1914 battle line
39 Comment, part 2
46 Brim
47 La-la lead-in
48 Trike rider
49 Some racehorses
50 Puffed up
54 Library Lovers Mo.
55 Natural pump outlet
57 Former U.N. chief U ___
58 Comment, part 3
61 Proctor's call
63 Cabinet dept.
64 "So ___ to offend . . ."
65 Phone book abbr.
66 Where many Sargents hang, with "the"
68 When repeated, an old TV sign-off
70 Spanish pronoun
71 Drink sometimes flavored with cinnamon
72 Whiz

74 Dirt in a dump truck, maybe
76 Isle of Mull neighbor
78 "The Torch in ___" (Elias Canetti memoir)
79 & 81 Landmark 1972 album by 3- and 126-Down
83 Actress Van Devere
87 TV series featuring the war god Ares
89 D-Day transports: Abbr.
91 Very narrow, in a way
92 Football Hall-of-Famer Herber
93 Dated
96 Russian assembly
98 Spanish eyes
100 Damone of song
102 Land on Lake Chad
103 Swear
105 Lexicographer's study
107 Comment, part 4
110 Sloughs
112 Cape in the Holy See
114 Colorful moths
115 Piña ___ (drinks)
116 Monetary unit of Panama
118 Where the Snake River snakes: Abbr.
119 Constellation near Cancer
120 Put out
121 Comment, part 5
125 Seventh-century year
129 Opera singer Mitchell of "Porgy and Bess"
130 Strand material
131 Afrique du ___
132 Had in view
133 Most dear

136 Ken and Lena of Hollywood
138 Belt and hose, e.g.
141 "I'm ___ here!"
142 End of the comment
145 Kind of call
146 Publication that clicks with readers?
147 Helping hands
148 A Sinatra
149 Some Romanovs
150 Honey bunch?
151 Entertain, as a child at bedtime
152 Real lulu

DOWN

1 Base for the old British East India Company
2 Indo-Europeans
3 With 126-Down, a noted humorist
4 Not so pleasant
5 Some hallucinogens, for short
6 Really clobber
7 Temporary
8 Recipe direction
9 Places for R.N.'s
10 Bubkes
11 Waste
12 Judge in 1990's news
13 Kill ___ killed
14 R.&B. singer Cantrell
15 Establishes
16 Electrical resistor
17 Subject of many a sad ballad
18 Couturière Schiaparelli
19 Something to break or shake, in phrase
20 Unduplicated
26 Up to, in ads
27 Slangy commercial suffix
32 Activate, as a switch

35 String group, maybe
37 Put oneself where one shouldn't
39 "Beam ___ . . ."
40 "___ no?"
41 Ride around
42 Order
43 "The Family Circus" cartoonist
44 Cousins of ospreys
45 Minute Maid Park player
46 Barely got along
50 One begins "The Lord is my light and my salvation"
51 Anthem start
52 Con game
53 Favoring bigger government, say
54 Kind of conservative
55 Bit of tomfoolery
56 With full force
59 Circus trainee
60 Butterfingers
62 Brian of early Roxy Music
67 Cinders of old comics
69 Straighten
73 Station along Route 66
75 Basis of a biblical miracle
77 Exuberant cry in Mexico
79 Now you see it, now you don't
80 NW Missouri city, informally
82 Cry one's head off
84 Opening for a coin?
85 Tuscany cathedral city
86 Ranch stock
88 Wrench's target
90 Sequel title starter
93 Latin dance
94 Feathered, say

SUNDAY

by Victor Fleming and Bonnie L. Gentry

95 Tulsa daily, with "the"
97 Show up
99 Trash pads?
101 Drink that's stirred
104 On-site supervisor?
106 Concocted
108 Night calls
109 What's expected
111 Midwest harvest
113 Noncellular phone
117 Wall St. figures
119 Lists
120 Led astray
122 Flexible reply
123 Plays peacemaker for
124 Bantu language
125 Not hearing
126 See 3-Down
127 Chant
128 Battle cry
132 Radar fig.
133 Toll
134 Baseball Hall-of-Famer Aparicio
135 Not this or that, in Spain
136 Medical suffix
137 Shoot up
139 Acerb
140 Italian bone
143 ___ dye
144 Golfer Michelle

ACROSS

1 See 131-Across
4 Root holders
10 End of "Lohengrin"
16 Minor player
19 Manning the quarterback
20 Good to go
21 Perfume bottle
22 Itinerary info: Abbr.
23 Yo-yo
24 Demonstration against a Miss America pageant?
26 Riddle-me-___
27 One making calls from home
29 Off one's feed
30 Tourist's aid
31 Fingerprint feature
33 Multiplying rapidly?
38 Legendary elephant eaters
40 Sinuous swimmer
41 It maddens MADD
42 Italian innkeeper
43 Loose rope fiber used as caulking
45 Ruckus
47 Shoebox letters
50 Grant-giving grp.
51 Collection of publications about historical advances?
58 Rush violently
59 Interstice
60 Northern Ireland politician Paisley and others
61 Dog it
63 Follower of Shakespeare?
65 Matter of aesthetics
66 Honored Fr. woman
67 Fab Four forename
68 One who accidentally blurts out "I did it!"?
75 De ___
76 Do-do connector
77 In excelsis ___
78 Perp prosecutors
79 ___ B'rith
80 Is indisposed
81 Use as a resource
82 Nobel-winning poet Heaney
87 Nose-picking and belching in the White House?
92 L.A.P.D. part
93 Work for eds.
94 Untilled tract
95 Coil inventor
96 Where people travel between poles?
100 "Little Birds" author
103 Twisted letter
105 Person who's not straight
106 Competitor's dedication to hard training?
111 Shaded spots
112 Carnation or rose
113 Gray spray
114 Come back again
117 Bird ___
118 Item to be checked on a census form?
123 Bit for an accelerator
124 Considerably
125 Taking prescription drugs, informally
126 Put something on
127 Ki ___ (Korea's legendary founder)
128 Antigua-to-Barbados dir.
129 What to see in a Chevrolet, in old ads
130 Got as a result
131 With 1-Across, an agreeable guy

DOWN

1 Course offerer
2 '06 class member, e.g.
3 Hairsplitter
4 One born on a kibbutz
5 "Splitting Heirs" actor
6 Patterned after
7 Tiger Stadium's sch.
8 Minor, at law
9 Like some hair
10 Recipient of much intl. aid
11 Opposite of tiptoe
12 Turkic language
13 Fruity frozen treat
14 Cyclades island
15 Unwelcome visitor
16 Healthful exercise, informally
17 Home of the John Day Fossil Beds National Monument
18 "The Quiet American" author
25 Bulldoze
28 Dig
32 4-Downs, e.g.
34 Really run
35 "Jenny" co-star, 1970
36 Feudal estate
37 Canines to beware of
38 "Zuckerman Unbound" novelist
39 Locale of Interstate H1
44 Teatro alla Scala locale
46 Players for prayers
48 Like some sees
49 Sister of Thalia
52 Contorted
53 Sometime sale site
54 Decided one would
55 Continuously
56 Male issue
57 Starchy foodstuff
62 In place of
64 With great strength
67 Take as an affront
68 Flyboys' hdqrs.
69 Pow!
70 Leave a mark on
71 Drain of color
72 Faith of fakirs
73 V.I.P. at V.P.I., say
74 Burkina ___
80 Stubborn sorts
83 Penguin variety
84 Nashville nickname
85 Where Lew Alcindor played
86 Critic's award
88 Touchy subject
89 Fails to be
90 Garlic relative
91 Whodunit title word
96 Gibes
97 Down Under denizens
98 Have covered
99 In
101 "___ robbed!"
102 More prone to pry

SUNDAY

by Mark Feldman

104 Flash light?
107 Pot-___ (French meat-and-vegetables dish)
108 Must have
109 Lyon is its capital
110 Under a spell
115 Watering aid
116 Some till fill
119 Abbr. after Sen. Judd Gregg's name
120 Nine-digit ID issuer
121 Org. that publishes American Hunter
122 Knock

85

$13 \times 2 = 26*$

ACROSS

1 Pitch in
7 Sight near an igloo
11 Show utter disrespect to
17 Something in France
19 Plastic surgeon's target
22 *Discount brokerage formed in 1996
23 *Site of a famous drawing?
24 Scorch
25 My dear man
26 Run the show
28 Ratio phrase
29 Hardly raining?
32 *Writer who coined the word "booboisie"
35 Wane
38 Fee follower
39 Biological rings
40 Satellite counterpart
41 *Deceased writer whose work was the basis for a hit 2005 film
44 Kiss, in "Harry Potter"
45 Former Span. money
48 Something a bride may have
50 Newsman Potter and others
52 Doll
54 Old man of the sea, to Homer
55 Pop
57 How 265-pound football Hall-of-Famer Larry Little was named?
59 Legal hearing
60 Bonus
61 1939 Best Picture nominee banned in the Soviet Union
63 Year Chaucer died
65 *Kids' cookie makers, informally
68 Folk duo ___ & Sylvia
69 Johnnycake
72 Porcelain piece
73 Alpine sight
76 Some takeout
77 Spy, at times
79 Damned doctor
82 First two words of "Waltzing Matilda"
83 Building contractor's study
84 These provide relief
85 ___ Kosh B'Gosh
86 Language whose name means "army"
89 *1970's–80's TV villain
92 Knick rival
93 French West Indies isle, informally
95 Bit of a comic
96 Peter the Great's co-czar
98 *It was retired in 2005
101 Chestnut
103 Make ___ for it
104 Capital of Belarus
107 As well
108 Daily ___, "Spider-Man" newspaper
113 *QB who was the 1963 Player of the Year
116 *World order
119 Dumps
120 "Mission: Impossible" types
121 Skip
122 Seven ___
123 Treat as a villain

DOWN

1 Its logo is four rings
2 Iced, with "up"
3 Waste
4 *Measure of brightness
5 Attorney's advice
6 Breviloquent
7 Peewee
8 Record producer ___ Adler
9 Latin 101 verb
10 Regard
11 Barefoot
12 "Gotta catch 'em all!" sloganeer
13 Its logo is five rings: Abbr.
14 How Holmes beat Ali in '80
15 How chicken à la king may be served
16 Scandinavian language, to natives
17 Milk purchases: Abbr.
18 In the main
20 Fill up
21 University of North Carolina
27 Prot., for example
30 Some college staff
31 Tree that's a symbol of sorrow
33 "Don't Bring Me Down" grp., 1979
34 Pesters
35 Continental abbr.
36 *It provided tires for Lindbergh's Spirit of St. Louis
37 Good relations
39 "Just ___!"
40 French Dadaist
42 Ones getting coll. counseling, maybe
43 Harry Bailly, in "The Canterbury Tales"
45 *Not for everyone
46 ___ blue streak
47 Kind of race
49 Go with
51 Setting for part of Kerouac's "On the Road"
53 Kind of symbol
55 Precipitate
56 What Indiana once pursued
57 River to the Danube
58 "A seductive liar": George W. Ball
60 Grp. with balls and strikes
62 Ending with cash
63 Singer Marilyn
64 Film executive Harry and others
66 #26 of 26
67 Fall behind
70 Brussels-to-Amsterdam dir.
71 Nice ones
74 Neighbor of Rom.
75 Lab safety org.?
78 Hot and heavy, e.g.: Abbr.
79 Crosswords, say
80 The Runnin' Rebels, for short
81 Mach 1 passer
83 Like Larry of the Three Stooges, surprisingly
84 Healthy amount
87 Football positions: Abbr.
88 Pioneering German auto
90 ___ boost

SUNDAY

by Derrick Niederman

91 Barbara on the cover of 15 TV Guides
93 "Apollo 13" actor
94 Symbol of perfection
97 *Beetles
98 Lee of the old Milwaukee Braves
99 Look inside
100 Quiet, now
102 Truth, old-style
105 Figure (out)
106 Common arthroscopy site
109 Mountain West Conference team
110 Actress Gershon
111 1990's Senate majority leader
112 Nav. designation
114 Zenith
115 Singing syllable
117 Zenith rival
118 Chou En-___

ACROSS

1 Pop group with a hit Broadway musical
5 "Dido and Aeneas," for an early English example
10 Three-time Masters winner
15 Smack
19 Pastelería offering
20 Had
21 Challenger's quest
22 Agitated, after "in"
23 Affectionate aquarium denizen?
25 Opposed to getting more angry?
27 Changes a mansard
28 Popular women's fragrance
30 Force in the Trojan War
31 French department
32 Glyceride, e.g.
33 Hatched
34 Monty Python member
37 Two-time L.P.G.A. Championship winner Laura
39 Grime fighter
40 Dark suit
42 Hub of a wheel
43 Grade enhancer
44 Does one's part
45 "Invasion of the Body Snatchers" invaders?
49 Trombonist Winding
52 Tiny amount
53 Preceder of Peter in a phonetic alphabet
54 Ear flap?
55 Listing
57 Less taxing
60 They're all that matter
62 A little flat?
63 At a slow pace
65 Evening thing
66 Sub
67 Wannabe surfers
68 Pluvial
69 Cot on wheels
70 "There's ___ for that"
71 Rhine feeder
72 Peach or beech
73 Panama, e.g.
76 "Miss Pym Disposes" author, 1946
77 Lettuce in the spring?
81 It's long in fashion
82 Actress Long and others
83 Beef cut
84 Discharged
86 Stink
90 It might raise a stink
92 ___-length
93 Ranchero wraps
94 Sine or cosine
95 Author of "Chaim Lederer's Return"
97 One offering compensation, maybe
98 Fit
99 Calm
102 Very scared insect?
104 Tainted tapioca?
107 Start of the Order of the Garter's motto
108 Bring down
109 Not done as well?
110 Switch attachment?
111 Puts on
112 Beat
113 Sty sound
114 Home, informally

DOWN

1 Patriots' grp.
2 Memory, sometimes
3 Invited
4 Sci-fi figures
5 Concert hall
6 Made pants?
7 Certain Prot.
8 Low-___
9 Stuff on tape
10 Union members
11 Number in C.B. lingo
12 Suffix with novel
13 Iran's Ayatollah ___ Khamenei
14 Actor William of "My Three Sons"
15 Desperado
16 Newscast segment
17 Sowing machine
18 Cremona product, for short
24 TV's Michaels
26 Stretch
29 Part of many a Civil War statue
32 Get out of
33 Blockhead
34 It's administered in H.S.
35 Capital whose Parliament house is called Fale Fono
36 The best time to elope?
38 Choice words
39 First or economy
41 Loot
43 Feather in one's cap
46 Hypnotist's directive
47 Deceiving
48 Old Nick
49 Young warmonger?
50 Others, in the Forum
51 Pour ___
56 Lyricist's need
58 Faithful servant in "As You Like It"
59 Lesser cut, usually
60 Not native
61 It fades in the fall
62 Play up
63 Pointer's reference
64 Primo
65 Oenone's husband, in myth
66 Like a defendant in court
68 Police car feature
69 Purplish
71 "So long"
72 Beat
74 Bit of skating practice
75 Marigraph activator
78 Take in too little
79 Rub the wrong way
80 Cubans' locations
81 Cousin of a herring
85 Went back and forth

SUNDAY

by Richard Silvestri

86 Kind of acting
87 Near
88 Tour de France cyclist Floyd
89 Newspaper piece
90 Like Captain Kidd
91 Modern-day rhymer

93 Olympic skater Cohen
94 Awaken
96 End of many a race
98 Way up
99 ___-Asiatic
100 King

101 Hazzard County lawman
103 Category in baseball's Triple Crown: Abbr.
105 Athletic supporter
106 Caught on to

ACROSS

1 Not generic fashion
6 Hurry
11 Complaints
16 Soldier's fare, for short
19 Accustom
20 Appropriate
21 Full-length
22 Anthem contraction
23 Parent's admonishment
26 Records that are easily broken
27 Greets
28 Catchers
29 Drink with a three-leaf logo
31 Water source
32 26-Across, e.g.
35 Disorder
36 Landon of 1930's politics
39 1986 Pulitzer-winning novel set in a cattle drive
43 Computer-animated hit film of 1998
44 Vein holder
46 "In principio ___ Verbum"
47 Hot, in Vegas
49 Delta hub
52 They're hooked
55 Satisfy
58 Paul Theroux novel made into a Harrison Ford film, with "The"
60 Hebrew name meaning "Hill of spring"
62 Biased

63 Solid South, once
65 Thus far
66 "___ my case"
69 Cheering loudly
71 Snap, e.g.
76 ___-free
78 Dangerous place
84 Painting and printing, e.g.
86 1982 #1 hit with the lyric "living in perfect harmony"
89 Nixon commerce secretary Maurice
90 Dickens boy
92 Certain book addendum
93 Zip
95 Rossetti's "___ Ancilla Domini"
97 ___ II, first man-made object to reach the moon
98 Baker's stock
100 Sign of affection
105 Form W-9 datum: Abbr.
106 Initial progress
108 Response to "am not"
109 Canon camera
111 Black ice, e.g.
112 About
114 Goes for the bells and whistles
119 Suffix with infant
120 TV announcer's exhortation
124 U.S.S.R. successor
125 Reds, once
126 Host of TV's "In Search Of . . ."
127 New Mexico county
128 Salon job
129 Candymaker Harry

130 Sends to Hades
131 Spring

DOWN

1 Gifts of greeting
2 One-two connector
3 Water mark?
4 Young's partner in accounting
5 Devastating
6 Un plus sept
7 Invite to one's home
8 Lyon who played Lolita
9 Word of encouragement
10 Gabriel Fahrenheit or Anders Celsius
11 Actor Young of the "Rocky" films
12 Specialist M.D.'s
13 Prefix with system
14 Causing more laughs
15 Strengthen
16 Soft rock?
17 Evangelist's cry
18 Imitation
24 Slimming procedure, briefly
25 One of two rivers forming the Ubangi
30 Personal, often
33 180-year-old in Genesis
34 Avoid
35 "Halt!"
36 Something to remember
37 Reveal
38 Two-timing
40 More trim

41 Adulterate
42 Minn. neighbor
45 Common Web site content
48 Olympics city after St. Moritz
50 Rapa ___ (Easter Island)
51 More trim
53 Pat
54 Puerto Rico, e.g.
56 Paramedic's need
57 Seth and Abel's mother
59 Pablo Neruda's "___ to Common Things"
61 Online brokerage since 1993
64 ___ Nostra
67 Curtain raiser?
68 Mug in a pub
70 Founder of the American Shakers
71 Duplicates, briefly
72 Bran material
73 Marmalade ingredient
74 Home of Carthage College
75 Superlative suffix
77 Little squirt
79 "Kid-tested, mother-approved" cereal
80 It can't be good
81 Part of a magical incantation
82 Smooths
83 Ronan ___, "God Bless America" singer at Yankee Stadium
85 Didn't lie?

by Seth A. Abel

87 Flower girl, sometimes
88 Some pool sites
91 Bookkeeper's mailing: Abbr.
94 Through
96 Salad morsel
98 Law school class
99 One interested in net savings?
101 Grp. founded in Washington on 4/4/1949
102 Pulverized
103 Creator of Genesis
104 Somewhat
107 Where a person might get into a habit
110 "___ say . . ."
112 Bill producers
113 Site for sore eyes?
115 Sci. class
116 Lord in France
117 Net
118 Part of a piggy bank
121 Originally
122 Kind of operation
123 "Let me think about that . . ."

ACROSS

1 Thwacked but good
7 Come to one's senses
13 Trial case
20 Needing crackers, say
21 Spotted cat
22 More than tanned
23 Is acquainted with a quartet of wildebeests?
25 Consummate skill
26 Have coming
27 Poetic contraction
28 Religious sch.
30 Clears for liftoff
31 What is that in Mexico?
33 Community character
36 Drill one more time
38 Early run?
40 Booby-trapped nudist resort?
43 Soul buddy?
46 Skin ___
48 Cornmeal creation
49 Like 60% of people
51 Prudent time to get to the airport
54 ___ Dinh Diem of Vietnam
55 Old guy, slangily
56 Young guy, slangily
57 Subject of some gossip
61 Busy
62 Poet ___ García Lorca
65 Had plenty
66 "Once in Love With ___"
69 Vegetarians' supermarket protests?
73 "Um" cousins
74 Sulking more
76 One who's fallen
78 Home of the world's second-oldest written constitution, after America's
79 Make it big
82 Traveling
86 Old Olds models
87 Record producer Brian
88 Belief in disbelief
91 Contractions
92 Outskirts of the outskirts
96 Italian, e.g.
97 ___-wolf
98 Transported a couple of Porta-Potties?
101 C.S.I. evidence
102 Zoom in on
105 Sought morays
106 Foolish talk
108 "Fanny Hill," supposedly
110 Hockey's Tikkanen
112 Fifth and Mad.
114 Skip it
117 City on the Smoky Hill River
119 Rose raised by a sardonic gardener?
123 Less considered
124 Title heroine of a hit 2001 French film
125 Diplomat Harriman
126 Emotional
127 Busybodies
128 Towers above

DOWN

1 Expressway
2 Trollope's "Lady ___"
3 Place for strikes or strokes
4 Dots on a map
5 Salon workers, for short?
6 Nimble
7 Pointed
8 Main threat?
9 Calc. prerequisite
10 Blood sharers
11 Old French coins
12 Results of piercing pain?
13 1972 treaty subj.
14 Available on the stock exchange
15 "And they went ___ in a Sieve": Edward Lear
16 Robin Williams-esque
17 Eastern European guy who loves both sexes?
18 Word turned into its own opposite by putting a T in front
19 Big name in ice cream
24 Shy person?
29 Candy billed as "The Freshmaker"
32 Heed
34 She was famously married 3/20/69 at the Rock of Gibraltar
35 Initials for two Belushis
37 Bagged leaves
38 Horizontal, perhaps
39 Oktoberfest serving
41 "Exodus" hero
42 Word on a wall, in the Bible
44 Vulture, e.g.
45 Beginnings
47 Symbol on the front of some bars
49 Halt
50 Mideast capital
52 Campaign dirty trick
53 Trumpeter on the "Kill Bill" soundtrack
55 "___ go!"
58 Sis, e.g.
59 Horned Frogs' sch.
60 Kind of pain
63 Key of "The James Bond Theme"
64 List for St. Peter
65 Fidgety
66 Horrifies
67 Cabbage
68 Christmas quilters' haze?
70 Number cruncher, for short
71 Ad follow-up?
72 "Wait ___!"
75 Poi source
77 Individually
79 One-spot
80 En route
81 Oval-shaped loaf
83 Alternative energy source
84 Speller's phrase

SUNDAY

by Lee Glickstein and Ben Tausig

85 Community ctr.
89 Prefix with realist
90 Teeny, slangily
92 Manhattan, for one: Abbr.
93 Follower of Manhattan

94 Milk source
95 Convalescent sites
98 Noble partner
99 Current resisters
100 Had too much
103 "The Prince of Tides" co-star

104 Certain 60's protest
107 Bouquet
108 When repeated, a dolphinfish
109 Abba of Israel
111 French weapon
113 Calif. force

115 Ill-gotten gains
116 Mound stats
118 Poetic preposition
120 Long
121 Place for a toothpick
122 Postgrad field

ACROSS

1 Major-league team with the most season losses, 120, in the 20th century
5 Fills positions for
11 A mouse moves over it
14 "Get ___!"
17 Former enemy capital
18 Kind of wrestling
19 House painting attire, maybe
22 Electrolysis particle
23 Whining from execs?
25 Be slightly turned on?
27 "Son of Frankenstein" role
28 Mint family plant
29 Rock guitarist Barrett
30 Flight
32 Pens and needles
35 "Summer of Sam" director
36 Day ___
39 Laid up
41 "Yikes!"
42 Fashionable gun?
47 Lose resilience
49 Ringside shout
50 Regard
52 Cheesy snack
53 Engineering project begun in 1898
55 Usher to, as a table
57 Princess of Power
58 Money in the bag, maybe
59 "Well, this pays the rent"
61 Bug
62 Whit
63 Deletes
66 "Then join you with them, like ___ of steel": Shak.
67 Assistants at a Kate Spade factory?
71 Valle del Bove locale
72 ___ Park, N.J.
74 NASA vehicle
75 Part of a winning combination
76 Irish-born actress McKenna
78 Washer setting
80 Like James Brown's music
82 Snoops
83 Someone sexy
85 60 shares, e.g.
87 Cordial
88 The Wildcats of the N.C.A.A.
89 New England hockey hero
90 Unit amount of sunlight seen?
92 Knotted up
94 Central
96 Suffix with Ecuador
97 Accident
100 Missouri city, briefly
102 Flit (about)
103 Equi- equivalent
106 Motivated
109 As recently as
111 Reunion no-shows?
115 Hemlock?
118 Go blading
119 Literary orphan
120 Swimming
121 Glacial ice formation
122 Three of a kind, in poker parlance
123 Suffix with bass
124 Scenic vistas, briefly
125 African antelope

DOWN

1 Stick
2 Isolate
3 Play garden produce like a horn?
4 New York's Mount ___ Hospital
5 No-no's opposite?
6 Letter-shaped fastener
7 Mine entrances
8 In a proper manner
9 Braved
10 High-hatter
11 Beer can feature
12 ___ right
13 W.W. II event
14 Shaggy sponsor of a sort?
15 Lodge
16 N.Y.C. arena
17 "The Laughing Cavalier" artist
20 Sprightly dances
21 Brief online message
24 A. A. for children
26 Place trailers are in
31 Wires
33 ___ land
34 Footnote word
37 Grenade part
38 Santa ___ (hot winds)
39 To whom "We'll always have Paris" was spoken
40 Time for crowing
43 Key with three sharps: Abbr.
44 Separation
45 "Voilà!"
46 Examination of an English royal house?
48 Phazyme alternative
50 Raison ___
51 Relieving knee pain?
53 Uninteresting
54 Cat's sniffer?
55 Kingdom of Broadway
56 Beat
60 Long jumper
62 Inconstant
64 Prevent from making a hit?
65 Gets some color
68 Wreck site
69 Supermarket chain
70 Nurse
73 Able to see right through
77 "Say as he says, ___ shall never go": "The Taming of the Shrew"
79 Gang land
80 Farm young
81 Old
83 "Gilligan's Island" dwellings
84 Attending to a task
86 F.D.R. plan
90 They meet in the middle

SUNDAY

by Joe DiPietro

91 ___-European
93 "Go, and catch a falling star" poet
95 City connected to Philadelphia by the Benjamin Franklin Bridge
98 Where kites may be found
99 Canon competitor
101 Sommer in the cinema
103 Ishmael's half-brother
104 Rap relative
105 Ready to be drawn
107 "One Good Cop" actress
108 Tiny time period: Abbr.
110 Jerk
112 ID's with two hyphens
113 It may be given from father to son
114 PC screens
115 Station personalities
116 Actress ___ Dawn Chong
117 Back again

ACROSS

1 Outstanding football player
7 Keep after further changes
13 Indian-related
19 Letter-shaped tesserae
20 Little sucker
21 He wrote "Even the worthy Homer sometimes nods"
22 Store I most like to shop at?
24 Ready for publication
25 Comic Auerbach
26 2600, 5200 and 7800, gamewise
27 Photo ___
29 Site of July 1944 fighting
30 Jack who hosted the 1950's game show "Dotto"
32 Mouse catcher, in Madrid
34 Actress Aniston, to friends
36 Missing from 22-Across
37 Melee in a Dumpster?
42 Fix up, as old floors
45 "Too bad"
46 1957 hit for the Bobbettes
47 Combine
48 Hang around
51 Missing from 119-Across
52 ___ Corner, Va. (Washington suburb)
53 N.R.C. forerunner
54 What you will
55 Cabbie's call
57 Worked (up)
58 Missing from 73-Down
59 Clothing retailer beginning in 1969
60 Flipper?
62 Most calm
65 Discounted by
66 Rouses
68 Seasonal beverage
69 Perennial best-seller subjects
71 Medieval chest
74 Dr. Egon ___ ("Ghostbusters" role)
77 Imagine
81 Signals
83 Missing from 13-Down
84 Busy travel day, typically
86 East German secret police
87 Baseball Hall-of-Famer Al
88 Actress Gardner
89 Glacial ridges
91 Missing from 61-Down
92 Where Zaragoza is
93 Blue Stater, more likely than not
94 Pioneering weather satellite
95 Federico of Clinton's cabinet
96 Novel
98 Place to wash clothes in old Rome?
100 U.S. News or YM
102 Gold units: Abbr.
103 Vater's boy
105 Memorable 1966 hurricane
106 "I Ain't Marching Anymore" singer
108 Cry of surprise
110 Overflowed
113 Arab capital
117 Senator's locale
119 Droid in an oil container?
122 Looked like Groucho
123 Some T-shirt designs
124 Arose
125 Pitcher's quote
126 Cops' weapons
127 Tone deafness

DOWN

1 Soprano Gluck
2 Astronomical meas.
3 Good news on a gloomy day, e.g.
4 Objections
5 Exhibit
6 Baja bruin
7 Missing from 37-Across
8 Forces
9 Apelike
10 Starbuck's order?
11 Dictionary abbr.
12 Prefix with -derm
13 A particular bit of typography?
14 Casting need
15 It's usually blue, green or brown
16 Certain eligibility requirement for Little League?
17 Amtrak service
18 Deceived
20 Where Kofi Annan received an M.B.A.
23 Finely honed
28 Attire with pics of sheep, maybe
31 ___ Martin (cognac)
33 Source of spices for old traders
35 Charlie Chan player on TV
37 Soaks
38 Thrown for ___
39 Super Bowl XXXVII winner, for short
40 Sheet of ice
41 Leanings
43 Go over
44 Communications orbiter
47 Get by
49 Pilots' info
50 Sales crew
52 Bolt holder
56 "Maybe this is fate"
58 "Be ___" ("Help me out")
61 Heeds humorist George?
63 Memory trace
64 Across
67 Jon with the 1992 hit "Just Another Day"
70 "___ of the D'Urbervilles"
71 "Lonely Boy" singer
72 Crowd sound
73 What you hear on a Chris Rock recording?
75 Faux "buttons"
76 Hoist again, as a sail
78 Whiz
79 Not abstaining
80 Type measures
82 Actress Aimée
85 Missing from 16-Down
89 Expiate
90 Airer of many games
95 Founder of Lima
97 Show to a seat, informally
98 1992 Elton John hit
99 Postgame productions
100 Cabbage

SUNDAY

by Brendan Emmett Quigley

101 Functioned
104 Four Holy Roman emperors
107 Missing from 98-Across
109 Passing mention?
111 Range: Abbr.
112 Quizzical sounds
114 OPEC member
115 Italian artist Guido
116 Saint from Kiev
118 Dripping
120 Mouths, zoologically
121 Org. receiving royalties for "God Bless America"

ACROSS

1 With 126-Across, author of the quip starting at 27-Across
6 Kind of race
10 "Come Back, Little Sheba" playwright
14 Modern home of the 10-Down
18 Product sold with a bag
20 "Hop ___!"
21 Tyros
23 Bill Clinton memoir
24 Nasty sort
25 Effecting a release
26 Blue
27 Start of a quip from Court and Society Review, 1887
30 V.I.P.
32 Literature Nobelist Morrison
33 What "Lucy in the Sky With Diamonds" may or may not be about
34 Quip, part 2
38 Edit
44 "An Affair to Remember" star, 1957
45 Berlioz's "Les nuits d'___"
46 Man of mystery
47 Layered
48 Project completion?
49 King Minos, for one
52 Site for Franklin Roosevelt
54 Matter of debate
55 Pageant prize
57 Quip, part 3
60 "It's about time!"
62 Lucre
63 Energizer or Duracell option
64 Low-value wad
65 Quip, part 4
70 "The Thief of Bagdad" actor, 1940
73 Ramallah grp.
74 Mystique
75 W.W. II wolf pack
79 Quip, part 5
83 "Rubber Duckie" singer of children's TV
84 See 112-Down
85 Winter pear
86 Brynhild's beloved
90 Granting grp.
91 It can be found in a tree
93 Cry with eyes lit up
95 4×4
96 Cold war winner
97 Huge, to Hugo
98 Quip, part 6
102 Lao-___
104 Dutch export
105 Dia's opposite
106 End of the quip
113 Try to win, in a way
116 Like a Swiss Army knife
117 One of a sailing trio
118 Time competitor, informally
120 Used a crowbar on, maybe
121 Election day: Abbr.
122 Fish that may someday spawn
123 Call after a hammer is hit
124 Agrippina's slayer
125 Prize since 1949
126 See 1-Across

DOWN

1 ___ law
2 Nutritious bean
3 Breakfast in a box
4 Flying start?
5 Common ink purchase
6 Tittle
7 It's read word for word
8 Fun house item
9 "Revolution From Within" author
10 Old inhabitant of 14-Across
11 With every hair in place
12 Ones dressed in black
13 F.D.A.-banned supplement
14 Match player?
15 Dramatic rebuke
16 Scout leader?
17 S O S responder: Abbr.
19 Satisfied subscriber, apparently
22 Part of a manger scene
28 Stem
29 Poet with the longtime NPR program "A Word in Your Ear"
31 Pencil holder, sometimes
34 Muscular watchdog
35 Sparked anew
36 "But on the other hand . . ."
37 Early sixth-century year
39 Put out
40 Stain
41 Actor Williams of "Happy Days"
42 Revolution, for one
43 Hammock supports
47 Sic on
49 Bills, e.g.
50 Exactly, after "to"
51 Court plea, briefly
53 Anne of comedy
56 Bygone Crayola color
58 Black piano key
59 Pearl City setting
61 Imbibe
62 Brigham Young University site
66 "Let's ___ There" (1980's NBC slogan)
67 Dim responses
68 ". . . ___ saw Elba"
69 Retired
70 Tired
71 Mark Twain/Bret Harte play
72 Game of chance
76 "Black Beauty" author
77 Link with
78 ___ Tranquillity
80 Offer that seems too good to be true, probably
81 Birthright seller

SUNDAY

by Mark Diehl and Kevin McCann

82 Lug
87 Floor (it)
88 Knoxville sch.
89 Get back on track
92 Begin something, in slang
94 Just firm enough
96 Lofty degree

98 It's a test
99 Element that quickly oxidizes in air
100 Artist with the 2002 #1 hit "Lose Yourself"
101 Winter fishing tool

103 Not attack head-on
106 Family viewing mark
107 "My ___!"
108 March slogan word
109 Dawning response

110 "Way cool!"
111 Strange: Prefix
112 With 84-Across, very simple
114 Had to settle
115 Bone head?
119 Application form abbr.

ACROSS

1 Mitsubishi S.U.V.
8 Knocked their socks off
15 Earth
20 Wake-up call, e.g.
21 It may be said after kissing the tips of one's fingers
22 Healing plants
23 What the peddler owes?
25 B-ball
26 Bust ___
27 Construction material in King Solomon's temple
28 National rival
30 Driver's aid
31 Maker of the first walkie-talkie
34 "All My ___ Live in Texas" (1987 #1 country hit)
36 Berate
38 Lt.'s subordinate
39 Top Tatar's tattler?
44 Jellied dishes in England
45 Place for a father-to-be: Abbr.
46 First name in gossip
47 Passes
49 Squad leaders: Abbr.
52 Way to the top
54 Shirt tag info
56 Not knowing what to do
59 "You're ___!" (Archie Bunker comment)
60 Advice for an understaffed yachtsman?
63 ___ seul (solo dance)
64 Change for a fin
66 Net alternative
67 Close pitches
69 Kind of acid
70 Unable to get loose
74 Site of a 1797 Napoleon victory
75 Cause of some spots
77 Screwball
78 Apple holder, maybe
80 St. Martin, e.g.
81 Result of whip-ping?
85 Architect William Van ___
86 Simmons competitor
88 Suffix with flex
89 Cartoonist who drew the Shmoo
90 Mimics
91 Some hotel visits
93 Summer coolers
95 Clamor
96 Spanish for "are"
98 Best-selling base-ball equipment?
102 Sec
105 Neverland
107 Common street name
108 At no charge
110 Classic New Yorker cartoonist ___ Irvin
111 100 centimes
114 ___ set (group of tools)
117 Early Beatles, affectionately
118 "The Goat, or Who is Sylvia?" writer
120 Packer fan's angry cry after an interception?
124 Massey of "Rosalie"
125 Slimmest election margin
126 Cupidity
127 Cake part
128 Balcony's edge
129 Gifts

DOWN

1 ___ Defarge of "A Tale of Two Cities"
2 Hells Canyon locale
3 "Quit your excuses"
4 All, in music
5 That, to Tadeo
6 Call
7 Ouija, e.g.
8 Blue dye
9 Dancing girl in "The Return of the Jedi"
10 "The ground ___ she trod": Milton
11 Urban carriers
12 Patterned fabric
13 Operation Exodus participant
14 "Every ___ king"
15 Literally, "big water"
16 Grp. with the 1977 platinum album "Out of the Blue"
17 Hoboes by nature?
18 Anti-Prohibitionist's cause
19 Ledger column
24 Burn
29 Repetitive sort
32 Delivery lines: Abbr.
33 Law man?
35 Unknown
37 Riga native
40 Show horse
41 Ring figure
42 Ox-eyed queen of myth
43 Means to ___
45 Fla. vacation spot
48 Black currant flavor in wines
49 Bush activities
50 Skeletal support in a sponge
51 Muppet seller's gender guideline?
52 Lao-___
53 1940's first lady
55 Woeful words
57 Flashback caption
58 Transfers
60 Cry made with one's arm behind one's back
61 Less than right?
62 Real-life boxing champ who appeared in "Rocky II"
65 Lubrication channel
68 VCR insert
71 Bottom-of-letter abbr.
72 Panpharmacon
73 Insomnia cause
76 O'Connor successor
79 Alley ___
82 Recipe abbr.
83 Fast server?
84 Island that's part of 90-Down: Abbr.

SUNDAY

by Ashish Vengsarkar

87 Big fat mouth
90 See 84-Down: Abbr.
92 Clash (with)
94 Floor wiper
95 Elevs.
96 Overseas train service
97 ___ Artois, beer from Belgium
99 "Mr. Belvedere" co-star
100 Hit man
101 Pawed
102 Attract
103 Blue-pencil
104 Impatient agreement
106 Start to a bit of bad news
109 Blaze
112 Opposite of under
113 Kid watcher
115 Suffix with electro-
116 Sarcastic comment
119 Little Rock-to-Memphis dir.
121 Seductive Longoria
122 New Deal inits.
123 Chess champion Mikhail

TURNABOUT IS FAIR PLAY

ACROSS

1 Fink on
7 ___ Reid (the Green Hornet)
12 Suffix with cannon
15 Coverage grp.
18 Yank out
19 Add zip to
20 Lyric poem
22 Result of a laundry room short?
24 Third tone of a musical scale
25 Yakked, yakked, yakked . . .
26 Assault verbally
27 Run down
28 Vitamin amts.
29 Nav. rank
30 Sr.'s test
32 Rolodex no.
33 Myrmecologist's interest
34 Josip Broz, familiarly
35 Ecol., e.g.
36 Magi's origin
39 Simple abodes
42 "___ Blu Dipinto di Blu"
43 What a turkey stuffer has?
47 Jacked up
49 Like many leases
50 Drink often served hot
52 ___ scale
53 "American Idol" judge
56 Team's burden
58 Do at the wrong moment
60 Strengthen
63 Group of notables
65 Jezebel's husband
68 Row C, maybe: Abbr.
69 Cousin of a herring
71 One with a six-yr. position
72 Solar wind particles
74 U.K. bestowal
75 Coughed up
77 Spectacles
79 Has a few
81 More informative
83 Where bills go
86 Clark role
87 Tommy Dorsey hit "Oh, Look ___ Now"
88 Tiny bit of time: Abbr.
90 Took it easy
93 Maximally sore
95 Test for a needed hosiery change?
100 Tee off
101 Burst open
103 Hospital supply
104 Iowa college
105 Defendant at law: Abbr.
107 Relative of atmo-
108 Locale in lilac-time, in an Alfred Noyes poem
110 Old telecom conglomerate
112 Don't just seem
113 ___ morgana (mirage)
114 Singsong syllable
115 Haberdashery item
118 Marsh wader
120 Hurried, on a score
122 Cause of a beach house phone glitch?
124 Place to play Ping-Pong
125 Like some dates
126 Longtime Disney chief
127 Many a dogsled driver: Abbr.
128 Daughter of Loki, in Norse myth
129 Blow away
130 Halloween bagful

DOWN

1 Internet browser button
2 Airline to Bogotá
3 Hits the sack
4 Pan lubricant
5 Not abstinent
6 Our base
7 "___ there"
8 John of Broadway's "Carousel"
9 Acre resident
10 Fife players
11 Spike TV, once
12 Evidence of a passer-by in a photo?
13 Playground retort
14 Cut off
15 Ostrich's pose?
16 Everglades swimmers
17 Beat in the market
19 "Get a Job" syllable
21 Lowdown
23 ___ of Paris
27 Vice president after George
31 1968 Peace Nobelist Cassin
37 Name for a farm dog
38 Blue shade
40 Hemingway's "The Nick ___ Stories"
41 ___ Valley, Calif.
44 Kind of prize
45 Civil-rights leader Roy
46 Wander in a library
48 Popular block puzzle first put out in 1969
51 Aussie's neighbor
53 Unrespectful sort
54 Macbeth's burial place
55 Off-road vehicle gearshift problem?
57 Eared plant
59 Brand of home perm kits
61 Cows and sows
62 Sandwich for a horse?
64 Way to serve chop suey
66 Look out for, say
67 Oscar title starter
70 G.P.A. spoilers
73 Toot
76 ___-pointe (ballet position)
78 Small songsters
80 Many college profs

by Fred Piscop

82 Marijuana
84 With 85-Down, old DC Comics spinoff
85 See 84-Down
87 Farmers' spreads
89 Alexander, e.g.
91 Unbending

92 This isn't it
93 Expense report item
94 Grunge rock hub
96 X-ray
97 Egg-shaped instrument

98 Noble headwear
99 Lamenting ones
102 Bank offering, for short
106 Way to go
109 United with
111 Churchill's "___ Finest Hour"

116 Seating datum
117 What's more
119 Additionally
121 It may be said to a doctor
122 Lotion letters
123 Plenty worked (up)

ACROSS

1 Slanted
7 Silly smile
13 "Le Rhinocéros" playwright
20 Protracted prayer
21 Relative of a rhododendron
22 Start of a hole
23 Job for a ballroom dance instructor?
25 Refuse to help in the garden?
26 Is in the Vatican
27 Sing ___ Daily, major Hong Kong newspaper
28 Altar in the sky
29 "Nonsense!"
31 Internet message
32 Discovery accompaniers
34 Job for a lingerie salesclerk?
38 Popeye, for one
39 Divine
41 Jimjams
42 Sainted pope called "the Great"
43 No. of People, say
44 Start of Idaho's motto
45 Anatomical enclosure
47 Banks on
50 Vegetable with sushi
52 Officer who may not be in uniform
55 Elects
56 Bus. runners
59 Job for a coffee shop employee?
64 Base approval
66 Shrinks' org.
67 Modern music genre
68 Blocks
70 Mucho
71 Mass. summer setting
72 "Family ___"
74 Decorate, as a 54-Down
75 It rolls on a Rolls
77 127-Down grp.
78 PC user's shortcut
80 Fearsome weapon
83 Martinmas's mo.
84 Grind
85 Miscellany
87 Job for a high school teacher?
90 Diamond of note
91 Bite
93 Suffix with super
94 Info at SFO
95 "Forget it"
98 Sermon subject
100 Man chaser?
103 Fix
105 "___ take arms . . ."
106 Queen of the fairies
109 Rosencrantz or Guildenstern, in "Hamlet"
112 Least bit
113 Job for an architect?
116 Roughly
117 Yawning
119 What a keeper may keep
120 Poetic ending with how
121 Idled
123 The Divine, to da Vinci
124 "With All Disrespect" essayist
126 Job for a business tycoon?
130 Supremely spooky
131 Skirts
132 Putter's near-miss
133 Jilts
134 Mixture of many spices, in Indian cookery
135 Ties a no-frills knot?

DOWN

1 Green
2 It has a tip for a ballerina
3 Rama and Krishna, e.g.
4 Was up
5 Quick approval: Abbr.
6 Appetite whetter
7 Baseball's Maglie
8 "The Compleat Angler" author Walton
9 Siege site of 1936–39
10 Flexible
11 Extra-wide spec
12 Farriers' tools
13 Most eager to go
14 Antipoverty agcy.
15 Moriarty, to Holmes
16 X Games airer
17 Job for a film photographer?
18 Multi-Emmy-winning NBC sportscaster
19 Bewhiskered animals
24 Subject heading for strategizers
30 In a tizzy
33 Party prep
35 Worrisome mechanical sound
36 Prime meridian std.
37 Kids' jumping game
40 Absolutely fabulous
46 Italian sweetheart
48 Farm measures
49 "___ Excited" (Pointer Sisters hit)
51 "This one's ___"
53 More cordlike
54 See 74-Across
57 Flub
58 Development sites
59 Subordinate deity, in classical myth
60 Modernize
61 Job for a dating service counselor?
62 Ascend
63 "You can't get out this way"
65 Lift
69 Harmony
73 Where some major arteries go
76 Medea, for one
79 Move, in Realtor-speak
81 Box
82 Certain specialty docs
86 See 108-Down
88 Competitor of State Farm
89 Handled
92 Disgraces
96 Hobbyist with toy trains, e.g.

SUNDAY

by Norma Johnson and Nancy Salomon

97 J.F.K. debater in 1960

99 Chinese restaurant sign

101 Help from on high

102 What's left

103 Steamy, maybe

104 "Hear, hear!"

107 Early NASA rockets

108 With 86-Down, popular serial comic strip beginning in 1940

110 Functional

111 Settles down for the night

114 Against a thing, legally

115 Cantilevered window

118 Dancer's dip

122 It might make you a sweater

125 Suffix with spiritual

127 The Cavaliers of coll. football

128 Hush-hush grp.

129 Mil. mail depot

ACROSS

1 How sale goods may be sold
8 Hardy bulbs
13 Hockey game starter, often
20 Contract
21 Even if, briefly
22 Humbled
23 Ann Landers, e.g.
24 Further shorten, maybe
25 Fooled around
26 Dirty coat
27 Hollywood stars, e.g.
29 Hang loose
31 Swim routine
32 Chaps
33 Henna and others
34 Helgenberger of "C.S.I."
38 Heroine of a Gershwin opera
39 Horse course
41 Swing around
45 Praise from a choir
47 "Here ___"
49 "Holy mackerel!" and others
50 -
52 Utilizes fully
53 -
55 Where to find an eBay listing
56 It's often left hanging
57 ___ Brazzi, star of "South Pacific"
58 Harvester ___
59 Personae non ___
62 Cur
63 Conforming to
67 Sympathetic
68 -

69 Hands down
70 Williams with a crown, once
77 Hits hard
78 Mr. Big, e.g.
79 High points
80 Suffix with Ecuador
81 Bilingual Muppet
84 Legendary
85 -
89 Soldier's accessory of old
90 -
91 Actress Gardner
92 Precisely
93 Hymn pronoun
94 Small racer
96 Honks off, so to speak
98 B. D. ___ of Broadway's "M. Butterfly"
99 Staff note
101 Henley who wrote "Crimes of the Heart"
102 Hopper
106 Irish revolutionary Robert
107 Had dinner at home
109 Natty sorts
113 Vulnerable to fire
115 Product label abbr.
117 Teases
119 Kind of family
120 Masonry, for one
121 Shows
122 Hands out, as homework
123 Some HDTV's
124 Haifa money

DOWN

1 Hieroglyphic figures
2 Huxtable boy, on "The Cosby Show"
3 Florence is on it
4 Trap contents
5 Some ducts carry them
6 Highway behemoth
7 Heavy hitters
8 "Haven't Got Time for the Pain" singer, 1974
9 Like non-oyster months
10 Some score notations, for short
11 Leafy green
12 "Thanks, pal"
13 Ancient
14 Soft-soap
15 Leather sticker
16 Carter of sitcomdom
17 Part of a score
18 Heavy
19 Interjects
28 Heave-hos
30 Go after, as a rebound
34 Hepburn, Garbo and Gable employer, once
35 Huntsville's home: Abbr.
36 Seoul soldier
37 Rocky Mountains line
38 Tip of Manhattan
40 Very expensive contest prizes?
41 Hera, to Persephone

42 Drug once available under the commercial name Delysid
43 Emma player in "The Avengers"
44 Fancy name appendage
46 Hebrew of old
48 Diamond cutter?
49 Series terminal
51 Macho way to fight
54 Old atlas abbr.
59 Former high-tech co.
60 "Citizen X" star, 1995
61 Response: Abbr.
64 Cousin ___ of "The Addams Family"
65 Name separator
66 Dept. store stuff
70 Ad ___ (how tariffs may be assessed)
71 Homes, for some
72 Norse goddess of fate
73 Heckler's missile
74 "I ___ bad moon rising"
75 Hand cleaners at the dinner table
76 Phoenician fertility deity
81 Bit of sch. writing
82 "How exciting!"
83 Halmstad's locale: Abbr.
86 "How was ___ know?"
87 Place for a duck
88 Hosp. readout
95 -
97 -

SUNDAY

by Harvey Estes

100 County with the White Sands National Monument
101 Blue
102 Howe who wrote "Pride's Crossing"
103 Weight
104 Hyperbola parts
105 "Hallucinogenic Toreador" artist
106 New York cardinal
108 First name in a dictionary
109 Hall-of-Fame catcher Carlton
110 Plains native
111 Apostle who wrote "Ye see how large a letter I have written"
112 Heathrow sights, once
114 Photog's image
116 Spank
118 Heavy-duty cleanser

96   SANDWICH MAN

ACROSS

1 Modern wall hanging
5 Military letters
9 Kind of case in grammar: Abbr.
12 Fruit of a flower
19 Place
20 Water carrier
21 Shetland turndown
22 Nail polish remover
23 Cheery fellow in the neighborhood?
26 One for the books
27 "You got that right!"
28 Slowly ascended
30 Class clown, e.g.
31 More furtive
32 Actress Kelly
33 Empties (of)
35 Bit of tax planning, for short
36 Excellent portrayal of a Gary Cooper role?
39 Hitch
40 Brainy
45 Work periods
46 Fireplace
47 Social breakdown
48 Turkish title
49 Answer men
50 "Let me repeat . . ."
51 Tattoo an anonymous source?
56 Dried coconut meat
57 Charlotte ___

58 "Holy mackerel!"
59 Night spot
60 Clears
61 Something to "call me" per an old song . . . or a hint to this puzzle's theme
65 Tin Man's malady
68 Let up
70 Turn red or yellow, say
71 Impermissible
72 Flat storage site
73 "The A-Team" actor on the cover of GQ?
76 Lines on a staff
77 Presenter of a likeness?
78 Start of a Latin conjugation
79 Minnesota college
80 Match
81 "Enough!"
84 Gemstone quality
86 Running in circles?
87 Father's song about a 79-Down character?
89 Bard's "before"
90 Pull (in)
91 "It's Too Late Now" autobiographer
92 All in ___ work
97 Mountain climber, e.g.
99 Saint whose feast day is December 25
102 1969 hit by the Who
103 Nuts
105 Get a bald advertising icon out of the slammer?

107 In pieces
108 Father figures
109 Cover girl Heidi
110 Razor name
111 AOL alternative
112 Sheffield-to-London dir.
113 Big name in games
114 Outdoor wedding rental

DOWN

1 Returnees from Mecca
2 Not laugh-out-loud funny, perhaps
3 Place for a programme
4 Dance in France
5 "This is right ___ alley"
6 Mediterranean isl.
7 Keep from overheating, in a way
8 Rococo
9 Recipe amount
10 Starr of the N.F.L.
11 Bach's "___, Joy of Man's Desiring"
12 Campus figs.
13 Candles in a menorah, e.g.
14 They may go under the arms
15 Response to a backstabber
16 Putting up a guy in the bath?
17 Among other things
18 Aristocracies
24 "Babi ___" (Yevtushenko poem)
25 They may make you sick

29 Kind of income
32 Extinct flightless bird
34 Security needs
36 Test before further studies, for short
37 Geom. line
38 Many a NASA employee: Abbr.
39 Showy bloom
40 Stone heap
41 Come after
42 Honored a monocled man at the Friars Club?
43 Diplomats
44 Wait
46 Game player's gleeful cry
49 View by computed tomography
51 Noted polar explorer
52 Charles, for one
53 Natural bristles
54 Wyo. neighbor
55 John on a farm
59 Angled
61 Attention-getting cry
62 Open ___ . . .
63 Typing test stat.
64 Election closer?
66 RC's, e.g.
67 Fashion plates, in British lingo
69 Low part of a high top
71 Place for a béret
72 Havana's home
73 Column material
74 "Typee" sequel
75 Idiotic
77 Pitcher
79 See 87-Across: Abbr.

SUNDAY

by Elizabeth C. Gorski

81 Turn red or yellow, say
82 Dunk
83 Singer Lopez
84 Achieve through trickery
85 ___ St.-Louis, Paris
87 Mabel who sang "Fly Me to the Moon"
88 Lighthouse signals
90 Aptly named author Charles
92 Film buff's channel
93 Key of Prokofiev's Piano Concerto No. 1
94 Mountain ridge
95 Pine
96 Overseas assembly
98 Mozart's ___ Symphony (No. 36)
100 Mail letters
101 College application nos.
102 "Joy of Cooking" author Rombauer
104 Sign of success
106 Kisser

97

MISSING LINKS

ACROSS

1 Fooling (around)
8 Open, in a way
13 7, on modern phones
17 Alternatively
21 "Way to go!"
22 Weeping daughter of Tantalus
23 Perfectly, after "to"
24 Must have
25 White ___ House
27 Moved to and fro
29 Adds to the pot, say
30 Each
31 "The Sound of Music" name
33 Hunting canine
34 Intermittently, after "off"
35 Small spray
37 Muse of mimicry
39 Singer Mann
40 Big name in faucets
41 N.L. East team, on scoreboards
42 Double ___ play
45 Sun. talks
46 Loop loopers
47 Streamlined
49 Some E.M.S. cases
50 Address
52 U.S. 1, for one: Abbr
53 Ultrapatriot
55 Ole Miss rival
56 Postgrad degs.
59 Orange ___ Bowl
66 Sign of love . . . or rejection
68 Heavenly hunter
69 Bruin
70 One given "unto us," in Isaiah
71 Sundae topper
72 Spur (on)
73 Defeater of R.M.N.
74 Latin twinklers
75 Monocle part
76 Easter ___ bunny
85 Airline rarity, increasingly
86 Had a lame-duck session, say
87 Part missing from a vest
88 Poet laureate before Southey
89 Fails to
91 Attending to the matter
92 Too, in Toulouse
95 Skater Slutskaya
97 Had
98 e ___ Bay
101 Comprehend
102 Answer to the riddle "The higher it goes, the less you hear it"
104 Stand
105 Early third-century year
106 Alternatives
108 Engine part
109 Nada
111 F.B.I. facility
114 Thickening agent
117 New ___ Latin
120 Head's opposite
121 Only: Fr.
122 Fanatical
124 Fab Four name
125 Whacks
127 Part of MGM
128 Tropical fruits
130 Like many benefit tournaments
132 Computer file suffix
133 University in Greenville, S.C.
134 Like the 1915 San Francisco Mint $50 gold coin
136 Flag ___ Day
139 Exhausted
140 Seconds
141 Words after "put an" or "see no"
142 Fit for consumption
143 Time long past
144 Cornerstone abbr.
145 "The Exorcist" actor, with "von"
146 :-) :-) :-)

DOWN

1 It's tied up in knots
2 Tractor powerer, maybe
3 Progress
4 Printemps, par exemple
5 Norwegian playwright
6 Relatives of AND's and OR's in Boolean logic
7 High school class
8 Big name in auto racing
9 Kind of acid
10 Where streets meet: Abbr.
11 Support
12 Noblewoman
13 Contents of some patches
14 i ___ Pod
15 Gas station abbr.
16 Darns
17 Body ___ language
18 Lentil or bean
19 Petitioner
20 Whirlpools
26 Big ___ time
28 Bond rating
32 MGM motto opener
35 Start of many Québec place names
36 Former Patriots QB Steve
38 Mountain nymph
41 Pub offerings
43 Something carbon monoxide lacks
44 Rep.'s opposite
47 Render speechless
48 German canal name
51 Nut in mixed nuts
52 Varig destination
54 Hush-hush govt. org.
56 Abdominal pouches
57 Down's opposite: Abbr.
58 Blue shade
59 Average guys
60 Spur (on)
61 Bone connector
62 Take into custody
63 Beauty queen's wear
64 "The Thin Man" pooch
65 Actress Martin, star of TV's "National Velvet"
67 Tape, say
71 Dollar, slangily
73 Shock
74 It's the law
77 Suffix with Congo
78 Bit of beachwear
79 Setting for part of "King Henry VI, Part 2"
80 Mideast bigwig
81 Himalayan sighting
82 Hindu titles
83 Harmony
84 Furniture wood
89 Follow relentlessly
90 Show a deficit
92 Reproducing without fertilization
93 Letters at sea
94 1956 trouble spot
95 Desire
96 Goal for a D.H.
98 Trivial Pursuit edition
99 Kind of tide
100 Latin "behold!"

by Derrick Niederman

103 Former CBS military show
106 Buck ___ eye
107 In a tangle
108 Chianti containers
110 Part of L.A.
111 "Go away!"
112 With respect to hearing
113 Lightheaded people?
114 Fleet of ships
115 Bola user
116 One who suspends an action, at law
118 Leandro's love, in a Mancinelli opera
119 Urban renewal target
121 Soap format
123 Hammarskjöld of the U.N.
126 U-shaped river bend
127 Civvies
129 A portion
131 When repeated, a top five hit of 1968 or 1987
133 Deception
135 Turndowns
137 Like 9 or 5
138 Former defense secretary Aspin

ACROSS

1 Big rays
7 A little dirty
11 Fly nets?
15 Deer hunter
19 Golden Crinkles maker
20 Product in a tub
21 Mosque overseer
22 A part of
23 Bare
24 In a ___, there's at least one fluid ounce of ___
27 In a ___, there's a volume of ___ that keeps it firm
29 Designer Alvar
30 Symbol of Ireland
31 "Sixteen Tons" singer's workplace
32 In a ___, there's plenty of sweet ___ to be harvested
36 Nonexistent
37 Come by
39 Root used in perfumery
40 In a ___, you can periodically catch a ___
46 Entry need, maybe
48 Part of FWIW
49 Stackable snackables
50 Burst of energy
51 See 5-Down
52 Pounding
53 In ___, you might see some ___ hanging around
55 The America's Cup trophy, e.g.
56 Trueheart of "Dick Tracy"
57 "Foucault's Pendulum" author
58 Kind of bran

59 Region holding ancient Ephesus
62 Nuptial agreement
64 Scattered
66 In a ___, there's no shortage of ___ to drink
68 Targets
72 Red, white and blue letters
73 Mend a seam, say
74 Sutcliffe of the early Beatles
75 Stage sign
76 Onetime host of "The Morning Show" and "The Tonight Show"
79 Iran-Iraq war weapon
81 In the ___, there's the greatest concentration of ___
85 Latin word on a cornerstone
86 That isn't it
87 Actress Kelly
88 Grim, as a situation
89 Dogfight enclosure
90 "Get Smart" group
91 In a ___, many a ___ is rolled
93 Rejecters of modern technology
95 Advance again
97 Co. that created the term "Buddy List"
98 In a ___, there's lots of ___ in the machinery
100 Lengthy time units
102 Spritzer mixer
106 R & B singer Marie
107 In ___, plenty of ___ is growing

111 In a ___, many a ___ is standing
114 Two-syllable unit
115 Aftershave sold in green bottles
116 Needle holder
117 Animal on Sri Lanka's flag
118 Stone used by pedicurists
119 Philosophies
120 Some Hindu music
121 Items sometimes seen on car tops
122 Sets forth

DOWN

1 Go from person to person?
2 Team building
3 When pigs fly
4 Occupy
5 With 51-Across, Caped Crusader portrayer
6 Site on St. Paul's first missionary journey
7 Violinist's need
8 Role in Verdi's "Falstaff"
9 Copper
10 He's flexible
11 Use a paper towel on
12 Punk music subgenre
13 Rule out
14 Bit of negative campaigning
15 Supporting structure
16 Measure of one's worth?
17 Easter Island mysteries
18 Oscar winner Lee
25 Bad lighting?
26 Setting of Margaret Mead's first book

28 Attacks with a lance
33 Collapse
34 Plant resembling Queen Anne's lace
35 Double curves
36 Missing persons
37 He-men's opposites
38 Cartoon feline
40 Looks hangdog
41 Burp
42 Tone
43 "Arabian Nights" monster
44 Mo. of Paul Revere's midnight ride
45 Nickname of Lincoln's youngest son
47 Make furrows in
51 Dam in a stream
52 Bit
54 Card game that uses jokers
60 Have bills to pay
61 Like fresh hay
63 Active from dawn to dusk
65 Guilder's replacement
66 Tough guy
67 Wine list column
69 Dark expression
70 War hero Murphy
71 Trifling
74 Nostalgic 1970's variety show
76 Large oval fruit
77 Short drawers?
78 Immunity provider
80 Onerous duty
82 Refinery input
83 Prefix with city
84 Chat room abbr.
87 Extinct kiwi kin

SUNDAY

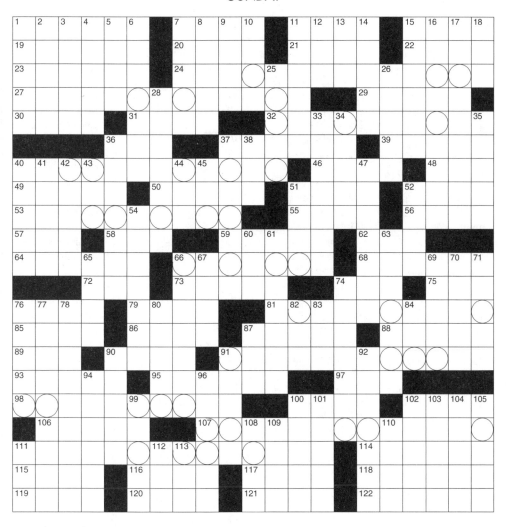

by Patrick Berry

90 Turkic tribal
   leaders
91 Animals used as
   food on "Lost"
92 Dishes the dirt
94 Some linen
96 Raven-haired
   heroine of
   a Poe tale

99 Eye site
100 End of a ballade
101 Starts off
102 Highest,
    as honors
103 The way of the
    world?
104 Two in one's
    hand

105 Fools
108 Wrigglers
109 Composer Satie
110 Stretched
111 Grp. in TV's
    "Criminal
    Minds"
112 Sch. group
113 Prayer ___

ACROSS

1 Most distant
7 Big Twelve team
13 Last of the Minor Prophets
20 First Ford
21 Philippine port
22 Nonrecurring publication
23 33.8 ounces?
25 Some honky-tonk music
26 Stephen of "The Crying Game"
27 Decoy site, maybe
28 Boil
30 Screen figure
31 Singers James and Jones
33 Friend of Dorothy, on "Sesame Street"
35 Disconnect
38 Stalwart plumber's credo?
43 Pharmaceutical chemist ___ Lilly
46 [Wham!]
47 End
48 Father of the Titans
50 Special attention, for short
53 Al ___
56 Ratchets (up)
57 Spoken
58 Pros
60 Teetotaling nun?
63 Straight
64 Saint in Brazil
66 Pops
67 Prefix with comic
69 Lawn tool
70 Long ago, long ago
71 Fur, e.g.
74 ___ Blaster (classic arcade game)
77 "Se ___ inglés?"
79 Make a bad copy of?
80 Winner's cry
81 Fiddle (around)
83 Oddly colored shoe?
88 Tide type
89 One line at passport control
91 U.S. highway with a ferry connection between Delaware and New Jersey
92 Language of India
94 Parts of apts.
95 Karate teacher
96 San ___, Tex.
98 Neth. neighbor
100 ___ rose
101 What the wet, baggage-laden passenger might take at the train station?
108 Former British royal
110 Newcastle's river
111 Old print
112 Actress Lena
114 And others
118 Calls a game
120 Western setting: Abbr.
121 One on the left
124 The ram in "A ram walks into a bar . . ."?
127 Rich green
128 Abet, in a way
129 Contract-negotiating pro
130 Garments at a 44-Down
131 Certain smokes
132 Chargers

DOWN

1 Eastern inn
2 Approaches in the Bible?
3 Think
4 Ending with how
5 Sloppy
6 Kind of shell
7 Light
8 Word before, after ___ or both before and after ___ "in"
9 Harmful
10 Spot
11 On the safe side
12 Kind
13 Oscar winner for "West Side Story"
14 Something to give an Alabama cheerleader?
15 Race part
16 John of "Freaky Friday," 1977
17 Rooster?
18 Human genus
19 Highway damaged by hurricane Katrina
24 Again
29 Most imposing
32 Venom carrier
34 Film character whose first name is Longfellow
36 Home of "Winged Victory"
37 About
39 Is into
40 Home of the N.C.A.A.'s Minutemen
41 California's ___ Valley
42 Recipe amts.
44 Outdoor party
45 Place for a 44-Down
49 Craftsperson
50 Enter
51 Aid for a detective
52 Like some C.S.I. evidence?
54 Game show contestant's option
55 Way to the top
59 Dirtbags
61 No-goodnik
62 Respect
65 Venus or Mars
68 Unit of hope?
71 Whisper sweet nothings
72 Dais delivery
73 Film company
75 Stray
76 "Not good!"
78 Behind
79 Quick
81 Quick
82 Title apiarist of film
84 Peeved
85 Soave or Orvieto
86 Bldg. planner
87 World capital on a gulf of the same name
90 At hand
93 Healthful food claim

SUNDAY

by Tony Orbach

97 1970 #1 song and album
99 Rd.
102 Investors' info
103 Hardens
104 Captain of the Nautilus
105 Fight
106 Put on the line
107 Mums
109 Month before febrero
112 Praise for toreadors
113 Home of the oldest university in the continental Americas
115 Lincoln and others
116 __ Park, old Coney Island attraction
117 Emphasized: Abbr.
119 NCO's charges
122 Tore
123 Some H.S. math
125 American __
126 Mr. Average

ACROSS

1 Prefix with -drome
5 Mogul
9 Philippine seaport
15 Mug
19 Low part of a hand
20 Pickup shtick?
21 "Haven't a clue!"
22 Duck: Ger.
23 Base leader
25 Parisian entertainment since 1869
27 "Likewise"
28 Shackles
30 Juicy, tart apple
31 It may be pushed before starting
32 Homestead Act unit
34 Sponsor at Indy
36 1 + 1 = 3, e.g.
37 River of Hesse
38 British ___
39 Western Hemisphere grp.
41 ___-Foy, Québec
42 "Time to go now!"
47 Pause that refreshes
50 Phrase of nonspecific attribution
52 Leaked, as from a container
54 Nashville-based awards org.
55 Diamond baron Cecil
56 1998 animated bug film
57 Nymph pursuers
59 "___ the ramparts . . ."
60 Tasting of wood, as some wines
63 Itch cause
67 Like some cottage cheese
68 Friend in a sombrero
71 Household scare
73 Natural sparkler
74 Bakery order
75 Hells Canyon locale
76 Not to mention
78 Tuneful city "by the sea-o"
79 Brought up the rear?
81 Stir up
83 Guiding light
86 Prince Valiant's firstborn
87 Directional aid
91 Teeth, slangily
93 L.A. hours
94 Slicker, umbrella, galoshes, etc.
96 Opening sound?
99 It's in the genes
100 Places for laces
101 Lure
105 Elevator stop
107 MoMA's home
109 Lifts
110 "Amadeus" star Tom
111 Steamed dishes
113 Place of sacrifice
115 "Ulysses" setting
116 Christmas decoration site
118 He was no dummy
121 Trojan ally in the "Iliad"
122 Sci-fi weaponry
123 Jean ___, creator of 56-Down
124 ___-majesté
125 Plain and simple
126 Does a dog trick
127 "This is going to get ___"
128 ___'acte

DOWN

1 It's worn
2 Worn
3 Rest
4 Place for pearls
5 Classic Liz Taylor part
6 President of Pakistan, 1978–88
7 Lily Tomlin's Edith ___
8 Many a Floridian
9 Skinny
10 Nutcases
11 Heater with a storage tank
12 Exiled Amin
13 Historic Virginia family
14 Kilns
15 Edvard Grieg work
16 Quick-acting intl. military unit
17 Dogie
18 Witnessed
24 Rye fungus
26 Raises a howl
29 Lean against
32 Screened terrier
33 White-collar workers?
35 No longer owed
38 Linda Ronstadt's "___ Easy"
40 ___-Cat
43 See here!
44 Some bedtime reading
45 Nelson in reruns
46 Onetime American Communist leader ___ Hall
48 Uncommon sources of music nowadays
49 Stick to
50 Setting for some Sherlock Holmes mysteries
51 Combining of companies making the same product
53 Zest
55 Travel guide
56 "The Clan of the Cave Bear" heroine
58 One little piggy
61 Bee: Prefix
62 On the canvas, informally
64 Lab vessel
65 Immigrant's course: Abbr.
66 Network on a 55-Down: Abbr.
69 Atty. ___
70 They're easy to dial on a rotary phone
72 Chuck
77 Winds in a pit
80 "What's the ___?"
82 Lake that's a source of the Mississippi
84 Big time
85 Potential lifesaver for a drowning person
88 Mars or Mercury
89 Ex-senator Sam
90 Site of swings and a sandbox

SUNDAY

by Manny Nosowsky

91 Restaurant chain founded in 1958 near L.A.
92 Edges
95 "Nothing is so much to be feared as fear" penner
97 Croaking
98 Boring result
102 It may lead to a breakout
103 Least friendly
104 Two fins' worth
105 Three-time N.F.L. M.V.P., 1995–97
106 Staggers
108 Bob Cratchit, in "A Christmas Carol"
110 "Ben-___"
111 Mets, Jets or Nets
112 Spur-of-the-moment
114 "___ of the D'Urbervilles"
115 Big John of golf
117 Literary monogram
119 Grooved on
120 Set

ACROSS

1 Percussion instrument
5 Hive makers
11 Easily passed
15 Junket
19 "Oh, uh-huh"
20 One with a mortgage
21 Dark region of the moon
22 Do followers
23 Meat, lettuce, cheese and tomato in a foot-long bun?
25 Huge
26 Destructive 1995 hurricane
27 Glare reducer
28 Graffiti on a jail wall?
31 Traffic monitors
36 O.K.
37 "P.U.!"
38 Actor Charleson of "Chariots of Fire"
39 Poplar tree
40 Lifeguard's purview
43 Like some penguin feet
45 Social activity on a military base?
47 Pastor who pitches?
49 Prefix with light
50 Irritated with
52 Nascar circuits
53 Early second-century year
56 Something struck
59 Legal
63 Support payment query?

70 Cataract site
71 Refrigerator brand
72 "Finding ___"
73 Cinnamon source
74 Tidewater collector
75 Director Gus Van ___
76 Amounts owed at a diner?
79 "CHiPs" star of 1970's–80's TV
82 Snowmobile steerer
83 Obsessed with
84 Defense initiative, for short
86 Bad musician's "body part"
91 Draft org.
94 Part voting aye?
99 Headwear for a building chief?
102 "S O S"
103 Bottle size
105 Cat-___-tails
106 Maria preceder
107 Dockworkers' org.
109 Shine, in product names
110 Island hoppers
112 Junk mail a trucker might get?
116 Auto needs
117 Killarney's land
118 Drink mixer
119 Where we be?
125 Insurer's calculation
126 Bygone despot
127 One who's left
128 Big source of corn
129 Legis. meeting
130 Radio, e.g.

131 Judge's declaration
132 Run things

DOWN

1 Dogfaces
2 Big Ten power-house, for short
3 Homestead Natl. Monument locale
4 Unified whole
5 Looie or hooey, e.g.
6 Approached
7 "Then what?"
8 Food label fig.
9 Chicago futures exchange, for short
10 Arizona tourist town
11 Changed
12 Pitch-raising guitar device
13 Verdi aria
14 Having all angles equal to 144 degrees
15 Counselor on "Star Trek: T.N.G."
16 Fix, as brickwork
17 "Somehow everything gets done"
18 Footed glass
24 Clichéd
29 Romance novelist Roberts
30 Electrification
31 Totally consumed
32 "Take ___" ("Congratulations!")
33 Extra capsule in a pill bottle
34 Film style
35 Loudness measure
41 N.Y.C. landing site

42 Latin 101 word
44 Not quite rhyming
46 "Just ___ about to . . ."
48 Trump daughter
51 Robert Burns's "___ Louse"
54 "The Sound of Music" family name
55 Philanthropist Hogg
57 "What'll ___?"
58 When repeated, start of a child's taunt
60 Where the first Ringling Brothers circus was staged, 1884
61 Nobelist Wiesel
62 Places to put your feet up
63 Facility
64 Kind of tree
65 Having parts to be filled
66 "The Matrix" hero
67 Radio iconoclast
68 Bop
69 Ball
74 Outlaw
77 Small songbird
78 One way to the Hamptons, for short
80 The first letter in 84-Across
81 Bums
85 Uruguayan uncle
87 "Woe ___" (humorous grammar book)
88 Loco
89 Sport with arm-waving

SUNDAY

by Patrick Merrell

90 Bubble makers
92 Fish throwaway
93 God with a crested helmet and spear
94 Sci-fi weaponry
95 It might end with a start

96 Rebels of the Southeastern Conference
97 Wary
98 Dudley Do-Right's love
100 Vital Russian route

101 Agitated
104 Stevedore
108 Emerged
111 Things counted by the second?
113 Signs
114 Genealogist's study

115 Nature film?
120 [per the original]
121 Size bigger than med.
122 It might be called in
123 Wise one
124 Rob Roy's refusal

ACROSS

1 Many applications
5 Miss
9 Tudor queen, informally
13 Rafting area
19 Final, e.g.
20 To be played in unison
21 Horse ridden by Hotspur in "King Henry IV, Part I"
22 Shrewdness
23 Jazzy James
24 Breakdown on a Hyundai assembly line?
27 Edit for TV, say
29 Birthplace of 41-Across: Abbr.
30 Reason for a flood of calls to the police dept., maybe
31 "Wheel of Fortune" purchase
32 Rev. Jesse on Sundays?
38 ___ florentine
39 Author Bagnold
40 Till bill
41 "Nemesis" novelist
45 Stickers
47 Old Roman's boast after a deer hunt?
52 Town north of Anaheim
53 Seat of Washoe County, Nev.
54 Runners at the corners, say, in baseball
55 Chow
56 Long in the tooth
57 Go on stage
59 Bluish gray
62 "Oh, give ___ home . . ."
63 Check for typos, e.g.
65 Some of Shakespeare's income?
69 Astroturf alternative
72 Truss
73 Popular vodka, informally
74 Newly mortared bricks and stones?
79 Decrees
83 With 74-Down, unanimity
84 Grisham's "___ to Kill"
85 Obstruct
88 Become unhinged
89 Words of confidence
91 Go ___ (start fighting)
94 Person making unauthorized reports
95 Oscar-winning Irene
96 November through April, to vacationers?
100 World Series game
101 Decorate with pointy figures
102 Unveil, in poetry
103 Instance
105 Mad staff: Abbr.
106 One needed to bestow a blessing on a golf club?
112 Leaves at a luau
114 Mad., e.g.
115 1950 World Cup host, with a stadium for 180,000+ people
116 Musical with the song "N.Y.C."
117 Advice to Claudius, in "Hamlet"?
123 Memorable 2004 hurricane
125 Spoke in a poke?
126 Spoils
127 Dubai or Houston
128 TV part
129 Gets rid of
130 Big petrol seller
131 Chop ___
132 Formerly, once

DOWN

1 "Is that a fact?!"
2 Supersized
3 Phase of life before retirement
4 Buss
5 "Beauty and the Beast" role
6 Words said with a raised hand
7 Reward for going home?
8 Pick up
9 Most insolent
10 Volkswagen model
11 Took notice
12 State of confusion
13 Far out
14 Coolers, for short
15 Commonly accepted as such
16 Comment after looking at one's cards
17 Submarine base?
18 NBC inits.
25 ___-frutti
26 Cambodia's Lon ___
28 Applications
32 N.B.A. legend Kareem Abdul-___
33 Oscar winner for "Separate Tables"
34 Driver's lic., e.g.
35 Adequate, old-style
36 Tablet
37 See 117-Down
42 Home of El Nuevo Herald
43 Wedding band, maybe
44 Travel items
46 Dishonest sort
48 Rejections
49 Jet part
50 Battery number
51 Out of place
53 Pharaoh, for one
58 ___-Rooter
60 Company on the move
61 Yellow ball
64 "Di quella pira," e.g.
66 Palindromic writer
67 Eggheady sort
68 Flop
70 Hit hard
71 Where "yes" is "ioe," pronounced in three syllables
74 See 83-Across
75 Like the emperor Atahualpa
76 Backs
77 Like baseball covers
78 Thanksgiving dishes
80 It starts in Yellowstone National Park
81 Barrel-shaped marine mammals
82 Meager
86 Sponge
87 Long bones
90 Splits hairs
92 On and after
93 Be under, as an officer
97 Ewe said it

SUNDAY

by David J. Kahn

98 Cold response?
99 High point
100 V.I.P.'s opposite
104 Meager
107 Africa's ___ Tomé
108 Future seed
109 ___ Circus
(ancient Roman
arena)

110 Big name in
trading cards
111 Put together
112 Hidey-hole
113 10,900-foot
European peak
117 With 37-Down,
popular book on
grammar

118 Laugh syllable
119 Tailback's stat:
Abbr.
120 Call for help
121 Symbol of
worthlessness
122 It's found
in seams
124 Celtic rival

ACROSS

1 Sharp cheese quality
4 Center of emotions
9 Mountain top?
15 ___ Club of old TV
18 Big record co.
19 Many, many
21 This puzzle's northern border?
22 Be in a hole
23 Access code?
25 Stockpiles
26 Fired up
27 Scruffs
28 Its clue reads "Unstable subatomic particle"
30 Treater's words
32 Key-signature preceder
33 Family subdivisions
34 Opposite of post-
36 Drying chamber
37 With 33-Down, quickly
38 More than devotion
40 Sine ___ non
41 Gary ___, Pultizer-winning Beat poet
42 Kind
43 Plays
44 Abrasive stuff
46 Spot for slop
47 Prevent from escaping
49 Breaches of faith

51 With 97-Across, bearer of edible triangular nuts
53 Land with monsoons
54 Not monaurally
58 Meat, in Madrid
61 Count with many titles
64 More faithful
65 Congresswoman Abzug and others
67 Vulnerable point
68 "Awww"-inspiring
69 It may be indicated by a stroke
70 Hot
72 An Untouchable
73 Mosaic flooring
75 Restaurateur Toots
76 Newport Beach sight
78 Where a bell ringer may stand
80 Ibsen play
83 Like some carol apparel
86 Within reach
87 Receiver's counterpart
90 Gave birth to
92 Drops
94 Fourth of 12: Abbr.
95 Eye openers?
96 Clark of country music
97 See 51-Across
98 Provided, as a line
99 ___ haddie (smoked fish)
100 Run for dear life?
102 Cold war draft

104 Williams's "Popeye" co-star
105 Attacked in a rage
106 Unpaired
107 Missed a golden opportunity
110 Disagrees
113 In shape
114 This puzzle's southern border?
115 Antarctica's ___ Coast
116 French pronoun
117 "___ bad!"
118 Hot
119 Water falls?
120 "___ a chance"

DOWN

1 It may glow in the dark
2 Crater creators, e.g.
3 Makeshift Frisbee
4 One taking a big bow
5 Suffix with Capri
6 Message in a bottle, maybe
7 Already chosen for play, say
8 Mass × velocity measurements
9 Sound in the middle of Italy
10 Unstable subatomic particle
11 Minute opening?
12 Beetle, e.g.
13 Hall-of-Fame pitcher Joss
14 Onetime
15 Spots for some shirts
16 Matching pair

17 "Here, maybe I can do it"
20 They're often dinged
24 Once called
29 Suffix with direct
31 RCA competitor
33 See 37-Across
34 Big name in sneakers
35 Like baba
39 Bay windows
40 Ancient Roman financial officer: Var.
41 Targeted, as with a mailing
44 Boom
45 Firms: Abbr.
48 "Sic et Non" author
49 Discuss business at a social occasion
50 Mansion staff
52 Bay
53 Hater
55 Rustic
56 Often-smoked fish
57 Metallurgists' supplies
58 Explorer at Labrador in 1497
59 French conductor Leibowitz
60 Red or Card
62 Satellite of 1962
63 Approval on "The Little Rascals"
66 Strong women
68 Licentious man
70 Blood carriers
71 Has trouble swallowing
74 Place of chaos
77 Cow annoyers

SUNDAY

by Joe DiPietro

79 Org. in TV's "Nash Bridges"
81 Adds as a bonus
82 State capital on the Tietê River
83 Started to melt
84 Home of many talk shows

85 Opposite of dominate
87 Supplier of candy and toys for kids
88 "Shane" actor
89 Lion, at times
91 It's used to check septic systems

93 Asian observance
95 Shareholder's income: Abbr.
98 Steakhouse selection
99 Cot alternative
101 Guitar great ___ Paul

103 They were once cloned
104 Chop up
108 Prefix with skeleton
109 Actor Wheaton
111 Yalie
112 Take in slowly

ACROSS

1 Relaxed
8 Co. that makes Band-Aids
13 Pivots
19 Dish ladled out hot or cold
20 Draw out
22 Dominant dogs
23 In myth, killer of his own mother, Clytemnestra
24 Chinese symbols on Santa's vehicle?
26 Do some tailoring
27 Snooker need
28 Fortuneteller's opening
29 Baseball's Moises
30 Paleontological wonder at a natural history museum
31 Part of old French Indochina
33 Punching devices
35 "March of the Penguins" director ___ Jacquet
36 8-Down, with "the"
37 Rolling rock
38 Itsy-bitsy door decoration?
43 Like some chiefs
45 Variety
46 Second string
47 Refuges
49 Spoke at great length
52 1994 sci-fi writer's memoir
56 Makings of a coup

57 Some 1960's coupes
58 "Get ___ get out"
60 Chemical ending
61 Home's counterpart
63 Sold out, in a way
67 In use
69 Hearst's San ___ castle
70 Delay
71 Scratch
72 Tremor
73 Relief provider
74 Dispatch boats
75 Spigot site
76 Common green house gift
77 A long, long time
79 "___ Rollo" (popular Mexican variety show)
80 Big test
83 Opposite of should
87 Whitish
88 "Don't get any ___"
90 ___-Caps
91 Hot dog
93 Sunburnt Santa?
97 Greek height
98 Dandy
101 River of Devon
102 Kind of terrier
103 ___ speak
104 Bog down
105 Big top?
107 Sight from Messina
109 It might leave tracks
110 "Peter Pan" writer
112 Santa reindeer-turned-zombie?
116 Fetch

117 Three in one
118 Celebrates
119 Woman in Sartre's "No Exit"
120 Texas city
121 Goodwill
122 Sauntered

DOWN

1 Cancels
2 One who might grab the bull by the horns
3 Gifts you only think about giving?
4 Hedingham Castle locale
5 Court minutes
6 Place to get a reaction in school?
7 Venusians, e.g.
8 Manger figure
9 Everything, on the Ems
10 Never, in Nürnberg
11 Early seventh-century year
12 Christmas gift easily identifiable by shaking?
13 Away's partner
14 Suffix with form
15 Kraft Nabisco Championship org.
16 Spiny cactus
17 Expired
18 Per se
21 Amazon's home
25 Cross-out
27 Handler of gifts for the kids on the "naughty" list?

32 Call at sea
34 Attest
37 Fleur-de-___
38 Mincemeat ___
39 Corner piece
40 Stretch (out)
41 Dorm overseers, for short
42 Popular record label
44 Adjusts, as laces
47 Pogo, e.g.
48 Italian tragic poet Vittorio
50 Stern parent's reply
51 Played some songs, say
53 Throws a Christmas tree?
54 "Encore!"
55 Hunter's meat
57 Star wearer: Abbr.
59 Christmas quaffs set atop a board?
62 Dot follower
64 Film buff's cable channel
65 Thrice, in Rx's
66 Grp. with the 1977 hit "Do Ya"
67 "Mazel ___!"
68 Melodic pieces
71 "Law & Order" figs.
73 Sell to a new audience, say
76 Rescues
78 Military trial, briefly
81 "___ the season to be jolly"
82 N.J. summer setting
84 G8 member

SUNDAY

by Brendan Emmett Quigley

85 Serengeti grazer
86 Christmas laughs
87 Tokyo-based carrier
89 Father Time prop
92 1962 Paul Anka hit
93 Precede
94 Stephen Hawking's alma mater
95 Comedian ___ Mac
96 Kansas City suburb
99 Brooks Robinson, e.g.
100 Squinted (at)
103 Like dishwater
104 1957 hit for the Bobbettes
106 Obligation
108 Genesis man
109 QB Hasselbeck
111 Hgts.
113 U.S.N. officer
114 Stephen of "V for Vendetta"
115 Samuel's teacher, in the Bible
116 Two qtrs.

(See Notepad)

ACROSS

1 Sharp competitor
4 "Do ___ to eat a peach?": Eliot
9 German link
12 Represent, as in legal matters
18 Ectomorphic
19 Worker with a chair
20 Be a make-up artist?
21 Red fluorescent dye: Var.
22 1954 film set in 16th-century Japan
24 Old cable inits.
25 They may get into a jam
26 Low digits
27 Elite groups
29 About
30 Many garden plantings
32 Most broad?
34 Wide shoe spec
37 1981 Alan Alda comedy, with "The"
42 Underground network
43 Diplomat Silas
45 Flip (out)
46 Jubilant
48 Barely beat
49 Director Welles
50 Stockholm flier
51 1982 Dudley Moore tearjerker
54 British gun
55 In a sardonic way
56 Blood line
57 Goldman ___
59 Pre-Q queue
60 Some accents
63 Bad beginning?
66 Prof.'s helpers
67 More manly-chested
70 Charged

71 "Yeah, that'll happen!"
73 "All the Things You Are" composer
74 Avian meat
75 Wordsworth works
76 1983 Charles Bronson thriller
79 Symbol
80 Fed. medical research group
81 Fey of "30 Rock"
82 Supremos
83 QB Favre
84 Child's activity?
86 Candy holder
87 Madrid Mrs.
88 Browns slowly
90 Roman man
91 "___ new?"
93 Fights
94 Pang
96 Tale
97 1990 sequel to "Chinatown," with "The"
101 Half of a 1955 merger: Abbr.
104 January 1 events
105 Colorado Indian
106 Ghost
107 Instruments with keys
109 Off
110 Christopher who wrote "Still Me"
112 1988 baseball flick
115 Emeritus: Abbr.
116 In an odd way
119 Magazine success
120 Cart
122 Subscription card option
127 Feminine suffix
128 The Caribbean's ___ Islands
130 Suffix with glass

131 1987 Peter Falk crime caper
133 "Quantum Healing" author
134 Some linemen: Abbr.
135 Heraldic silver
136 Towel embroidery
137 Reasons
138 Summer clock setting: Abbr.
139 Entangle
140 Gridiron figs.

DOWN

1 Incomes
2 Pause in verse
3 Cape ___, Mass.
4 "___ Said" (Neil Diamond hit)
5 Knock out, say
6 Start of a spell
7 Tail end
8 "Love Story" author Segal
9 Last month
10 1995 Hugh Grant farce
11 Rock stats
12 Auspices
13 With 81-Down, tradition suggested by this puzzle's theme
14 Bygone despot
15 1970 Jack Nicholson picture
16 ___ lark
17 Thing in court
18 Original title of Beethoven's "Fidelio"
19 Rafter's wood
22 Crooks
23 Dover delicacy
28 Not liquidy
31 Begins courting
33 Cable staple since 1979
35 Organic compound

36 Choosing-up word
38 "___ needle pulling thread" ("The Sound of Music" lyric)
39 Flamenco cheer
40 Rob Roy's refusal
41 Co. shares
44 Overthrowing, e.g.
47 Twisty curve
52 Temper
53 Old IBM PC's
54 Price reader
56 Turkish V.I.P.'s
58 Feuding (with)
59 Gas station adjunct, often
60 It may go for a couple of bucks
61 Dashboard feature
62 1932 romance with Maurice Chevalier
63 Actor with a mohawk
64 Kind of harp
65 Elegy
67 Laugh sound
68 Not play it straight
69 Peewees
71 Kind of test
72 War stat
73 Metric wts.
76 Baseball's Martinez
77 Part of E.S.L.: Abbr.
78 Bank offering
79 It's surrounded by white
81 See 13-Down
83 Some cricketers
85 Popular smokes
86 1999 film set in the Persian Gulf
88 ___ choy
89 Parisian way
91 Flamingo, e.g.
92 Speedway letters

SUNDAY

by Elizabeth C. Gorski

93 Huge financial loss
94 It'll give you a lift
95 Instruction to a chauffeur
96 Gagarin in space
98 Golf's Michelle
99 ". . . ___ quit!"
100 Springy dance
101 Joint proprietors
102 Cold-blooded pets
103 Horse handler
106 Unload
108 Like a Cyclops
111 Most loathsome
113 1545 council site
114 No more than
117 Arm parts
118 Jewish orgs.
121 Concert gear
123 Bring in
124 Org. for women drivers
125 Copycat
126 Actress Daly
128 Junk bond rating
129 "I see!"
132 "___ me?"

The New York Times

SMART PUZZLES
PRESENTED WITH STYLE

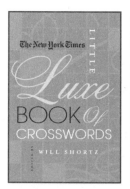
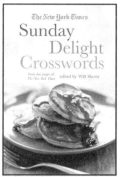

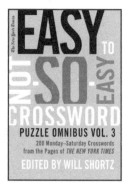

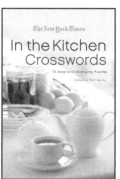

Available at your local bookstore or online at www.nytimes.com/nytstore

 St. Martin's Griffin

Answers

1

```
OCTANTS  STEREOS
PLATOONSERGEANT
PORTRAITPAINTER
OOZED  VAT  STYLI
STAN  BEGIN  SOAP
EIN  TELECOM  UNE
RETOOLED  MITRED
   HHOUR  SINGH
BOEING  AUNTIEEM
ORA  SALINES  ARI
TIPI  SARRE  SRAS
ANERA  RIO  MATSU
NOMOREILOVEYOUS
ICANTSAYFORSURE
CONSIST  SWEATED
```

2

```
MMMMGOOD   OFFED
AAAMEMBER  PRONE
TELLSALIE  TERRA
TWA  THATSTOOBAD
HERR  ADIOS  NAGS
ASIAN  IERE  DEE
UTAHAN  STTERESA
    ATOR  SSNS
EXPLODES  ENVIED
XER  ICET  APPLE
PROB  CHERI  SAAB
LOTUSEATERS  NIE
OXEYE  LOVESCENE
REGIS  LIONTAMER
EDENS  TRESPASS
```

3

```
ETTU     SEAMOSS
DIRTS   CASTANET
INUIT  MONTAIGNE
TESLA  AFTERNOON
HASITINFOR  MIRO
 RESURGES  HANES
  RETILE  ZINGS
   ONESHOT
 TERRA  LARSEN
DALEY  TERRINES
EREV  JOEMONTANA
TAKELEAVE  GATOS
ENTRUSTED  LINOS
STRESSES  ELIZA
TOASTEE    SKED
```

4

```
LAMB  OWLET  ILLS
ASEA  RHODE  NOOK
DIAL  GEOMETRYII
LANDMARKS  ROAST
ENTWINES  PEAL
   ISSUE  RADISH
SPANS  NEMOS  SHE
WETSUIT  EDUCTOR
ANA  GROSZ  ROSES
GAGMAN  AZTEC
  LANA  TARRAGON
AWARD  KINESCOPE
SANTAMARIA  OTIS
AGCY  TRENT  LUNT
PEER  MOSEY  APES
```

5

```
STRATA  OBSTACLE
TEASEL  PETUNIAS
ATRIAL  EVENINGS
GREASE  NEPALESE
EARNER  ALS
     GUNS  MADAM
PLAYDEAD  CANINE
LINEONESPOCKETS
ADDLES  HUSHHUSH
TOILS  RUNT
     CAT  AMPULE
ISOTONIC  RAINED
MARIPOSA  ILLINI
PREDATES  CELTIC
SAMEHERE  ASSENT
```

6

```
A I R G U I T A R ■ ■ C O C A
S N O O P D O G G ■ L A P A Z
T E S T A T O R S ■ A M E M O
A R I ■ T A T E ■ ■ Z O N E ■
I R E S ■ G E E ■ A Y M A R A
R O T C S ■ D R O P S I N O N
E R H A R D ■ S H O U L D N T
■ ■ E R I E S ■ M O S E S ■
F I R E L A N E ■ R A T H E R
A N I T A L O O S ■ N E U R O
S A V A N T ■ L E A ■ A T M S
■ H E C K ■ I N D S ■ C I I
C O T T A ■ I T S A P L A N E
O L E I N ■ T H E M A S S E S
M E R C ■ ■ E S S A Y T E S T
```

7

```
■ ■ S T U D I O R E M A K E S
■ ■ J U N I O R P A R T N E R S
W A S T E N O T W A N T N O T
U N H ■ S T N S ■ ■ S E N D A
R U I N ■ S O F A S ■ D E E R
S A B E R ■ N O S E S ■ L D S
T R A V I S ■ R E A P S ■ ■
S Y R I A N S ■ A L L E G R O
■ ■ S T O O P ■ S A T E E N
A G S ■ A W R A P ■ T A N T E
S O A P ■ S T R O M ■ E D I E
S O C A L ■ O L E G ■ A R Y
A G R E E T O D I S A G R E E
Y O U S A I D I T N O T M E ■
S O M E P L A C E E L S E ■
```

8

```
■ S T A T I O N S ■ A M P S
I H A D A D R E A M ■ B O I L
N E V E R A G A I N ■ B O Z O
T R E ■ A H A ■ L O R E N Z ■
O P R Y ■ O N D O P E ■ W A S
W A N E ■ A Z U R ■ S T A P H
■ ■ M O N A D S ■ P O L I O
B E T E L S ■ ■ B U N K E D
E L A N D ■ S T A I N S ■ ■
R A D I I ■ H O S S ■ I S N T
T S P ■ S C A T H E ■ L A I R
■ T O W H O M ■ A C T ■ M E A
M I L E ■ U P I N T H E S K Y
A C E S ■ P O S T E R I O R S
P S S T ■ O H I D U N N O ■
```

9

```
I N C A H O O T S ■ R A M P S
A I R W O R T H Y ■ I M A R I
S T A N D F I R M ■ P E R I L
I R T ■ S E T I ■ R O S C O E
M A I D ■ O I L C A N ■ E R N
O T O E S ■ S L O T ■ B A T T
V E N I C E ■ A R E Y O U O K
■ ■ C A R D I N D E X ■ ■
B L U E M O O N ■ R A C I S M
B A K R ■ D I M S ■ N A R C O
Q T R ■ D E T A I L ■ R E I N
P E A P O D ■ N E E T ■ L E I
I F I L L ■ P I G G Y B A N K
T E N E T ■ C L E A R A N C E
S E E D S ■ T A L L O R D E R
```

10

```
Q U I D P R O Q U O ■ G E T A
U L T R A S O U N D ■ O X E N
I T S I N T H E R E ■ O P E N
V I A ■ ■ L S A T ■ D O T O
E M T S ■ M A T T S ■ A S H Y
R A R A ■ A L E E ■ K N E E S
E T A T ■ S A D D L E D ■ ■
D E P I C T ■ ■ I N E V E R
■ ■ N O S C O R E ■ V E N I
J E S S E ■ O N A N ■ I N S T
A M A H ■ G N A W S ■ L E N Z
C O T E ■ A C T H ■ ■ R A I
O T O E ■ S E E I F I C A R E
B E R T ■ E R A D I C A T E S
I S I S ■ S T R E S S T E S T
```

11

```
CUDDLE ■ TARPAPER
ANORAK ■ AGUILERA
MIMING ■ RUSTLERS
STINK ■, RESTSTOP
HANK ■ LAYSISTERS
ARAMEAN ■ ABA ■
FINERIES ■ URGED
TAC ■ ATWATER ■ ELI
SNEAD ■ PROGRAMS
■ NIN ■ INHERED
POLICEDOGS ■ MIRA
AVEMARIA ■ HENRI
MAMABEAR ■ RUNGIN
PLOTLINE ■ ILDUCE
ASNEEDED ■ GASPED
```

12

```
CHATSUP ■ TRAUMAS
RADIOFREEEUROPE
ITSACOINCIDENCE
STORK ■ OMANI ■ GAS
TERA ■ CRETE ■ MORT
ORB ■ GEESE ■ QUOTA
■ HARSH ■ CURSER
RESIZES ■ CHOKERS
EXUDES ■ LAITY ■
DINER ■ TISCH ■ PSI
STDS ■ CHESS ■ COAT
OFO ■ ALANA ■ CHILI
NEWAGEMOVEMENTS
JENNIFERANISTON
ASSENTS ■ SEXTANT
```

13

```
                THINK
THOSE ■ TAD ■ IRONON
HIKES ■ ORR ■ SEEMTO
ITALS ■ SENATESEAT
NOPLACETOGO ■
KNIT ■ AAH ■ LOGICAL
■ SOAR ■ ANI ■ ASAMI
■ CEL ■ ENAMORED
■ OUTSIDETHEBOX
ENLISTED ■ ABA
WEAVE ■ NYC ■ ARNO
ERNESTO ■ OIL ■ OMIT
■ OVERFLOWETH
DREAMWORKS ■ FARSI
EILEEN ■ MEA ■ FITIN
ECHOES ■ ARY ■ STANK
THINK
```

14

```
PASSBY ■ LASCASAS
ENTIRE ■ EDNABEST
STENOS ■ TOOLCASE
THEIDIOTBOX ■ PUG
LIPSYNCHED ■ MOAN
ELLE ■ DEES ■ VERGE
SLY ■ WEAR ■ JESTER
■ IRENECARA ■
TRACED ■ BAMA ■ MEG
SEVEN ■ PERE ■ MAYA
ORES ■ MILESTONES
NOR ■ DAVIDCARUSO
GUIDEDOG ■ ASIMOV
ATLENGTH ■ ATTIRE
SELFTEST ■ NEATEN
```

15

```
SLIPRINGS ■ TEAMS
LEMONTART ■ AXMAN
INALATHER ■ CAPRA
DOME ■ GEEKCHIC
BRANT ■ HONKYTONK
YENTA ■ URGE ■ ARAB
■ APPLYTO ■ SARA
RUT ■ EEL ■ HUG ■ EAR
ANIT ■ SAGETEA ■
TINA ■ EBAN ■ ADAMS
ROCKSTARS ■ RANAT
ANTEHALL ■ SONO
CRUSE ■ LASTSTRAW
EERIE ■ ONAVERAGE
SPENT ■ ODDSMAKER
```

16

```
S P A C E C A D E T S ■ A S H
N O T E L L M O T E L ■ R T E
O R A L H I S T O R Y ■ M A S
B O X ■ I O T A ■ M E T E R S
S U I T ■ S E G A ■ R O N D O
■ S A U D ■ L E M S ■ M I A S
■ R A J ■ S A L T B A T H
G A G A R I N ■ T O U R N E Y
I L L N E V E R ■ W B A ■ ■
R O A D ■ E W E S ■ B D R M
L E R O I ■ S F P D ■ Y E O H
Y V E T T E ■ R I E L ■ G R O
M E D ■ A S I A N F U S I O N
A R A ■ L A V I E E N R O S E
N A T ■ L I O N T R A I N E R
```

17

```
A P T ■ P A R ■ ■ S P I R A L
L A H D I D A H ■ L O N E L Y
I N E U R O P E ■ A R C S I N
C A S C A R A S ■ S T A T E N
E M I T T E R S ■ H E M A N ■
■ A S S E R T ■ R E N E G E S
■ ■ S I D E S T R E E T
L A N E S ■ S E A ■ S A S S Y
I C E S K A T E R S ■ ■
B E T T E R S ■ M O P S U P
■ S P I L T ■ B A R R A G E S
H O R M E L ■ A M B U L A N T
A V I A T E ■ L E A N O N M E
R E C T O S ■ I N T E N D E R
P R E E N S ■ T E D ■ A N N
```

18

```
P A S T A S A L A D ■ T S P S
A R M O R P L A T E ■ W E R T
D E E P S E A T E D ■ O N E A
S A W T E E T H ■ U N E A S Y
■ ■ E N D E ■ I C E D T E A
B O N N I E ■ E M E R G E N T
A P U ■ C R E M E ■ D E P T H
C E D E ■ S L A T S ■ D A D O
K R I S S ■ M I A T A ■ G A M
P A S T O R A L ■ R I B E Y E
E S T E F A N ■ C A M O ■ ■
D E C L A W ■ R O T E N O N E
A R A L ■ B O O K E D I T O R
L I M E ■ A B N E G A T O R S
S A P S ■ R E A D Y T O E A T
```

19

```
F R A N Z K A F K A ■ N A T S
L I M E S T R E E T ■ E T U I
I C E C A S T L E S ■ E T N A
T E N K ■ P I P E D R E A M
E D D ■ S P A N I A R D S ■
■ S H A P E N ■ C O T T A
D I S P O S E S ■ P A W S A T
A L T E R E R ■ B A R E T T A
H E R E T O ■ C A R T L O A D
S T A D T ■ P A R C E L ■
■ P R O T E S T E R ■ C A M
D O P E N A N C E ■ C I T I
A V I A ■ S T A N L A U R E L
V E N D ■ S A R D I N E C A N
E R G S ■ E X A S P E R A T E
```

20

```
J A C K K N I F E ■ I D E A L
A L A N L O M A X ■ S O C K O
V A R I E G A T E ■ B A S I E
A B A T E ■ B I G O N ■ E H S
M A V S ■ L U G E D ■ G I S
A M A ■ B E M U S E S ■ A T E
N A N T E S ■ E I T H E R O R
■ O N T V ■ S O O T ■ ■
M A D E I R A S ■ J O C O S E
A X E ■ N A V A J O S ■ L E V
R O T ■ D A V E Y ■ M I C E
A L E ■ D E V A S ■ L E V E R
C O N D O ■ O N T H E S I D E
A T T I C ■ O N E O N O N E S
S L E E K ■ M A R E S N E S T
```

21

J	O	S	H	E	D	■	J	E	R	O	B	O	A	M
A	P	P	E	A	R	■	I	S	A	B	E	L	L	A
C	E	L	E	R	Y	■	M	O	B	I	L	I	T	Y
K	R	I	L	L	■	Z	E	T	A	S	■	V	A	N
F	E	N	S	■	T	E	N	E	T	■	M	I	R	O
I	T	T	■	R	Y	D	E	R	■	Y	E	A	S	T
S	T	E	P	U	P	■	Z	I	P	P	Y	■	■	■
H	A	R	R	I	E	D	■	C	U	R	E	A	L	L
■	■	I	N	B	O	X	■	P	E	R	D	U	E	■
P	O	E	M	S	■	V	E	E	P	S	■	R	C	A
U	R	S	A	■	G	E	R	R	Y	■	P	E	R	P
N	I	P	■	C	O	C	O	A	■	M	O	N	E	Y
J	O	R	J	A	F	O	X	■	L	A	M	A	Z	E
A	L	I	E	N	A	T	E	■	A	M	E	L	I	A
B	E	T	T	E	R	E	D	■	V	A	S	S	A	R

22

S	E	A	L	I	N	■	S	C	R	I	P	T	S
A	L	B	I	N	O	S	■	P	H	A	R	A	O	H
P	I	C	T	U	R	E	■	E	U	T	E	R	P	E
I	N	T	H	R	E	E	■	R	M	S	■	I	S	A
D	A	V	E	E	G	G	E	R	S	■	M	E	E	T
■	■	■	■	R	E	L	Y	■	F	E	T	C	H
■	B	E	R	S	E	R	K	■	C	U	R	A	R	E
T	O	I	L	E	T	S	■	C	A	J	O	L	E	D
A	N	D	E	R	S	■	Z	A	N	I	E	S	T	■
P	A	E	S	E	■	P	A	R	A	■	■	■	■	■
A	P	R	S	■	M	A	K	E	A	S	C	E	N	E
S	A	D	■	G	O	B	■	E	N	A	B	L	E	R
B	R	O	K	E	R	S	■	R	I	N	G	S	I	N
A	T	W	O	R	S	T	■	S	T	A	B	I	L	E
R	E	N	A	M	E	S	■	E	A	S	E	L	S

23

M	A	K	E	S	A	G	R	E	A	T	G	I	F	T
E	D	I	T	O	R	I	A	L	W	R	I	T	E	R
G	E	N	E	R	A	L	D	E	L	I	V	E	R	Y
A	L	G	■	A	B	A	S	E	S	■	E	R	R	■
B	I	T	E	R	S	■	■	■	A	N	A	I	S	■
I	N	U	S	E	■	D	E	P	O	S	I	T	E	D
T	E	T	E	■	L	I	V	E	L	I	N	E	S	S
■	■	■	L	O	V	E	S	E	T	■	■	■	■	■
S	P	A	R	E	P	A	R	T	S	■	E	L	E	A
E	A	S	E	M	E	N	T	S	■	B	R	A	Y	S
M	I	S	T	S	■	■	■	S	E	N	S	E	S	■
■	S	O	I	■	A	C	O	R	N	S	■	T	H	U
G	A	R	R	I	S	O	N	K	E	I	L	L	O	R
E	N	T	E	N	T	E	C	O	R	D	I	A	L	E
L	O	S	E	S	O	N	E	S	T	E	M	P	E	R

24

A	L	D	A	■	S	C	A	G	■	■	L	U	F	T
F	O	O	T	L	O	O	S	E	■	B	E	T	A	S
T	I	N	H	E	L	M	E	T	■	U	N	T	I	E
A	N	T	E	S	U	P	■	W	A	R	I	E	R	■
■	■	■	A	L	T	O	■	A	L	T	E	R	S	■
D	I	A	R	I	E	S	■	R	M	O	N	T	H	S
A	C	U	T	E	S	T	■	M	A	N	T	R	A	P
W	A	N	■	■	■	■	■	■	■	I	K	E	■	■
E	N	T	I	C	E	D	■	S	C	A	L	P	E	L
S	T	I	M	U	L	I	■	A	R	T	I	E	S	T
■	■	S	E	P	S	I	S	■	N	E	O	N	■	■
■	■	E	M	O	T	E	S	■	R	E	N	T	A	L	S
L	E	A	S	E	■	E	Y	E	P	I	E	C	E	S
T	I	M	E	R	■	C	A	M	E	C	L	E	A	N
S	T	E	S	■	T	H	O	R	■	S	S	R	S

25

C	O	C	O	A	B	E	A	N	S	■	S	H	A	H
O	R	A	N	G	E	T	R	E	E	■	C	A	T	E
O	N	T	H	E	S	T	A	G	E	■	A	N	T	A
P	O	T	E	N	T	A	T	E	■	O	R	D	E	R
■	■	■	R	T	E	■	■	V	I	O	L	I	S	T
C	A	S	■	R	D	A	S	■	C	H	A	N	T	S
A	N	T	S	Y	■	E	C	C	E	■	T	H	E	E
S	N	A	P	■	T	O	I	L	S	■	T	A	D	A
T	A	I	L	■	I	N	F	O	■	P	I	N	T	S
A	B	R	A	D	E	■	I	T	E	R	■	D	O	E
S	E	C	T	O	R	S	■	S	E	M	■	■	■	■
P	L	A	T	H	■	C	E	S	T	S	I	B	O	N
E	L	S	E	■	R	A	D	I	A	L	T	I	R	E
L	E	E	R	■	G	L	I	T	T	E	R	A	T	I
L	E	S	S	■	S	E	T	S	E	Y	E	S	O	N

26

```
A T T H E O P E R A ■ E P H S
C R A Y O L A B O X ■ S L A P
H O L E S I N O N E ■ T E R R
O M E N ■ N I N ■ L A D I D A
O P R A H ■ C I S S Y ■ A L I
S E S ■ A L B E E ■ R O D I N
■ ■ A U G U S T ■ G E N E
H A N D S E T ■ I M P O S E D
A M O I ■ ■ T E N T E D ■ ■
D O N T S ■ O L M A N ■ C P L
A R F ■ D A N N O ■ N E A L E
S E A L I N ■ O T S ■ R E A S
E T T E ■ A E R I A L I S T S
A T A N ■ I N T O X I C A T E
T O L D ■ S C E N E T H R E E
```

27

```
S E S T E T ■ T A J M A H A L
E X H A L E ■ S Q U I R E L Y
A P E M E N ■ Q U I C K I E S
B E L L E ■ B U I C K ■ F R I
O L L A ■ M E A N Y ■ L E O N
A L A ■ Z O R R O ■ V E R S E
R E C H A R G E ■ M I T ■ ■
D E S E X E S ■ N U D I S T S
■ ■ L I S ■ P A R E N T A L
O A S I S ■ R O D E O ■ A M A
X B O X ■ R E M I X ■ A R A M
C U R ■ Q A T A R ■ M A T R I
A S T E R O I D ■ H E R O I N
R E I N S U R E ■ A M O U N T
T R E S T L E S ■ W O N T D O
```

28

```
G E L L E D ■ ■ A B L E S T
A Q U A V I T ■ C R I M E A
S U M M O N E R ■ R O S I N S
J A P A N E S E ■ E A T S A T
E T E R N I T Y ■ A D E S T E
T E R R E N C E ■ G E N I E S
■ ■ A S B E S T O S ■ ■
■ C O S T S ■ A S T O N ■
■ M A I T R E D S ■ ■
V A L L E E ■ R E D S T A R T
I R I S E S ■ A P O L O G I A
A L B E R T ■ W A T E R L O O
C E R E A L ■ L I T E R A T I
O N E D G E ■ R E V E R E S
M E S S E S ■ ■ D E S E R T
```

29

```
■ F E L L S ■ T H E C O M I C
B O R E A L ■ H O N O L U L U
B R O N Z E M E D A L L I S T
L A S T Y E A R ■ M E A R A ■
■ ■ ■ P I E C E S ■ ■
F L A T D E N I A L ■ R A J A
R E P A I R I N G ■ V E N A L
A I R M A S S ■ E C O C I D E
G L O P S ■ S O D A W A T E R
S A N A ■ P U S H E S P A S T
■ ■ A R E T E S ■ ■
■ S E A T O ■ L A U R E L E D
T E R R I B L E T R A G E D Y
A L L C L E A R ■ A Y E A Y E
M A E S T R O S ■ S E R F S ■
```

30

```
S P O R T S B R A S ■ D I S H
H A V E A H E A R T ■ O N T O
I T A L I A N I C E ■ T S A R
M E L A L L E N ■ P U T O N S
■ ■ T O O T ■ C O L L U D E
A F F I R M ■ C O N N E C T S
P A R O S ■ J U L I A ■ I R E
P L A N ■ R O B O T ■ C A I N
A L T ■ C E D A R ■ N A N A S
R E E L E D I N ■ J O S T L E
I N R A N G E ■ R U T H ■ ■
T I N D E R ■ L A S T M I L E
I D I D ■ A N E S T H E S I A
O O Z E ■ P O E T L A R I A T
N L E R ■ E S S A Y T E S T S
```

31

A	G	A	P	E	■	W	A	S	H	A	B	L	E	S
R	O	L	L	O	■	E	M	A	I	L	L	I	S	T
I	N	P	E	N	■	B	E	R	T	L	A	N	C	E
D	E	A	D	■	L	E	N	D	S	A	N	E	A	R
N	F	C	■	R	E	D	D	I	■	C	A	P	E	■
E	L	I	■	A	V	I	S	■	M	A	H	R	E	S
S	A	N	D	P	I	T	■	N	I	L	E	■	■	■
S	T	O	O	P	T	O	■	U	S	E	R	I	D	S
■	■	■	P	E	E	R	■	T	R	U	S	T	I	N
R	I	S	E	R	S	■	S	M	U	T	■	S	S	E
E	N	O	S	■	■	F	E	E	L	S	■	N	E	E
A	L	L	T	H	E	R	A	G	E	■	B	O	A	Z
M	O	V	E	A	L	O	N	G	■	P	A	U	S	E
E	V	E	R	S	I	N	C	E	■	A	T	S	E	A
R	E	D	S	T	A	T	E	R	■	C	H	E	S	T

32

S	I	S	■	E	R	M	A	■	E	B	B	E	T	S
I	N	T	E	R	I	O	R	■	P	E	O	R	I	A
A	F	R	A	I	D	O	F	T	H	E	D	A	R	K
M	O	I	S	T	E	N	■	R	E	V	I	S	E	S
■	K	E	R	R	■	G	O	D	E	L	■	■	■	■
S	U	E	D	E	■	C	O	U	R	S	E	P	R	O
U	P	S	■	A	G	A	S	S	I	■	S	E	E	M
S	T	O	W	■	A	S	P	E	N	■	S	A	G	A
H	O	U	R	■	S	T	E	R	E	O	■	R	A	N
I	N	T	E	G	R	A	L	S	■	V	A	L	L	I
■	■	C	L	A	N	S	■	R	E	P	O	■	■	■
S	P	O	K	A	N	E	■	S	A	R	A	N	A	C
C	O	M	I	N	G	T	O	A	M	E	R	I	C	A
T	R	A	N	C	E	■	A	V	I	A	T	O	R	S
V	E	R	G	E	S	■	R	E	S	T	■	N	E	T

33

K	O	P	U	N	C	H	■	G	I	G	O	L	O	S
I	R	O	N	O	R	E	■	E	V	I	D	E	N	T
P	I	T	C	R	E	W	■	T	E	N	D	S	T	O
S	N	L	■	D	E	E	J	A	Y	■	S	A	H	L
B	O	U	T	■	D	R	U	G	■	B	E	L	■	■
A	C	C	R	A	■	S	S	R	S	■	U	R	G	E
Y	O	K	E	L	S	■	T	I	E	O	N	E	O	N
■	■	■	P	O	W	E	R	P	A	C	K	■	■	■
G	O	F	I	G	U	R	E	■	T	H	E	M	G	S
A	V	I	D	■	M	I	L	O	■	S	P	A	R	E
T	E	X	■	C	A	N	S	■	T	R	E	X	■	■
E	R	I	N	■	S	I	X	T	U	S	■	T	A	P
M	A	N	A	G	E	D	■	A	L	L	R	I	S	E
E	G	G	R	O	L	L	■	P	L	A	I	N	E	R
N	E	S	C	A	F	E	■	E	A	T	D	I	R	T

34

S	T	R	E	S	S	T	E	S	T	S	■	P	A	L
I	H	A	V	E	N	O	I	D	E	A	■	A	C	E
F	O	R	E	W	A	R	N	I	N	G	■	L	I	S
T	R	I	■	E	G	O	S	■	■	G	O	O	D	S
E	N	T	E	R	■	■	■	S	P	Y	W	A	R	E
D	Y	E	S	■	B	I	W	A	■	E	L	A	N	■
■	■	P	A	G	A	N	I	N	I	■	T	I	S	■
■	C	O	N	C	E	N	T	R	A	T	I	O	N	■
W	O	N	■	H	O	T	E	L	M	A	N	■	■	■
O	M	E	N	■	D	A	L	Y	■	G	E	M	S	■
R	E	Q	U	I	E	M	■	■	D	E	C	O	Y	■
S	O	U	N	D	■	■	I	S	A	O	■	H	U	S
T	V	A	■	E	A	S	T	E	R	N	M	O	S	T
E	E	R	■	S	W	I	S	S	C	H	E	E	S	E
D	R	T	■	T	E	X	A	S	H	O	L	D	E	M

35

L	I	N	C	■	S	P	I	K	E	J	O	N	Z	E
O	N	E	O	■	M	I	N	I	S	E	R	I	E	S
A	D	E	N	■	U	N	I	T	P	R	I	C	E	S
D	I	D	N	T	G	E	T	■	G	E	E	S	E	■
■	S	L	O	W	L	Y	■	W	H	E	N	■	■	■
■	P	E	T	E	Y	■	G	A	U	N	T	L	E	T
D	O	N	E	E	■	Q	U	I	T	S	■	E	X	E
E	S	O	S	■	S	U	I	T	S	■	T	A	P	A
L	E	S	■	F	O	A	L	S	■	W	A	F	E	R
I	D	E	A	L	I	S	T	■	F	I	N	E	R	■
■	■	D	A	L	I	■	B	A	N	Z	A	I	■	■
S	A	G	E	T	■	F	R	I	G	A	T	E	S	■
W	I	N	E	C	O	O	L	E	R	■	N	I	N	E
A	D	A	M	A	N	D	E	V	E	■	I	N	C	A
N	E	W	S	R	E	A	D	E	R	■	A	G	E	S

36

S	M	A	S	H	E	R	O	O	■	D	E	C	O	R
N	O	F	O	O	L	I	N	G	■	A	G	A	P	E
I	N	F	I	E	L	D	E	R	■	D	O	M	E	S
P	R	I	G	■	■	M	E	S	S	T	E	N	T	■
P	O	R	N	O	■	R	O	S	E	■	R	I	T	A
Y	E	M	E	N	■	U	R	S	A	M	I	N	O	R
■	■	E	S	S	I	E	■	S	E	P	T	E	T	■
A	S	S	■	P	A	N	■	E	O	N	■	O	D	S
S	H	O	V	E	L	■	K	E	N	A	N	■	■	■
S	I	L	I	C	A	G	E	L	■	C	U	S	P	S
E	V	I	L	■	M	A	Y	S	■	E	T	H	A	N
M	A	C	L	E	I	S	H	■	■	C	O	R	E	■
B	R	I	A	R	■	B	O	N	A	P	A	R	T	E
L	E	T	G	O	■	A	L	A	B	A	S	T	E	R
Y	E	S	E	S	■	G	E	T	S	R	E	A	D	Y

37

	G	A	M	E	■	■	D	I	E	T	S	O	D	A
B	E	L	I	E	D	■	O	N	C	E	A	D	A	Y
O	N	E	D	G	E	■	N	O	O	N	T	I	M	E
X	X	X	I	■	A	T	T	N	■	N	I	N	E	■
■	■	■	S	L	I	P	■	M	I	N	■	■	■	■
R	O	A	D	K	I	L	L	■	A	S	Y	L	U	M
I	D	E	M	A	N	D	A	R	E	■	■	E	N	O
L	E	I	S	■	E	Y	E	■	■	O	T	I	S	■
E	T	O	■	■	E	S	W	I	T	S	W	I	T	H
Y	O	U	N	M	E	■	I	N	A	S	E	N	S	E
■	■	O	A	R	■	T	A	B	S	■	■	■	■	■
■	G	U	N	K	■	A	H	S	O	■	S	K	I	M
P	E	R	F	E	C	T	■	■	O	N	E	I	D	A
E	L	L	E	R	B	E	E	■	S	O	T	T	E	D
A	S	S	E	S	S	E	S	■	■	H	E	A	D	■

38

I	N	F	I	N	I	T	E	■	N	U	M	B	E	R
N	O	R	S	E	M	E	N	■	O	T	E	L	L	O
S	P	A	R	T	A	N	S	■	H	E	R	O	E	S
E	L	I	A	■	C	E	N	T	I	■	M	O	V	E
C	A	L	E	■	S	T	A	R	T	■	A	P	A	R
T	C	E	L	L	■	S	R	A	■	S	I	E	T	E
S	E	R	I	E	S	■	E	M	B	E	D	D	E	D
■	■	■	E	T	C	■	S	A	X	■	■	■	■	■
I	N	P	E	R	S	O	N	■	R	E	D	R	A	W
N	O	R	M	S	■	V	I	A	■	D	E	U	C	E
A	T	O	P	■	B	E	R	M	S	■	E	N	C	L
R	A	V	E	■	E	N	V	O	I	■	P	A	R	L
U	S	E	R	I	D	■	A	R	T	I	S	T	E	S
S	T	R	O	V	E	■	N	A	U	S	E	A	T	E
H	E	B	R	E	W	■	A	L	P	H	A	B	E	T

39

H	O	T	S	P	O	T	■	B	I	O	P	I	C	S
A	P	R	I	O	R	I	■	A	C	T	A	B	L	E
H	E	A	D	S	I	N	■	L	E	T	S	E	A	T
A	N	N	E	H	E	C	H	E	■	A	T	A	R	I
■	■	■	S	C	E	N	T	O	F	A	W	O	M	A	N
A	T	L	A	S	T	■	L	U	N	A	R	■	■	■
C	H	A	R	T	■	W	E	L	D	S	■	P	E	A
D	O	T	S	■	D	A	I	L	Y	■	G	U	L	P
C	U	E	■	T	I	N	N	Y	■	R	U	B	L	E
■	■	T	O	N	T	O	■	P	O	L	E	A	X	■
M	A	J	O	R	G	E	N	E	R	A	L	S	■	■
E	R	U	P	T	■	D	E	M	O	N	I	C	A	L
S	E	N	D	O	F	F	■	I	L	O	V	E	L	A
A	N	T	O	N	I	O	■	L	I	K	E	N	E	D
S	T	A	G	I	E	R	■	E	X	E	R	T	E	D

40

C	E	R	A	M	I	C	S	■	K	O	J	A	K
E	X	O	N	E	R	A	T	E	■	A	N	A	M	E
S	Q	U	A	R	E	P	E	G	■	P	E	N	I	N
T	U	N	■	L	A	S	E	R	G	U	I	D	E	D
L	I	D	S	■	D	I	V	E	R	T	■	J	L	O
A	S	H	E	N	■	Z	E	T	A	■	■	■	■
V	I	O	L	A	T	E	■	S	N	L	■	M	E	A
I	T	L	L	D	O	■	■	D	A	B	O	M	B	■
E	E	E	■	A	R	R	■	H	E	R	E	T	I	C
■	■	■	R	A	C	E	■	D	A	H	L	S	■
E	D	A	■	V	I	T	A	L	S	■	K	E	E	P
V	E	N	U	S	D	E	M	I	L	O	■	A	Z	O
A	M	A	T	I	■	D	E	C	O	R	A	T	O	R
D	O	I	N	G	■	G	R	E	E	N	B	E	L	T
E	S	S	E	N	■	■	A	S	S	O	O	N	A	S

41

```
S I T A S P E L L ■ A D E L E
A P O L L O X I I ■ R E L A X
P A R T Y G I R L ■ M A C Y S
I N T ■ ■ ■ T R I P E ■ A S P
D A S A N I S ■ S O D ■ P A O
■ ■ L O C ■ A T T ■ A I N U
S T R A T E G I C R O U T E S
W H E N I W A S Y O U R A G E
A R B I T R O N R A T I N G S
P E E S ■ A L E ■ S I G ■ ■
S A L ■ A P B ■ A T E A L O T
E D A ■ A S R E D ■ ■ A Z O
A K R O N ■ E L D E S T S O N
T I M I D ■ A L L S E E I N G
S T Y L E ■ K E E P S A K E S
```

42

```
H O M E F R E E ■ D A Y S P A
O N A S L A N T ■ I M O N I T
G E T S A W A Y ■ R I B O S E
W H E A T ■ P I N S ■ W H A
A E R I F Y ■ E N D T I M E S
R A I S E U P ■ A L A M O D E
T R A ■ E N A M I ■ D U B ■
S T L O ■ G R A D S ■ S I G H
■ W S W ■ B L O C K ■ L O I
A G I T A T O ■ F O R C E P S
L E T E R R I P ■ P A R T O N
G O N ■ T E L E ■ M A R S H
O D E D O N ■ A N T E D A T E
R E S O R T ■ L I A R L I A R
E S S E N E ■ S E X S E L L S
```

43

```
H U S K E R S ■ A M I D S T
E X H I B I T A ■ M E T E O R
Y O U D A M A N ■ M O E S H A
D R T ■ Y E S D E A R ■ P A L
A I T S ■ S E R I N ■ C A V A
Y A L E U ■ S E E ■ A R I E L
S L E E V E ■ T I A M A R I A
■ H U L K H O G A N ■
W E R E L I V E ■ O H I O A N
O P E R A ■ A G R ■ L A N C E
B I L E ■ O S I E R ■ L E T O
E T A ■ I N S A L E S ■ T U G
G O T O L D ■ N O T A H O P E
O M E N I V ■ T A R R A G O N
N E S T E D ■ D O G G O N E
```

44

```
T H I S J U S T I N ■ G A O L
W I N T E R T I D E ■ O L G A
I D O N T G E T I T ■ I L L S
G E N ■ S E M I ■ J E N N E T
■ S A S S ■ L U I G I ■
S I C E M ■ C E D E ■ G A B
I M A N ■ S L U G G I S H L Y
G E T A C H A R G E O U T O F
M A S T E R K E Y S ■ D E V A
A N C ■ L I E D ■ B A R E R
■ R A I N S ■ M C A N ■
A R A W A K ■ B A L D ■ O B J
C O D A ■ A V E R A G E J O E
T A L K ■ G O L D M E D A L S
S M E E ■ E L L I P S O I D S
```

45

```
R A B B I T S ■ G A M E L A W
A Q U A R I A ■ I N A P I L E
S U L T A N A ■ B A T H T U B
P A R T N E R ■ S C A R I N G
E T U I ■ D I C O T ■ A N S E
R I S E N ■ N A N ■ H I T E M
S C H R O D E R ■ R U M O R S
■ M E N A C E R ■
B A D M A N ■ C O O L C A T S
E C R U S ■ S A N ■ S H I R T
L E S T ■ T A S T Y ■ A R E O
A R E A R U G ■ R E P O M A N
Y O U T U B E ■ A C E T A T E
E S S E N E S ■ C C R I D E R
D E S S E R T ■ T H E C A R S
```

46

B	A	B	A	W	A	W	A	■	M	I	S	A	I	M
O	R	A	L	E	X	A	M	■	O	H	E	N	R	Y
N	O	T	A	B	E	N	E	■	S	O	C	C	E	R
N	U	T	S	■	S	T	R	E	E	P	■	H	S	T
E	S	L	■	■	T	I	N	Y	■	B	O	I	L	
T	E	E	S	■	P	O	C	O	■	V	E	R	G	E
■	S	O	N	I	A	■	A	L	S	O	R	A	N	S
■	F	A	S	C	I	N	A	T	I	N	G	■		
J	E	T	P	L	A	N	E	■	A	D	I	E	U	
A	S	H	O	E	■	G	M	C	S	■	E	A	S	T
M	I	E	N	■	K	O	B	E	■	L	S	U		
P	A	N	■	A	N	D	A	L	L	■	H	A	T	S
A	S	I	A	G	O	■	S	I	A	M	E	S	E	S
C	O	L	L	E	T	■	S	C	H	E	N	K	E	L
K	N	E	A	D	S	■	Y	A	R	D	S	A	L	E

47

B	I	S	H	O	P	S	■	B	A	P	T	I	S	T
A	N	T	E	S	U	P	■	A	L	U	N	S	E	R
T	H	E	T	H	R	I	L	L	I	S	G	O	N	E
H	O	E	■	A	E	R	O	B	E	S	■	T	E	M
T	U	L	L	■	R	A	N	O	N	■	T	Y	C	O
U	S	E	A	S	■	L	G	A	■	N	E	P	A	L
B	E	D	S	H	E	E	T	■	M	O	R	E	S	O
■	H	A	S	D	I	B	S	O	N	■				
R	A	M	O	N	E	■	M	A	U	N	A	L	O	A
A	N	O	U	K	■	D	E	R	■	S	T	A	N	D
T	I	N	T	■	T	R	A	C	I	■	E	M	E	R
A	M	I	■	O	R	E	G	A	N	O	■	P	D	A
T	A	K	E	M	Y	W	O	R	D	F	O	R	I	T
A	T	E	I	N	T	O	■	T	R	I	R	E	M	E
T	O	R	S	I	O	N	■	S	A	D	E	Y	E	S

48

T	A	P	S	■	S	W	I	S	S	C	H	A	R	D
H	I	R	T	■	W	I	N	E	C	O	O	L	E	R
A	R	E	A	■	A	N	T	A	R	C	T	I	C	A
L	I	S	T	O	N	■	E	W	O	K	■	B	O	W
I	N	T	E	L	■	B	R	A	D	■	G	I	R	L
A	G	O	O	D	M	A	N	Y	■	G	U	I	D	O
■	F	L	U	B	S	■	B	A	S	K	E	T		
S	T	A	M	I	N	A	■	D	U	S	T	E	R	S
T	I	M	I	N	G	■	B	A	S	T	A	■		
T	R	A	N	E	■	D	O	I	H	A	V	E	T	O
H	E	R	D	■	C	O	B	S	■	N	H	L	E	R
O	D	E	■	B	A	L	D	■	S	K	O	R	T	S
M	O	T	H	E	R	L	O	D	E	■	L	O	R	I
A	U	T	O	D	E	A	L	E	R	■	S	P	A	N
S	T	O	P	S	T	R	E	E	T	■	T	O	D	O

49

C	O	S	E	T	■	■	L	I	E	S	T	O
A	P	E	X	E	S	■	E	V	A	N	S	T	O	N
P	E	N	P	A	L	■	M	I	S	S	P	E	L	L
E	N	S	U	R	E	■	E	N	T	I	R	E	L	Y
L	E	O	N	I	D	■	R	E	P	T	I	L	E	■
L	A	R	G	E	S	■	G	R	O	U	T	E	R	■
A	R	I	E	S	■	L	E	I	S	■	■			
■	S	A	R	T	R	E	■	E	T	C	H	E	R	■
■	■	A	N	D	S	■	Y	A	X	E	S			
■	A	R	C	A	D	I	A	■	S	C	R	A	P	E
■	T	E	R	R	I	E	R	■	O	L	D	M	A	N
C	O	L	O	R	A	N	T	■	N	E	W	I	S	H
E	M	I	N	E	N	C	E	■	I	C	A	N	S	O
S	I	N	I	S	T	E	R	■	C	A	R	E	E	R
S	C	E	N	T	S	■	■	R	E	E	D	S		

50

S	I	L	E	N	T	X	■	A	S	T	A	R	T	E
T	H	E	F	O	R	E	■	T	H	R	E	E	R	S
D	O	G	F	O	O	D	■	T	I	E	C	L	I	P
E	P	I	■	P	O	O	C	H	E	S	■	E	O	N
N	E	R	F	■	P	U	R	E	R	■	Y	A	L	E
I	S	O	L	A	■	T	A	G	■	R	E	S	E	W
S	O	N	A	T	A	■	T	Y	P	E	S	E	T	S
■	■	T	E	C	H	■	M	A	H	I	■			
R	E	N	T	A	C	O	P	■	C	A	T	N	I	P
O	N	E	A	M	■	K	I	X	■	B	I	O	M	E
S	T	A	X	■	S	K	E	G	S	■	S	T	E	R
A	R	R	■	P	H	A	R	A	O	H	■	U	M	P
R	A	P	A	N	U	I	■	M	R	A	P	R	I	L
I	N	A	B	I	N	D	■	E	T	I	E	N	N	E
O	T	R	A	N	T	O	■	S	A	M	E	S	E	X

51

```
T R I E D A C A S E ■ V A C A
D A I L Y D O Z E N ■ I D A S
S P I K E D H A I R ■ O A R S
■ ■ O R I E L ■ O I L M E N ■
C A W ■ S C R E E N T E S T S
O P A H ■ T E A M ■ A T A ■ ■
R I T E A I D ■ U N L I N K S
O P E N T O ■ ■ ■ A I R D R Y
T E R R A N E ■ E M A I L E R
■ ■ C Y R ■ B C D E ■ S E M I
A T O M I C B O M B S ■ R E A
W H O O S H ■ P E R O N ■ ■ ■
A R L O ■ A P P E A L E D T O
S E E R ■ D O E S N T W O R K
H E R E ■ S I D E D I S H E S
```

52

```
M E D A L ■ A R I A S ■ S A F E H A V E N
A M I N E ■ R O O N E ■ A L E X A N D R A
Y E S Y O U R X L N C ■ D O M I N I O N S
A R C T I C ■ Y A L L ■ S E A T O ■ O O H
■ ■ H I S T ■ E U R O ■ ■ ■ I G N ■ ■ ■
B A L I ■ B U R N E D I N F E G ■ A D A S
U C O N N ■ N U S ■ E N G A G E ■ S E R A
L N D G E N E R E S ■ ■ R A N S O M E R ■
B E E ■ R E D A C T ■ L O A N ■ P L A T O
■ ■ A V R I L ■ E C A R D ■ G A I N O N ■
S E A L I O N ■ X P D N C ■ C O R N D O G
A L L I E S ■ S K I E D ■ T O T H E ■ ■ ■
L I C E S ■ B T E N ■ A M A R N A ■ I A M
I C A N T S E E ■ ■ U N K N O W N N T T ■
N I T E ■ N A R I T A ■ E E E ■ K O R A N
E T R E ■ L M N T A R Y M A T H ■ R E D S
■ ■ ■ A S P ■ S O M A ■ ■ ■ S E A T ■ ■ ■
L A Z ■ E A R T O ■ L B O S ■ A T H E N A
A S S E R T I O N ■ O B C T P R O B L E M
M A K E S R O O M ■ A E T N A ■ L A M I A
A P P L E I S L E ■ D R O S S ■ L Y O N S
```

53

```
L A P S E S ■ A M B L E D ■ R A M P A G E
I C E A X E ■ S E R I E S ■ I M M O V E D
R E P R O A C H M O T E L ■ P E D X I N G
A S S A D ■ L E O N ■ R O N ■ ■ L I E ■ ■
■ H U M A N I T A R I A N R E P A I D ■ ■
E R A ■ S O P ■ R E S O R T ■ A R A ■ ■ ■
R I F F ■ O P S ■ ■ S W E E T ■ I M S E T
G O T T A R E P E A T A N D R U N ■ O N E
S T E M S ■ D U M B ■ N A X O S ■ F U S E
■ ■ R E C T ■ R A I N ■ ■ L E T I N O N ■
R E P A I R I N G D I R T Y L A U N D R Y
A C A D I A N ■ L O W E ■ S P A S ■ ■ ■ ■
C A R E ■ C A S C A ■ B O R A ■ A L G E R
E S T ■ R E P L A C E T A B L E C L O T H
R H Y M E ■ T I R E D ■ A F T ■ Y O R E ■
■ I B M ■ D E T E S T ■ A U K ■ D E A ■ ■
R E P L A Y S I T O N T H E L I N E ■ ■ ■
A T E ■ F U N ■ ■ P E L F ■ I V A N I ■ ■
T H E M O O N ■ R E P E L S A L V A D O R
S A T U P O N ■ B E R T I E ■ S E D A T E
O N E M P T Y ■ S W E E P S ■ U S E R I D
```

54

```
S E C T ■ A D O L P H ■ T I L L ■ C A R B
E L L A ■ S O N O R A ■ I S A Y ■ A L O U
R A I S E T H E P O T ■ E N T R E N O U S
B L O T T O ■ F E E D T H E K I T T Y ■ ■
■ ■ ■ E R U P T S ■ S R I ■ ■ S E N ■ ■ ■
U S C ■ E N S I L E ■ O N C E ■ D E B T S
N I A ■ ■ D I V A S ■ S W A M I ■ S U E T
M E L D S ■ S O L T I ■ I R O N S ■ C P U
A G L O W ■ O R N A T E ■ ■ S H A K E N ■
N E T G A I N ■ M A T C H T H E A N T E S
■ H E N N A S ■ G R E ■ S I R R A H ■ ■ ■
B R E A K T H E H O U S E ■ S T O K E U P
R E B R E W ■ R O N D O S ■ ■ N I O B E ■
I V E ■ R O W E L ■ E V A D E ■ A N D O R
N U T S ■ S A N Y O ■ E L A T E ■ D A M ■
G E S T E ■ D A T A ■ R E M A I L ■ S T S
■ ■ ■ E D S ■ ■ O H O ■ ■ N E L L I E ■ ■
D R A W T H E F L U S H ■ ■ E N T E R S ■
M E S A V E R D E ■ C U T T H E C A R D S
V E E R ■ E N I D ■ A M A Z O N ■ I M A N
S L A T ■ P O C O ■ R E B U T S ■ L A S S
```

55

```
A L L A T ■ ■ H E M I C ■ ■ D A P P L E
M E A N E R ■ P A C I N O ■ P A P E R E R
I N T O N E ■ I R O N O N ■ I M P R O V E
D I V I N G B E L L E ■ T A K E S ■ S A C
N I N ■ I O T A ■ P O R E ■ ■ ■ P E N T ■
F I A T ■ S W I N E F L U E ■ S P L A T S
C T N ■ A T E E ■ S E A R S ■ C A E N ■ ■
C E S A R E ■ S A T A N ■ A R C A D E S ■
■ ■ C I R C ■ B O R N E F R E E ■ C A T ■
A P R I L ■ O A R ■ ■ E L A T E D ■ O R R
L A U D ■ S U M A C ■ R O S I N ■ A N T A
P E N ■ S T R A D A ■ I T S ■ F I S H Y ■
H A N ■ C A S T E L O T S ■ T A L L ■ ■ ■
A N I M A T E ■ ■ C A R E T ■ R A S C A L
■ N A P E ■ W R I T E ■ R A S P ■ H C L ■
A N G L E S ■ E I T H E R O R E ■ R E E D
S O L E ■ B P O E ■ E T O N ■ A S T ■ ■ ■
S R A ■ P R A T T ■ W E S T W A R D H O E
E M P E R O R ■ A V I A T E ■ L I N I N G
T A S T E R S ■ C A L V E D ■ S T E R E O
S L E A Z Y ■ ■ T Y L E R ■ ■ T R E S S
```

56

```
WAIF SETTO  CRAB  LENT
ALTI AFOUL  SHULA CLAY
IDENTIFIEDITASAGSHARP
TORNADO STRIPES LANCE
   THRO OAF  ROI
WROTEITDOWNFROMMEMORY
EUROS  DAN   INON  TAO
ESTD FIST SANER SATYR
USEOFTWOHANDSANDANOSE
NEG IRON YODEL  ENT
STANDON LECID HASIDIM
  AGO MASON RARE ONO
WHILEPLAYINGBILLIARDS
HADAT ADORE ABLY REOS
OIL  USAF SLO  SAMOA
AREQUIEMFORHISPETBIRD
  UTE  MAI   ELAL
CLEAN MOANING AREARUG
BYTHEROLLINGOFTWODICE
EROO EDGES LOTTA ZEST
RANG PEAS  ESSEX ENDS
```

57

```
FONTS SUPS  DRAB  TOSS
INOIL THAT  OENO DARNS
CINCO YOGACLASS OXBOW
HOCKTHEHERALDANGELS
ENESCO STRIDE USA
   ALKA OAS   PLOWMEN
AFRAIDOFTHEDOCK  ERO
DCL  DOFF DISH  HANS
ACA INRI BRUSH AUDIT
LEWISANDCLOCK ECHOER
SAN VIP AEC ALE WPA
HITMEN MAKESPOCKSFLY
OLMOS POLYP RACE DOL
TAOS COMO MESO  ICE
AMC GREATWHITESHOCK
TAKEAIM HES   STEM
   LUC COACTS WISETO
BOCKSUPTHEWRONGTREE
GRAPH AIRSTREAM OATES
PAREE BNAI  EDYS STENT
AWED  UGHS  DESK HESSE
```

58

```
OLAF YUP  BARO SHE SRA
MASERATI OVERSEAS HED
NOSYORINQUISITIVE AMO
IST DRLAURA GONE SPAR
CEO FIN MIDEASTERN
WINDOWCOVERINGS KOOKS
ODORS HRE ISAY  INF
ESSO TIER POL ORDEALS
 MSEC WALKEUNE ABIE
ISH TAKERSOUTPOSTGAME
SCOREPADDISTAUNPEELED
LATEWORDNCERUPEON LYS
ALEC TEYNNERS  KNOB
MELROSE SWF PEND RAGE
 FUN  HTML OTE GABLE
STOIC HEADOFTHEPRISON
CARTESIANS APE  LAD
ANDS CARD STIRSUP ATT
RKO DOTSINTHENIGHTSKY
EEG BLUENILE EMISSION
DDS LDS SHOR TIN EASE
```

59

```
CANE MENSA  BRAVA AGAR
ARAT ICAHN  RUPEE MERE
SIGH NOPRIORESSRECORD
ASSISI UMM DETOX  MED
BEACHCOMBINE  BITES
ANT EAVE SIEG RISOTTO
   CARESSMANUFACTURER
SRA SNOW YEOW  RYES
PEEPS NATO  SODAS
REVOLTS PIPETTESQUEAK
EYETOOTH VID SAYUNCLE
PALETTEAROUND LEAFLET
  HEAVE MAAM  TRACT
ETNA LEIA ROSA  ETS
GREGORIANCHANTEUSE
GETEVEN STOP ORTO WOW
 SCRUB  SUPERBOWLINE
APO LOADS REV  BSIDES
MASSEUSEHYSTERIA BETS
ASTI NEMEA  IRISH ELEE
PSST DAISY  TYSON LYNX
```

23A – CURIOUS, 34A – CURTAINS, 89A – WARDEN, 104A – STARS,
15D – ROUND, 45D – KETTLES, 48D – ANSWER, 57D – KENNEL.
SOLUTION QUOTE: WALKERS OUTDISTANCE RUNNERS.

60

```
SAMOSA  SLAPDASH  AGITA
PEAHEN  NILEBLUE  TONES
ANDMAKEITSNAPPY   ENACT
REA SLEPTON  HESS  ESSO
TIM CENSER  TAR  CUSP
ADELA  RACY   FINELY
  APOP  SNAPPER ONION
BIGDEAL  NEHRU  ITGO
EVIL SAVEME ANIN LSAT
LOVES YAXIS  RETIREE
TRE PAINTS  HASSLE CEL
 INASTIR QUOTA PROVO
ACTI ISLA UPHOLD ONEG
NASL  ALCEE  ARIADNE
ALOES  FATLESS  DENS
 IMSURE  ARPA  ATRAS
ECRU SSN AGORAS  AVE
ASTR MICA ANILINE DEA
ILIAD DEFICITSPENDING
LIMNS ONETASTE ASIAGO
STEEL LESSTHAN REELED
```

61

```
CHARTER  THAT   INUSE
THENERVE HOLE   NIGER
WRONGTOEVERSPLITTHEM
OUR LOIS GOTO THE PIU
KEEPER  BONE  BEERCANS
 ISTOBESELDOMLYUSED
AEC  JAL   ROSE   RTS
ISMOREORLESSOK   AAA
GUINNESS WHONEEDSTHEM
UNREAL  READERS  LEOVI
ADA  SOSO   OSLO  PES
NETTY  SPORTIN  GIJANE
AREIMPORTANT CARRACER
   MAR  ARENTNECESSARY
CSI  ELIO   LOO   CBS
TOENDSENTENCESWITH
ELEGISTS  LEAR  LOAFER
OLD EKE ATAD IDLE AYE
ALLTIMEWORSTMISTAKES
RESET  SORE  ANNEALED
STUDS  PLOD  NOTEPAD
```

62

```
ERITREA  ITSLATE  PAGES
VETOERS  NATASHA  AROMA
INCOMETAXRACKET  SIDED
COHN  UNSER  FOSSE  LEI
TIESINTO  TAO  HOMERS
SRS  THENOELPRIZE  ASST
     TEL  KNEE  DOALLS
GRIM  CHIT  SAIN  ETAS
ORIN  CHEESEURGERS  MUS
MANHOLES  WIT  DISSECT
ANKARA  SPRITES  SOURCE
HOOTERS  HUN  TENSIER
ALF  LOOMINGDALES  ICEE
ADES  CELS  ICON  MEAD
 IDEALS  OHOH  SEQ
SISI  LEAKFORECAST  RDA
GOATEE  NFL  LOWSPEED
TDS  NEATO  LOPER  ACED
MATTE  FATHEROFTHERIDE
ATEAM  ALTERER  AMMETER
JERRY  RESTSON  SOIREES
```

63

```
WNBA  GERE  ACME  MOMENT
OEUF  OLIN  SLIP  AMALIE
WARRENFACTIONS  RACINE
SPRITE  SRI  POT  CHOSEN
   CAAN  YES  LESHAN
  BATTENPRACTICE  WYES
ICON  GIT  LLANOS  HARA
MINSTREL  AMA  NABOKOV
ATE  RAVENMANIAC  YOUDO
MYDEAR  ION  VUE  APTER
  TIERACK  CASSINI
ITSON  AGE  FAN  TOEING
SHANE  PARTONSHOTS  COM
LANDERS  ALA  ALOEVERA
ANDI  ATBATS  ATL  IRAN
MESS  CARRIONCHARGES
  OVERIT  MET  SOMN
ESCROW  ECO  HIE  DANIEL
STADIA  FISSIONLICENSE
SORELY  ENTO  NOON  SOPS
OPERAS  REED  SSTS  ERNS
```

64

```
(P)WATCH  OPENSEA  HOT(P)
SAHARA  ERRATUM  OLAV
ISOMER  NOTRARE  OSTE
ZOOMS  MOVEIT  REHEAT
ENTITLE  ESTE  ICANSO
      ASA  AMOCO
SPERMBANK  ARA  ESPO
CACAO  SNAPOPEN  ZHOU
ALOTOF  ASOF  LEGREST
GENERIC  BOFF  NEARTO
  REVISAL  LEGO  REF
(P)PCS  EIGHTBALL  AIR(P)
KIA  EMIT  ALTOIDS
NEPALI  SABE  ISEENOW
ICERINK  FLAP  HAVETO
FERN  UNCLETOM  NEVIN
ESSO  TOO  SPICERACK
    GETIT  ENS
POINTB  FOOD  DATSUNS
INDOOR  FEVERS  HANOI
COLD  EDUCATE  YELLED
KNEE  AERATED  ETOILE
(P)ERS  KEEPERS  PANTS(P)
```

65

```
PLEBE  CLANG  FRET  SAP
DONALD  EIGER  LETO  PLO
QUAKIERSTATE  OSCULATE
BECK  NOAHS  HOI  CARAT
ALTER  DRESSIERDRAWERS
CLERIC  LINDY  EON
HAD  COSBY  OLDEST  ORES
  FORTE  SWEATIERVEST
TOO  DOGMA  RYAN  CESTA
TRIG  OLEARY  PARTON
HULL  BITTIERPILL  BOND
IMPALA  NARNIA  URIS
SPUME  POCK  TOANY  YEA
BUMPIERCROPS  WEEKS
EPPS  RETIRE  KERRI  FED
   SLO  MENDE  STEELY
COCKIERSPANIELS  SUDAN
AVAIL  DOS  ONEUP  RONA
COSMICAL  BOXIERSHORTS
TIE  COIF  BRINK  IMPART
IDS  ANNA  SONGS  MESAS
```

66

```
A L E W I F E   F L E W I N   M A R L I N
R E N A M E S   I O L A N I   E R O I C A
I A N T H E T E R R I B L E   G A B L E R
O N E T O T E N   N C A A   B A B I Y A R
S E A S   E T D   I S T O O   N O G O
O D D   H O M E O F T H E B R A E   F E W
    C O O   R O O       I N H E A T
M A D I S O N   N E P A L   E Y E S H O T
A G R A   L O N E S O M E D O E   T E R I
A R I   F A R O   R O T I   S P R A I N
N E E D Y   A L B A T R O S S   G O L F S
D E R A I L   T O M E   C H A S   L I T
P O E M   O P E N I N G M O E S   D E C A
A N D O R R A   E D D I E   S P R A Y E R
    U N H A N D   L E S   E O N
S A C   E N D I N G M A C H I N E   W C S
T R A M   A F I R E   E A T   S H I H
O C T O P U S   C O M A   K A S H M I R I
O H I O A N   Y O U O N L Y L I E O N C E
G E O R D I   E L N I N O   I L L T E L L
E R N E S T   H E D R E N   C O D E R E D
```

67

```
H I D E H O   L A T E R O N   P R E S S U R E
O C E L O T   E X O T I C A   R O T H I R A S
W E N T S T R A I G H T U P   O B E I S A N T
E S T O P   A H S   L E S S   A A N D E
    N I N N Y   S A W A S L I G H T L O S S
S C H   T U G   A P G A R   O T O E S
T O O K A B E A T I N G   P L U R A L S
A V R I L   M O N I E S   F O A L   E D I T
S E A T   A S A N   S P R I N T   S P O S A
I N C H E D A H E A D   F E L L S H A R P L Y
S S E   P E L L   D O H   B E Y   E M O T E S
    M O S T   W E R E H O T   A L I S
O N E A C T   C A L   P A Z   T A P A   C R I
L E D T H E R A L L Y   G O T H A M M E R E D
O A S T S   R A K E I N   O I S E   S O T O
G L E E   B A N S   P I L A T E   A S C I I
Y E L L S A T   G A V E U P G R O U N D
    C R E T E   S E G O S   L E M   S A O
R E A C H E D A N E W L O W   D A N S E
A N N U L   L O R E   I A N   D E E R E
S U S P E N S E   G A I N E D M O M E N T U M
P R E P P I E S   O R V I L L E   M A I N S T
S E L A S S I E   T S E T S E S   C L E A T S
```

68

```
R A I L S A T   D R I L L   A P O G E E S
A L T O O N A   E A S E S   C A R O U S E
D I S G U S T O F W I N D   C L A I R O L
S A Y I T   L I L T   R E A C T
    C H A R L E S I N D I S C H A R G E
A H S   E S T A S   C O P S E   L A O S
N O T O N C E   Q T I P S   N O N U S
G O L F D I S C O U R S E   I R O N O R E
S H U T   A V I A   P R E T E N D S
T A K E   S I R E N S   A R I A S
  S E R M O N O N T H E D I S M O U N T
    A N I L S   E X U D E S   L E A P
A P O S T A T E   S A M E   N A N A
L I F T E R S   T R U M P D I S C A R D S
I N G O D   R E A P S   S P O R T E D
S N A P   F A I R Y   O S L I N   O M E
T A B L E O F D I S C O N T E N T S
    I N S T S   O D E A   A C T A S
C I A G A T E   B L O O D D I S C O U N T
T I G H T E R   B E R R A   R O T U N D A
R I O T E R S   S A S S Y   E C S T A S Y
```

69

```
L I F T S   A L G A   A G A P E   U S S R
A P R I L   S E E S   R E P O S   S O L O
B O O T E E I N T H E B E A S T   A D O S
    L E A F   S E C   T S O S   A V E
T H E P R I N T S O N T H E P O P P E R
S E E D Y   C O O   U E Y   P H O N E
A C R   C A N   M K T S   G S H A P E D
T H E T A U R U S I N T H E H A I R
    S A B L E   T R O Y   M A D E   P O T
C H A S E D   G R E W   R I L E   G O B I
L I T T L E R E A D W R I T I N G H O O D
O K I E   S O N Y   H U N S   D O O L E Y
P E P   M A Y O   A I T S   M I D S T
    J A C K A N D T H E B E N S T A L K
I S A I D S O   A W E S   A L G   B A A
M A M B A   D N A   M R T   M O L D Y
T H E E M P E R O R S N U K E L O W E S
H A N   S E X Y   H O E   D I R E
E R I S   R U M P L E D S T I L T S K I N
R A T E   P L O T S   A L E C   A T O N E
E N Y A   S T P A T   T I N E   L O N G E
```

70

```
A R I   E L I O   W H A M   S H E D D
S U L A   M I N X   H I L O   S C A R E [ON/OFF]
P I L L S B U R Y B A K E [ON/OFF]   P A L A C E
I N T O T O   E M O T E S   D I N E S I N
R E R E A D S   O K A   I N T R U D E
E D Y   P I K E R   D A T I V E   R E S
  W H E E L [ON/OFF] O R T U N E   C [ON/OFF] E R S
A U D I   S E N   S A N T E   B I C
C R E P T   T O B A G O   F E N D E D [ON/OFF]
T A P E R [ON/OFF]   R A G   I S A A C   L I E
E N O   U S E T H E [ON/OFF] S W I T C H   U R I
D I S   S P U E S   H A S [ON/OFF]   E N D E R
[ON/OFF] C E N T E R   T E A S E T   S E E S [ON/OFF]
  A M C   B E E C H   N I E   I S T S
L A R G E   S A W N [ON/OFF] S H O T G U N
E C O   L A R E D O   O R L O P   S W F
[ON/OFF] C A M P U S   M O M   E M P O W E R
A R R E A R S   B A I L E E   A E R O B E
R U S T L E   D E S S E R T A N D C [ON/OFF] E E
D E A R E R   [ON/OFF] S E T   E T U I   H E R S
O S T E R   S T A S   D A D A   D S T
```

71

```
EPOPEE   NED    TEETHES
MARINES  ICES   POWERADE
QUICKCENTURY  AGELIMIT
ULNAE  QURANDURAN  PRES
AVG   AUTO   RES   PLA
DISABLE   SCAN   NEEDLE
  QUILTBYASSOCIATION
OCCURS  RESTS  DON  SOTS
PARA   TOAT   HOTEL
QBERTANDROEPER  VIABLY
ROPIEST  OLDER  SEABLUE
STEAMS  QUESTBATHROOMS
  PIVOT   NAPE   LIEN
INIT  SIP  IMAGO  CRISTO
QEDHOTCHILIPEPPERS
SALEMS   POTS   RESHOOT
 OSS  MOO   LEIS   URU
RAVI  QANDABEARS  OATER
APERTURE  QUITYOURSELF
MITERING  INRE  NASTASE
AGONIZE    TEX   ROOTED
```

72

```
PRIEST   BOSS   EVER  WOK
RONDOS   CRATE   DELAWARE
UNCELEBRATED   IRISHSEA
DIOR   TAO   RAMBO  HIHAT
ENGLISHCHANNEL  SOLIDS
  ERE   KEN   STEELMEN
BRR  ASSERT   NOODGES
AHEM  ORBITS  SCAN  TAU
CELIBACY  CHICKEN  ROSE
HAYFORK  ELOI   AUNTS
 FAMOUSCROSSINGS
MOSES   SOHO   NAUTICA
APED  TAGTEAM  HANNIBAL
GEL  AIDA  EDISON   CARP
ICEDTEA   SHOERS   RDS
 COLUMBUS  EEK   UPI
CATNAP  ONEARMEDBANDIT
ORION  ORALB  DOI  SOME
ABORTIVE  JULIUSCAESAR
CONSIDER  USURP  OTTERS
HRS  CANS  KEGS  NESSIE
```

73

```
CUSS  LOKI  ABOMB  KAFKA
OSHA  IWIN  RANEE  ILIAD
DEARSANTA  THEANSWERIS
 BRITISHWAITINGLINE
YESES   EFS   AYS   WAH
 NOES   ATRIAL   PALE
SECONDPERSONSINGULAR
EEEE  STAY  ISH  EUCLID
ARYL  VNECK  PROWSE
TAOIST  OOLA  AMAT  WES
OPRAHWINFREYSMAGAZINE
NEE  TOTE  KILO  EVONNE
 MIRAGE  NANCY  WOES
CALICO  ATA  ITOO  INAT
DRINKWITHJAMANDBREAD
LOVE  MENACE  SASE
IDE  BRA  COM  ENATE
 WORLDWIDEWEBPREFIX
RAINYSEASON  NONVERBAL
BORIC  INLET  SHOE  OILY
ILENE  TEARS  ARMS  SATE
```

74

```
ASEA  RIDER  SHARE  ABIT
SENDSANOTE  HONOR  CONE
PROJECTMANHATTAN  CRUX
CUR  NIH  STARTER  DEIST
AMMO  EEL  SPIN  MOSSES
 DISCOUNTSENIORS
LAMENTABLE  ANTI  PAO
AMISS  NEEDLES  TETHERS
PARSEC  DESERTCOLORADO
 AAH   ALERT   ECOL
ESL  MINUTENEWYORK  ERE
ATTN  ILOSE   DEP
RECORDBADTRACK  STUPOR
PROVERB  DESPOND  TRADE
SNL  CALX  PLURALIZED
 SAKEFOROLDTIMES
DAPPLE  APOP  EPH  TEAR
RURAL  ICETEAS  FEM  DIO
ARID  ENTRANCESERVANTS
MAZE  CROAT  TAKESPLACE
ALES  TERSE  STADT  ASHY
```

75

```
INAWE  SOS  ALES   TOPPS
NASAL  IRA  LUCY  FACEIT
SITTINGBULLION  SKEWER
TRIEDON  DEIGN  THEATRE
 RET  MISSIONMANNERS
SEAL  AFUSS  ACRO  RES
CABOOSES  AUNT  PPP
RUNOFTHEMILLION  RANAT
ADE  FER  AIMAT  CHICAGO
MERIT  OLIO  GOSSIPED
 MOUNTAINPASSION
MRPEANUT  DELA  NOISY
PARAGON  GIJOE  TUE  NHA
STENO  NOTIONFORPROFIT
 TOG  NOSY  SETSFREE
ADO  DALE  AMISH  FADS
DEPOSITIONSLIP  EWE
OMITTED  RIPEN  GRANDMA
BEATAT  PONYEXPRESSION
EATERY  INTO  EGO  TEMPT
SNERT  COHN  SAW  ESSES
```

76

```
A F R O   M R M O M   I C A N   O J O S
S E A R S   O U T I E   N A M E   V I N O
K R Y S T A L B A L L   S T A B L E M E N
T A E   O R D E R   M I E N   A R S O N
O L D F O G Y   A N N A G R A M M   H U E
    A G O   B R I O C H E   L A M O N T
W A R R E N P E A C E   T R E X   O R C S
E L I   R E T E L L   S V E L T E
B I G G R E E N   O S S A   N E Z
E V E R E T T   J E R R Y R I G G S
R E L I C T   P A L E R M O   R A K I S H
  D O U G G R A V E S   D I G I N T O
R I D   L A S T   B A S E N J I S
D O R E M I   E S P R I T   U N E
P E S O   A M O R   P A I G E T U R N E R
E V E N T S   R E C E I V E   A P E
T A B   S K I P T O W N E   A P R I C O T
S L U N G   S H I N   R A D I O   A B A
H E S I T A T E R   A P R I L R A I N E S
O R C A   R O U E   T R A D E   R O A S T
P A H S   P O S E   M E T E R   U L E E
```

77

```
B E S T S   J A M B   S E N D   T O I L S
A S C O T   A P E R   H U E S   U P L I T
S T A N D U P S T R A I G H T   R H O N E
E E L   N A E S   D R E I   S N I V E L
R E P O M A N   E D E N   G E T R E A L
  M I R   A N D S   E P O C H   I G A
C L E A N M Y P L A T E   A N T E A T E R
E L A N D   A N E M O N E S   O O F
N A S   M I N E R S   D E S E R T R O S E
T N T   Y O G A S   Y O K E L   H I N N Y
R E E L O U T   S E W   E L E C T E E
A R R O W   Z E R O S   R A C E R   H E B
L O S A N G E L E S   C U L T I C   E R A
  N B A   E V A G A B O R   H A G E N
R E A D U P O N   D O M Y H O M E W O R K
E L S   S E D A N   N A S A   E E O
S E A F I R E   O B E Y   B A K L A V A
P A R E N S   G R U B   M O E N   L E W
E N U R E   S E T M Y S I G H T S H I G H
C O L D S   P R O P   U C L A   D U B A I
T R E E S   Y E N S   V E E R   S T I N T
```

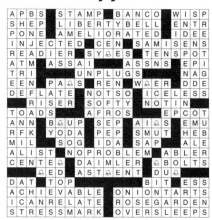

78

```
G L O   G O A L S   S T E A M   D I N
R E V   A L L I E   S T R A T I   A R N O
A S E   L I L A C   T I A R A S   M I T T
M A R I A V O N T R A P P   P R E V U E
M B A S   E W E   A L E S   P R I C E R S
A R R A S   V I A L   W E I G H I N
R E M O D E L L I N G   H A N S E N
  I M E A S Y   S P O R T   T U B
B A C K   M A N E   S E E M   E O C E N E
A D A R   A D A   A C E S   D A H L I A
D O R A L   S I N G A P O R E   S A L T S
E N D U E D   O I L Y   E L S   F E E T
M A I T A I   P O L E   A S I T   E R R S
S I N   C H O K E   A L O H A S
A W A K E N   O F F D U T Y C O P S
C L A M M E D   E P O S   M A N I C
D E C R I A L   O V E R   S A C   S E E R
I S O M E R   H E R E F O R D S H I R E
P S A T   T I R A N A   A L E R T   O C A
I N C H   I N U R E S   C A N O E   T E M
N A H   N A M E D   T R A M P   A D S
```

79

```
A P B S   S T A M P   B A N C O   W I S P
S H E P   L I B E R T Y B E L L   E N T R
P O N E   A M E L I O R A T E D   I D E E
I N J E C T E D   C E N   S A M I S E N S
R E A D I E R   S Y B E S   T E N S P O T
A T M   A S S A I   A S S N S   E P I
T R I   U N P L U G S   N A G
E E N   P A A S   R E N   W A E R   D D E
D E F L A T E   N O T S O   I C E L E S S
  R I S E R   S O F T Y   N O T I N
T O A D S   A F R O S   E P C O T
A N N   B A U P   S E P   A I A S   E M U
R F K   Y O D A   P E P   S M U T   H E B
M I L   S O G   I D A   S A P   A L E
A L I S T   N O P R O B L E M   A B L E R
C E N T E A   D A I M L E R   A B O L T S
  A E D   A S T A E N T   D U A
D A T   T O P   B I T   E S S
A C H I E V A B L E   O N I O N T A R T S
I C A N R E L A T E   R O S E G A R D E N
S T R E S S M A R K   O V E R S L E E P S
```

80

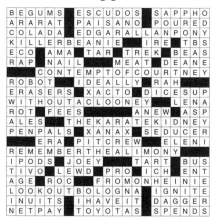

```
B E G U M S   E S C U D O S   S A P P H O
A R A R A T   P A I S A N O   P O U R E D
C O L A D A   E D G A R A L L A N P O N Y
K I L L E R B E A N I E   I R E   T B S
E C O   A M A   T A R   T R E K   B E A S
R A P   N A I L   M E A T   D E A N E
  C O N T E M P T O F C O U R T N E Y
R O B O T   I D E A L L Y   R A H
E R A S E R S   X A C T O   D I C E S U P
W I T H O U T A C L O O N E Y   L E N A
R O T   F E E S   A N E W   A S P
A L E S   T H E K A R A T E K I D N E Y
P E N P A L S   X A N A X   S E D U C E R
  E R A   P I T C R E W   E L E N I
R E M E M B E R T H E A L I M O N Y
I P O D S   J O E Y   T A R T   B U S
T I V O   L E W D   P R O   I C H   E N T
A G E   R O C   F R O M O N H E I N I E
L O O K O U T B O L O G N A   I G N I T E
I N U I T S   I H A V E I T   D A G G E R
N E T P A Y   T O Y O T A S   S P E N D S
```

81

```
I L I A C   A F T S   P U M A   I M A C S
W A N N A   G A Z E   O R E L   T A R R Y
I V A N T H E T E R R I B L E   S R T A S
N A N A N A N A   A R A B   I N T E N T
  A R T H U R C O N A N D O Y L E
V S H A P E S   T O O T   L O U R
E T O N   A U T O   O M E N S   Q B S
N A P O L E O N B O N A P A R T E   U L E
N Y E   A C U T E R   L T R S   S A I N
    G T O S   H A I G   A T K I N S
S A M U E L T A Y L O R C O L E R I D G E
P I U S X I   L E A P   O S I S
A R C H   E L A M   A D J O I N   A D D
T E K   E L V I S A A R O N P R E S L E Y
E D S   T A I N T   C B E R   A P S E
  M A S C   T H O R   T O P T H I S
  C H R I S T O P H E R R E E V E
P U E B L O   R A I N   N E A T I D E A
R O L L E   L A U R E N C E O L I V I E R
A M O U R   E L L S   P E R F   T E N E T
T O T E S   O B I T   R O O F   E S T E S
```

82

```
P R E S   M O R O S   G U N   M O R K
A E S O P   S A I N T   O N E S E A S O N
R A M B L I N R O S E   P A S T E L H U E
A M E B A S   S T P A U L   T O O L A T E
    E Y R E   E D N A   O N C E
S N E R D   C A N C E R C U R E   A G E R
L A X   A C U T E   D I E S   D E B O N E
O P I A T E   W A C   P S I S   B L O T S
T A T L E R   I R A T E   A C C R E D I T
  E A S E   L E N O   O R O   O R E
O W N S   B A L D I N G P A T E   B L E D
N I M   3 R 3   G I R L   S W F F
T E A M M A T E   C A V E D   T I E B A R
I S S U E   O L E O   E S E   E N R O B E
M E S S E D   S A M E   T R A D E   Y E N
E L E C   O V E R E X P O S E   G E S T E
    A L T I   C O P A   S A L E
S T A T U E S   A N I M A L   S A L A M I
L A M E B R A I N   R E S U M E S P E E D
A P P L E S E E D   E L I T E   S O R R Y
B E S S   D R Y   D A N Z A   T O L L
```

83

```
B A G S   P R I S O N   S L O B S   R H E A S
O R E O   C O N T R A   E A R L E   H E L L O
M Y O U T P U T I S D O W N B U T   E A S E L
B A R R I S T E R   A R A C E   S T O R A G E
A N G E L   R I O   A G E   B U R S T
Y S E R   M Y I N C O M E I S U P I T A K E A
T E E M   T R A   T O T   P A C E R S
P O M P O U S   F E B   A O R T A   T H A N T
S H O R T P O S I T I O N   T I M E   E N E R
A S N O T   R E S   T A T E   N A N U   E S O
L A T T E   A C E   F I L L   I O N A
M Y E A R   C L A S S   C L O W N   T R I S H
  X E N A   L S T S   A A A   A R N I E
S A W   D U M A   O J O S   V I C   N I G E R
A V O W   T E R M   O N T H E L O N G B O N D
M I R E S   O R A L E   I O S   C O L A D A S
B A L B O A   I D A   L E O   S O R E
A N D M Y R E V E N U E S T R E A M   D C I I
  A B B I E   D N A   S U D   M E A N T
C L O S E S T   O L I N S   A U T O P A R T S
O U T T A   H A S I T S O W N C A S H F L O W
S I R E N   E Z I N E   A I D E R S   T I N A
T S A R S   R O S E S   R E A D T O   O N E R
```

84

```
M A N   S C A L P S   A C T I I I   C O G
E L I   A L L S E T   F L A C O N   A R R
N U T   B E A U T Y P R O T E S T   R E E
U M P I R E   I L L   M A P   R I D G E
  I N A S T A T E O F P R O F U S I O N
R O C S   E E L   D W I   P A D R O N E
O A K U M   A D O   E E E   N E A
T H E L I B R A R Y O F P R O G R E S S
H U R T L E   G A P   I A N S   L O A F
  A N A   A R T   S T E   R I N G O
A B S E N T M I N D E D C O N F E S S O R
F A C T O   A S I   D E O   D A S
B N A I   A I L S   T A P   S E A M U S
G R O S S N A T I O N A L C O N D U C T
  L O S   M S S   L E A   T E S L A
S K I A R E A   N I N   E S S   L I A R
C O N T E S T A N T W O R K E T H I C
O A S E S   H U E   A S H   R E E C H O
F L U   P R O F E S S I O N B O X   I O N
F A R   O N M E D S   E N R O B E   T S E
S S E   T H E U S A   R E A P E D   Y E S
```

85

```
  A S S I S T   S L E D   S P I T O N
Q U E L Q U E C H O S E   H O O K N O S E
T D W A T E R H O U S E   O K C O R R A L
S I N G E   S I R   E M C E E   I S T O
    S L E E T Y   H L M E N C K E N
  A B A T E   F I E   A R E O L A E
A M F M   C S L E W I S   S N O G   P T A
R E G I S T R Y   N E D S   S U G A R
P R O T E U S   L A N C E   I N A P T L Y
  O Y E R   P E R K   N I N O T C H K A
M C D   E Z B A K E O V E N S   I A N
C O R N B R E A D   E W E R   T B A R
C H I N E S E   T A P E R   F A U S T U S
O N C E A   C O D E   B U L L P E N S
O S H   U R D U   J R E W I N G   C E L T
  S T B A R T S   G A G   I V A N V
M X M I S S I L E   O L D S A W
A R U N   M I N S K   T O O   B U G L E
Y A T I T T L E   U N R E S O L U T I O N
E Y E S O R E S   S E C R E T A G E N T S
  D E P A R T   S E A S   H I S S A T
```

86

```
ABBA  OPERA  SNEAD  BUSS
FLAN  DUPED  TITLE  APET
CUDDLEFISH  ANTIMADDER
REROOFS  ESTEE  ARMADA
   ORNE  ESTER  CREATED
PALIN  DAVIES  CLEANER
SPADES  NAVE  PLUS
AIDS  PODDEDPLANTS  KAI
TAD  OBOE  HUSK  ATILT
EASIER  ATOMS  STUDIO
TARDILY  PLANE  STANDIN
HODADS  RAINY  GURNEY
ANAME  AARE  TREE  HAT
TEY  BUDDINGHEADS  MAXI
NIAS  RUMP  SPEWED
MALODOR  HAMPER  ANKLE
SERAPES  RATIO  ASCH
ATONER  TONED  APPEASE
SHUDDERBUG  OFFPUDDING
HONI  ABASE  RARER  EROO
ADDS  TIRED  SNORT  NEST
```

87

```
LABEL  HASTE  BEEFS  MRE
ENURE  USURP  UNCUT  OER
IDONTLIKEYOURTONE  LPS
SAYSHITO  NETS  NESTEA
TAP  VINYL  AILMENT
ALF  LONESOMEDOVE  ANTZ
LEAF  ERAT  ONAROLL
ATLANTA  ADDICTS  SLAKE
MOSQUITOCOAST  TELAVIV
ONESIDED  BLOC  TODATE
IREST  AROAR
COOKIE  SCOT  SNAKEPIT
CAREERS  EBONYANDIVORY
STANS  TINYTIM  LEXICON
NOTAONE  ECCE  LUNA
EGGS  LOVINGCARESS  SSN
TOEHOLD  ARESO  EOS
HAZARD  ASTO  UPGRADES
ILE  DONTTOUCHTHATDIAL
CIS  ENEMY  NIMOY  OTERO
SET  REESE  DAMNS  FOUNT
```

88

```
PASTED  AWAKEN  ATTACHE
INCODE  CALICO  BRONZED
KNOWSFOURGNUS  MASTERY
EARN  TWAS  SEM  DEICES
ESO  ETHOS  RETEACH
ABC  BAREINNMINED  BRO
BRACER  POLENTA  ASIAN
EARLYISH  NGO  GRAMPS
DUDE  MISTRESS  ORNATE
FEDERICO  ATEALOT
AMY  MEATBUYCHANTS  ERS
POUTIER  APOSTATE
POLAND  GOPLACES  AWAY
ALEROS  ENO  CYNICISM
LABOR  BOONIES  ETHNIC
SHE  BORNETWOLOOS  DNA
ENLARGE  EELED  YAP
MEMOIR  ESA  AVES  ROPE
ABILENE  WRYBREDFLOWER
HASTIER  AMELIE  PAMELA
INTENSE  YENTAS  DWARFS
```

89

```
METS  STAFFS  PAD  HIM
HANOI  INDIAN  OLDJEANS
ANION  SUITCOMPLAINING
LUSTALITTLEBIT  YGOR
SALVIA  SYD  LAM  STYLI
LEE  SPA  INBED  EGAD
GATINSTYLE  SAG  OLE
DEEM  NACHOS  ASWANDAM
SEATAT  SHERA  RANSOM
ITSAJOB  IRK  FIG  XSOUT
ARIB  PURSESAIDES  ETNA
MENLO  LEM  TAC  SIOBHAN
GENTLE  FUNKY  PRYERS
HOTSTUFF  ODDLOT  WARM
UNH  ORR  RAYPERVIEW
TIED  FOCAL  EAN  HAP
STJOE  GAD  ISO  DRIVEN
ONLY  MISSINGCOUSINS
DRINKOFDISASTER  SKATE
JANEEYRE  NATANT  SERAC
SET  OON  SCAPES  ORYX
```

90

```
ALLPRO  RESAVE  TRIBAL
LTILES  MINIVAC  HORACE
MYFAVORITEMART  EDITED
ARTIE  ATARIS  OPS  STLO
NARZ  GATO  JEN  IAN
BATTLEOFBIN  RESTAIN
ALAS  MRLEE  MIX  LINGER
TOM  TYSONS  AEC  ESTATE
HOPIN  HET  ANNE  THEGAP
SPATULA  SEDATEST  LESS
STIRS  NOG  DIETS
ARCA  SPENGLER  DREAMUP
NODSAT  CARL  EVE  STASI
KALINE  AVA  ARETES  VIC
ARAGON  DEM  TIROS  PENA
UNUSUAL  TOGASPRINGS
MAG  KTS  SOHN  INEZ
OCHS  OHO  TEEMED  CAIRO
OTTAWA  BOTOFTHEBARREL
LEERED  IRONONS  SPRANG
ADRATE  TASERS  ASONIA
```

91

O	S	C	A	R		A	R	M	S		I	N	G	E		P	E	R	U
H	O	O	V	E	R		T	O	I	T		N	E	O	P	H	Y	T	E	S
M	Y	L	I	F	E		O	G	R	E		C	A	T	H	A	R	T	I	C
S	A	D		I	N	A	M	E	R	I	C	A	T	H	E	Y	O	U	N	G
		C	E	L	E	B		T	O	N	I		L	S	D					
A	R	E	A	L	W	A	Y	S	R	E	A	D	Y		R	E	D	A	C	T
K	E	R	R		E	T	E		M	R	X		L	A	M	I	N	A	R	
I	L	E		C	R	E	T	A	N		D	I	M	E		I	S	S	U	E
T	I	A	R	A		T	O	G	I	V	E	T	O	T	H	O	S	E		
A	T	L	A	S	T		P	E	L	F		A	A	A		O	N	E	S	
		W	H	O	A	R	E	O	L	D	E	R	T	H	A	N				
S	A	B	U		P	L	O		A	U	R	A		U	B	O	A	T	S	
T	H	E	M	S	E	L	V	E	S	T	H	E		E	R	N	I	E		
A	S	A	B	C		B	O	S	C		S	I	G	U	R	D		N	E	A
L	I	N	E	A	G	E		A	H	A		U	T	E		N	A	T	O	
E	N	O	R	M	E		F	U	L	L	B	E	N	E	F	I	T	S	O	F
				T	S	E		E	D	A	M		N	O	C	H	E			
T	H	E	I	R	I	N	E	X	P	E	R	I	E	N	C	E		W	O	O
V	E	R	S	A	T	I	L	E		N	I	N	A		U	S	N	E	W	S
P	R	I	E	D	O	P	E	N		T	U	E	S		S	A	M	L	E	T
G	O	N	E		N	E	R	O		E	M	M	Y		W	I	L	D	E	

92

M	O	N	T	E	R	O		W	O	W	E	D	E	M		T	E	R	R	A
A	R	O	U	S	E	R		O	O	H	L	A	L	A		A	L	O	E	S
D	E	B	T	O	F	A	S	A	L	E	S	M	A	N		H	O	O	P	S
A	G	U	T		C	E	D	A	R		A	L	A	M	O		T	E	E	
M	O	T	O	R	O	L	A		E	X	S		Y	E	L	L	A	T		
E	N	S		T	H	E	R	A	T	O	F	K	H	A	N		E	E	L	S
			S	E	M		R	O	N	A		E	N	A	C	T	S			
S	S	G	T	S		T	B	A	R		C	A	R	E		A	T	S	E	A
A	P	I	P		U	S	E	B	O	A	T	H	A	N	D	S		P	A	S
F	I	V	E	O	N	E	S		C	O	M		D	U	S	T	E	R	S	
A	C	E	T	I	C		S	E	C	U	R	E	D		R	I	V	O	L	I
R	U	B	E	L	L	A		N	U	T		R	O	A	S	T	P	I	G	
I	L	E		W	E	L	T	C	R	E	A	T	I	O	N		A	L	E	N
S	E	R	T	A		I	B	L	E		C	A	P	P		A	P	E	R	S
		T	R	Y	S	T	S		A	D	E	S		H	U	E				
E	S	T	A		P	O	P	U	L	A	R	M	I	T	T	S		D	R	Y
U	T	O	P	I	A		E	L	M		C	O	S	T	F	R	E	E		
R	E	A		F	R	A	N	C		P	L	I	E	R		L	A	D	S	
A	L	B	E	E		T	A	K	E	M	Y	B	R	E	T	T	A	W	A	Y
I	L	O	N	A		O	N	E	V	O	T	E		A	V	A	R	I	C	E
L	A	Y	E	R		P	A	R	A	P	E	T		T	A	L	E	N	T	S

93

R	A	T	O	U	T		B	R	I	T	T		A	D	E		H	M	O
E	V	U	L	S	E		S	E	A	S	O	N		R	O	N	D	E	A	U
F	I	R	E	I	N	T	H	E	I	R	O	N		M	E	D	I	A	N	T
R	A	N	O	N		R	A	N	T	A	T		D	I	S		R	D	A	S
E	N	S		G	R	E		T	E	L		A	N	T		T	I	T	O	
S	C	I		E	A	S	T		L	E	A	N	T	O	S		N	E	L	
H	A	N	D	I	N	T	H	E	B	I	R	D		H	O	I	S	T	E	D
		O	N	E	Y	E	A	R		S	A	K	E		M	O	H	S		
S	I	M	O	N		P	L	O	W		M	I	S	T	I	M	E			
N	O	U	R	I	S	H		W	H	O	S	W	H	O		A	H	A	B	
I	N	D		S	H	A	D		S	E	N		I	O	N	S		O	B	E
P	A	I	D		E	Y	E	W	E	A	R		T	I	P	P	L	E	S	
		N	E	W	S	I	E	R		T	I	L	L		R	H	E	T	T	
		A	T	M	E		N	S	E	C		C	O	A	S	T	E	D		
A	C	H	I	E	S	T		N	O	S	E	I	N	T	H	E	S	O	C	K
I	R	E		D	E	H	I	S	C	E		S	E	R	A		C	O	E	
R	E	S	P		A	E	R		K	E	W		I	T	T		A	R	E	
F	A	T	A		T	R	A		T	I	E	T	A	C		H	E	R	O	N
A	G	I	T	A	T	O		S	A	N	D	I	N	T	H	E	L	I	N	E
R	E	C	H	A	L	L		P	I	T	T	E	D		E	I	S	N	E	R
E	S	K		H	E	L		F	L	O	O	R		T	R	E	A	T	S	

94

I	T	A	L	I	C		S	I	M	P	E	R		I	O	N	E	S	C	O
N	O	V	E	N	A		A	Z	A	L	E	A		T	E	E	S	H	O	T
L	E	A	D	I	N	G	L	A	D	I	E	S		C	O	M	P	O	S	T
E	S	T		T	A	O		A	R	A		P	A	H		E	N	O	T	E
A	H	A	S		P	A	C	K	I	N	G	S	L	I	P	S		T	A	R
F	O	R	E	T	E	L	L		D	T	S		L	E	O	I		I	S	S
		E	S	T	O		S	A	C		T	R	U	S	T	S	I	N		
	U	D	O		N	A	R	C		O	P	T	S		M	G	M	T		
D	U	M	P	I	N	G	G	R	O	U	N	D	S		Y	E	S	S	I	R
A	P	A		E	M	O		O	P	P	O	S	E	S		L	O	T	S	A
E	D	T		F	E	U	D		I	C	E		T	Y	R	E		A	C	C
M	A	C	R	O		P	O	L	E	A	X	E		N	O	V		R	U	T
O	T	H	E	R	S		W	O	R	K	I	N	G	C	L	A	S	S	E	S
N	E	I	L		T	A	N	G		E	T	T	E		E	T	A			
		N	O	M	A	T	T	E	R		S	I	N		O	W	A	R		
R	I	G		O	R	T	O		M	A	B		C	O	U	R	T	I	E	R
R	A	P		D	R	A	W	I	N	G	R	O	O	M	S		O	R	S	O
A	G	A	P	E		I	N	N		E	E	R		S	A	T		D	I	O
T	R	I	L	L	I	N		R	U	N	N	I	N	G	B	O	A	R	D	S
E	E	R	I	E	S	T		E	V	A	D	E	S		L	I	P	O	U	T
D	E	S	E	R	T	S		M	A	S	A	L	A		E	L	O	P	E	S

95

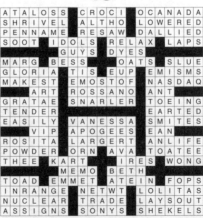

A	T	A	L	O	S	S		C	R	O	C	I		O	C	A	N	A	D	A
S	H	R	I	V	E	L		A	L	T	H	O		L	O	W	E	R	E	D
P	E	N	N	A	M	E		R	E	S	A	W		D	A	L	L	I	E	D
S	O	O	T		I	D	O	L	S		R	E	L	A	X		L	A	P	S
			G	U	Y	S		B	E	S	S		D	Y	E	S				
M	A	R	G		B	E	S	S			O	A	T	S		S	L	U	E	
G	L	O	R	I	A		T	I	S		E	U	P		E	M	I	S	M	S
M	A	K	E	S	T		E	M	O	S	T	O	F		N	A	S	D	A	Q
		A	R	T		R	O	S	S	A	N	O		A	N	T				
G	R	A	T	A	E		S	N	A	R	L	E	R		T	O	E	I	N	G
T	E	N	D	E	R									E	A	R	T	E	D	
E	A	S	I	L	Y		V	A	N	E	S	S	A		S	M	I	T	E	S
		V	I	P		A	P	O	G	E	E	S		E	A	N				
R	O	S	I	T	A		L	A	R	G	E	R	T		A	N	L	I	F	E
P	O	W	D	E	R		O	R	N		A	V	A		T	O	A	T	E	E
T	H	E	E		K	A	R	T		I	R	E	S		W	O	N	G		
				M	E	M	O		B	E	T	H								
T	O	A	D		E	M	M	E	T		A	T	E	I	N		F	O	P	S
I	N	R	A	N	G	E		N	E	T	W	T		L	O	L	I	T	A	S
N	U	C	L	E	A	R		T	R	A	D	E		L	A	Y	S	O	U	T
A	S	S	I	G	N	S		S	O	N	Y	S		S	H	E	K	E	L	S

96

```
HDTV  USAF  OBJ  ROSEHIP
AREA  PAIL  NAE  ACETONE
JOLLYMRROGERS  STATUTE
ILLSAY  CREPTUP  AMUSER
SLYER  MOIRA  RIDS  IRA
      GOODMRDEEDS  SNAG
CEREBRAL  STINTS  INGLE
ANOMIE    AGA    SWAMIS
ISAID  BRANDMRX  COPRA
RUSSE  YOWEE    BANDB
NETS  MRINBETWEEN  RUST
  EASED  RIPEN  TABOO
CDROM  MODELMRT  EGBDF
SIMILE  AMO    STOLAF
AGREE  DROPIT  FINENESS
LAPS  MYBOYMRBILL
ERE  REEL  MILNE  ADAYS
SCALER  EUGENIA  IMFREE
MANIACS  SPRINGMRCLEAN
ASUNDER  PAS  KLUM  ATRA
NETZERO  SSE  SEGA  TENT
```

97

```
MESSING  UNCAP  PQRS  ELSE
ATTABOY  NIOBE  ATEE  NEED
CHRISTMASTREE  WIGWAGGED
RAISES  PER  TRAPP  SALUKI
ANDON  SPRIG  ERATO  AIMEE
MOEN  ATL  CROSSWORD  SERS
ELS  SLEEK  ODS  SPEECH
  RTE  JINGO    BAMA  MAS
JULIUSCAESARSALAD  SMACK
ORION  UCLAN  ASON  CHERRY
EGG  JFK  ASTRA  LENS
SEALSOFFKEYCHAINSAWDUST
  MEAL  REMET    ARM  PYE
DOESNT  ONIT  AUSSI  IRINA
OWNED  GSTRINGSUPSETBACK
GET  AJET  EASEL  CCI
  PLANBS  CAM  ZILCH  LAB
AGAR  GUINEAPIG  TOE  SEUL
RABID  STARR  CHOPS  METRO
GUAVAS  PROAM  EXE  FURMAN
OCTAGONAL  FOOTBALLFIELD
SHOT  MORE  ENDTO  EATABLE
YORE  ESTD  SYDOW  SMILEYS
```

98

```
MANTAS  RACY  WEBS  PUMA
OREIDA  OLEO  IMAM  INON
REVEAL  SINGAPORESLING
PNEUMATICTIRE  AALTO
HARP  MINE  SUGARMAPLE
  NIL  STOPIN  ORRIS
METROSTATION  VISA  ITS
OREOS  SPASM  WEST  ACHE
PUNCHCARDS  EWER  TESS
ECO  OAT  IONIA  IDO
STREWN  BREWERY  AIMSAT
  USA  RESEW  STU  CUE
PAAR  SCUD  MOTHERLODE
ANNO  THIS  MOIRA  NOWIN
PIT  KAOS  BOWLINGALLEY
AMISH  RELOAN  AOL
WASHATERIA  EONS  SODA
TEENA  GREENPASTURES
FORESTPRESERVE  IAMBUS
BRUT  ETUI  LION  PUMICE
ISMS  RAGA  SKIS  STATES
```

99

```
ICIEST  KANSAS  MALACHI
MODELA  ILOILO  ONESHOT
AMERICANLITER  RAGTIME
REA  POND  SEETHE  ICON
ETTAS  ELMO  UNLINK
THESHOWERMUSTGOON  ELI
  POW  DEMISE  URANUS
TLC  DENTE  AMPS  VERBAL
YEAS  SOBERSISTER  TRUE
PAULO  DADAS    SERIO
EDGER  ERST  COAT  ASTRO
  HABLA  FORGE  YAHOO
FUTZ  OLIVELOAFER  NEAP
ALIENS  NINE  TAMIL  RMS
SENSEI  ANGELO    GER
TEA  ANYPORTERINASTORM
  FERGIE  TYNE  SEPIA
OLIN  ETALII  UMPS  PST
LIBERAL  BUTTEROFAJOKE
EMERALD  ENABLE  CLOSER
SARONGS  SALEMS  STEEDS
```

100

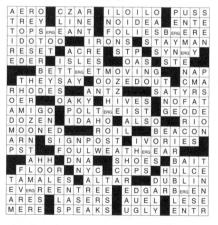

```
AERO  CZAR  ILOILO  PUSS
TREY  LINE  NOIDEA  ENTE
TOPSERGEANT  FOLIESBERGERE
IDOTOO  IRONS  STAYMAN
RESET  ACRE  STP  SYNERGY
EDER  ISLES  OAS  STE
  BETTERGETMOVING  NAP
THEYSAY  OOZEDOUT  CMA
RHODES  ANTZ  SATYRS
OER  OAKY  HIVES  NOFAT
AMIGO  POLTERGEIST  GEODE
DOZEN  IDAHO  ALSO  RIO
MOONED    ROIL  BEACON
ARN  SIGNPOST  IVORIES
PST  FOULWEATHERGEAR
  AHH  DNA  SHOES  BAIT
FLOOR  NYC  COPS  HULCE
TAMALES  ALTAR  DUBLIN
EVERGREENTREE  EDGARBERGEN
ARES  LASERS  AUEL  LESE
MERE  SPEAKS  UGLY  ENTR
```

101

```
GONG  SWARMS  ACED   TRIP
ISEE  LENDEE   MARE  REMI
SUBSTANDARD   EPIC   OPAL
    TINT   CONNOTATIONS
RADARGUNS  NOD  UGH   IAN
ABELE  POOLAREA   ORANGE
POSTDATING  ADMINISTER
TWI   SOREAT   OVALS
  CVII    OIL   ALLOWED
EXCOMMUNICATION    NILE
AMANA  NEMO  BARK  BASIN
SANT   COUNTERBALANCES
ESTARDA  SKI    INTO
   ATEST   TINEAR    NBA
PROPORTION  SUPERVISOR
BELPME  ONELITER   ONINE
AVE  ILA  GLO  SEAPLANES
SEMICIRCULAR    TAGS
ERIN  COLA  DISLOCATION
RISK  TSAR  EMIGRE  IOWA
SESS   SEND  RECESS  RULE
```

102

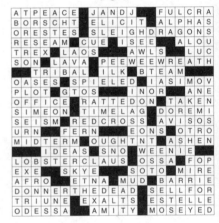

```
GELS  GIRL   BESS   RAPIDS
EXAM  ADUE   ROAN   ACUMEN
ETTA  SONATASTANDSTILL
RECUT   RUS   UFO     ANI
JACKSONINTHEPULPIT
ALA  ENID  TEN    ASIMOV
BARBS  VENISONVIDIVICI
BREA  RENO  TWOON   EATS
AGED  ENTER   SLATY  MEA
REREAD   SONNETPROFITS
  GRASS  TIE   STOLI
VIRGINMASONRY   UKASES
ONE  ATIME   DAMUP  SNAP
ICAN   TOWAR  MOLE  CARA
CARIBBEANSEASON  POKER
ENSTAR   OPE  CASE   EDS
  PARSONFORTHECOURSE
LEI   AVE   RIO   ANNIE
WATCHYOURSTEPSON   IVAN
OINKED  LOOT  PORT  TELE
ERASES  ESSO  SUEY  ERST
```

103

```
NIP   BOSOM   SKICAP   PTL
EMI  ATONOF  CANADA   OWE
OPENSESAME  HOARDS   LIT
NAPES   TE ND OWN   ITSON ME
GCLEF  GENERA  PRE   OAST
ATA  ID OLATRY  QUA  S NY DER
S OR T  DRAMAS  PUMICE  STY
  SEALIN   TREASONS
BEECH  LAOS  IN STEREO
CA RNE  LEOTOLSTOY   TRUER
BELLAS  WEA KS POT  LO VA BLE
ONEAM  ALLTHERAGE   NESS
TERR AZ ZO  SHOR   YACHT
  DOORSTEP   GHOSTS
GAY  NOTFAR  PASSER   HAD
OMITS  APR  DI LA TORS  ROY
TREE  FED  FINNAN  ELOPE
SALTII   DUVALL   FL EWAT
ODD  BLEWIT  TAKESISSUE
FIT  MEXICO  ADELIE   ILS
TOO  STOLEN  DRIPS   NOT
```

104

```
ATPEACE  JANDJ   FULCRA
BORSCHT  ELICIT  ALPHAS
ORESTES  SLEIGHDRAGONS
RESEAM  CUE  ISEE   ALOU
TREX  LAOS   AWLS    LUC
SON  LAVA  PEEWEEWREATH
  TRIBAL  ILK   BTEAM
OASES  SPIELED  IASIMOV
PLOT  GTOS    INOR   ANE
OFFICE  RATTEDON   TAKEN
SIMEON  TIMELAG  DOREMI
SEISM  REDCROSS  AVISOS
URN  FERN   EONS   OTRO
MIDTERM  OUGHTNT  ASHEN
  IDEAS  SNO  WEENIE
LOBSTERCLAUS  OSSA  FOP
EXE   SKYE   SOTO  MIRE
AFRO  ETNA  MUD  BARRIE
DONNERTHEDEAD  SELLFOR
TRIUNE  EXALTS  ESTELLE
ODESSA   AMITY  MOSEYED
```

105

```
RCA   IDARE  UND  ACTFOR
LEAN  BARBER  LIE  EOSINE
SEVENSAMURAI  TNN  GUAVAS
TOES  OLIGARCHIES    INRE
ANNUALS   HAMMIEST    EEE
FOURSEASONS  ROOTS  DEANE
FREAK  ELATED  NIP  ORSON
SAS  SIXWEEKS  STEN  WRYLY
  AORTA   SACHS   MNOP
BROGUES  MAL  TAS  HAIRIER
RANAT  DREAMON  KERN   EMU
ODES  TENTOMIDNIGHT  ICON
NIH  TINA  LEADERS  BRETT
COOKING  TIN  SRA  BRAISES
  UOMO   WHATS   BOUTS
THROE  YARN  TWOJAKES  CIO
BOWLS  UTE  SPIRIT  MOOGS
AMISS  REEVE  EIGHTMENOUT
RET  QUIRKILY   RENEWAL
  HAUL  BILLMELATER  ENNE
CAYMAN  INE  HAPPYNEWYEAR
CHOPRA  RGS  ARGENT  HERS
CAUSES  DST  SNARE   YDS
```

The New York Times

Crossword Puzzles

The #1 Name in Crosswords

Available at your local bookstore or online at nytimes.com/nytstore

Coming Soon!

Little Pink Book of Crosswords	978-0-312-65421-4
Little Black & White Book of Holiday Crosswords	978-0-312-65424-5
Every Day with Crosswords	978-0-312-65426-9
Clever Crosswords	978-0-312-65425-2
Weekends with Will	978-0-312-65668-3
Relaxing Sunday Crosswords	978-0-312-65429-0
Cozy Crosswords	978-0-312-65430-6
Sunday Crossword Puzzles Vol. 36	978-0-312-65431-3
Large-Print Crossword Puzzle Omnibus Vol. 11	978-0-312-65487-0

Special Editions

Brilliant Book of Crosswords	978-0-312-59004-8
Little Black (and White) Book of Sunday Crosswords	978-0-312-59003-1
Will Shortz's Wittiest, Wackiest Crosswords	978-0-312-59034-5
Little Luxe Book of Crosswords	0-312-38622-2
Double Flip Book of Crosswords and Sudoku	0-312-38635-4
Crosswords to Keep Your Brain Young	0-312-37658-8
Little Black (and White) Book of Crosswords	0-312-36105-X
The Joy of Crosswords	0-312-37510-7
Little Red and Green Book of Crosswords	0-312-37661-8
Little Flip Book of Crosswords	0-312-37043-1
How to Conquer the New York Times Crossword Puzzle	0-312-36554-3
Will Shortz's Favorite Crossword Puzzles	0-312-30613-X
Will Shortz's Favorite Sunday Crossword Puzzles	0-312-32488-X
Will Shortz's Greatest Hits	0-312-34242-X
Will Shortz Presents Crosswords for 365 Days	0-312-36121-1
Will Shortz's Funniest Crossword Puzzles Vol. 2	0-312-33960-7
Will Shortz's Funniest Crossword Puzzles	0-312-32489-8
Will Shortz's Xtreme Xwords	0-312-35203-4
Vocabulary Power Crosswords	0-312-35199-2

Easy Crosswords

Easy Crossword Puzzles Vol. 11	978-0-312-60826-2
Easy Crossword Puzzles Vol. 10	0-312-54171-6
Volumes 2–9 also available	

Tough Crosswords

Tough Crossword Puzzles Vol. 13	0-312-34240-3
Tough Crossword Puzzles Vol. 12	0-312-32442-1
Volumes 9–11 also available	

Sunday Crosswords

Finally Sunday Crosswords	978-0-312-64113-9
Crosswords for a Lazy Sunday	978-0-312-60820-0
Stress-Free Sunday Crosswords	0-312-56537-2
Big Book of Sunday Crosswords	0-312-56533-X
Forever Sunday Crosswords	0-312-54167-8
Sunday Delight Crosswords	0-312-38626-5
Sunday in the Sand Crosswords	0-312-38269-3
Simply Sunday Crosswords	0-312-34243-8
Sunday in the Park Crosswords	0-312-35197-6
Sunday Morning Crossword Puzzles	0-312-35672-2
Everyday Sunday Crossword Puzzles	0-312-36106-8
Sunday Brunch Crosswords	0-312-36557-8
Sunday at the Seashore Crosswords	0-312-37070-9
Sleepy Sunday Crossword Puzzles	0-312-37508-5
Sunday's Best	0-312-37637-5
Sunday at Home Crosswords	0-312-37834-3
Sunday Crosswords Vol. 35	0-312-59034-2

Omnibus

Garden Party Crossword Puzzles	978-0-312-60824-8
Easy to Not-So-Easy Crossword Puzzle Omnibus Vol. 4	978-0-312-60825-5
Lazy Day Crossword Puzzle Omnibus	0-312-56532-1
Weekend in the Country	0-312-38270-7
Crosswords for Two	0-312-37830-0
Crosswords for a Relaxing Weekend	0-312-37829-7
Easy to Not-So-Easy Crossword Puzzle Omnibus Vol. 3	0-312-54172-4
Crosswords for a Lazy Afternoon	0-312-33108-8
Lazy Weekend Crossword Puzzle Omnibus	0-312-34247-0
Lazy Sunday Crossword Puzzle Omnibus	0-312-35279-4
Ultimate Crossword Omnibus	0-312-31622-4
Tough Crossword Puzzle Omnibus Vol. 1	0-312-32441-3
Crossword Challenge	0-312-33951-8
Crosswords for a Weekend Getaway	0-312-35198-4
Biggest Beach Crossword Omnibus	0-312-35667-6
Weekend Away Crossword Puzzle Omnibus	0-312-35669-2
Weekend at Home Crossword Puzzle Omnibus	0-312-35670-6
Holiday Cheer Crossword Puzzles	0-312-36126-2
Crosswords for a Long Weekend	0-312-36560-8
Crosswords for a Relaxing Vacation	0-312-36694-9
Will Shortz Presents Fun in the Sun Crossword Puzzle Omnibus	0-312-37041-5
Sunday Crossword Omnibus Vol. 10	0-312-59006-7
Sunday Crossword Omnibus Vol. 9	0-312-35666-8

Easy Crossword Puzzle Omnibus Vol. 6	0-312-38287-1
Crossword Puzzle Omnibus Vol. 16	0-312-36104-1
Supersized Book of Easy Crosswords	0-312-35277-8
Supersized Book of Sunday Crosswords	0-312-36122-X
Previous volumes also available	

Portable Size Format

Everyday Easy Crosswords	978-0-312-64115-3
Puzzle Doctor Presents Crossword Fever	978-0-312-64110-8
Poolside Puzzles	978-0-312-64114-6
Sunny Crosswords	978-0-312-61446-0
Mild Crosswords	978-0-312-64117-7
Mellow Crosswords	978-0-312-64118-4
Mischievous Crosswords	978-0-312-64119-1
Wake Up with Crosswords	978-0-312-60819-4
Simply Soothing Crosswords	978-0-312-60823-1
Simply Satisfying Crosswords	978-0-312-60822-4
Simply Sneaky Crosswords	978-0-312-60821-7
Soul-Soothing Crosswords	0-312-59032-6
Crosswords in Bed	0-312-59009-1
Crosswords by the Seaside	0-312-56534-8
Easy, Breezy Crosswords	0-312-56535-6
Ferociously Fun Crosswords	0-312-56538-0
Fearsomely Frightful Crosswords	0-312-56539-9
Fascinatingly Fierce Crosswords	0-312-56540-2
Will Shortz Presents the Dangerous Book of Crosswords	0-312-56536-4
Coffee and Crosswords: Whipped Wednesday	978-0-312-60799-9
Coffee and Crosswords: Thirsty Thursday	978-0-312-60800-2
Coffee and Crosswords: Mocha Monday	0-312-54164-3
Coffee and Crosswords: Tea Time Tuesday	0-312-54165-1
Stress-Free Crosswords	0-312-54166-X
Tame Crosswords	0-312-54168-6
Wild Crosswords	0-312-54169-4
Ferocious Crosswords	0-312-54170-8
Ready, Set, Solve! Crosswords	0-312-38623-0
Crosswords 101	0-312-38619-2
Tension-Taming Crosswords	0-312-38624-9
The Crossword Connoisseur	0-312-38627-3
The Puzzlemaster's Choice	0-312-38271-5
In the Kitchen Crosswords	0-312-38259-6
Think Outside the Box Crosswords	0-312-38261-8
Big Book of Easy Crosswords	0-312-38268-5
Real Simple Crosswords	0-312-38254-5
Crosswords By the Bay	0-312-38267-3
Crosswords for Your Coffee Break	0-312-28830-1
Sun, Sand and Crosswords	0-312-30076-X
Crosswords for Your Beach Bag	0-312-31455-8
Crosswords to Boost Your Brainpower	0-312-32033-7
Cuddle Up with Crosswords	0-312-37636-7
C Is for Crosswords	0-312-37509-3
Crazy for Crosswords	0-312-37513-1
Crosswords for a Mental Edge	0-312-37069-5
Afternoon Delight Crosswords	0-312-37071-9
Crosswords Under the Covers	0-312-37044-X
Crosswords for the Beach	0-312-37073-3
Will Shortz Presents I Love Crosswords	0-312-37040-7
Will Shortz Presents Crosswords to Go	0-312-36695-7
Favorite Day Crosswords: Wednesday	0-312-59033-4
Favorite Day Crosswords: Tuesday	0-312-37072-5
Favorite Day Crosswords: Monday	0-312-36556-X
Crosswords in the Sun	0-312-36555-1
Expand Your Mind Crosswords	0-312-36553-5
After Dinner Crosswords	0-312-36559-4
Groovy Crossword Puzzles from the '60s	0-312-36103-3
Piece of Cake Crosswords	0-312-36124-6
Carefree Crosswords	0-312-36102-5
Fast and Easy Crossword Puzzles	0-312-35629-3
Backyard Crossword Puzzles	0-312-35668-4
Brainbuilder Crosswords	0-312-35276-X
Stress-Buster Crosswords	0-312-35196-8
Super Saturday Crosswords	0-312-30604-0
Café Crosswords	0-312-34854-1
Crosswords for Your Lunch Hour	0-312-34857-6
Easy as Pie Crossword Puzzles	0-312-34331-0
Crosswords to Soothe Your Soul	0-312-34244-6
Beach Blanket Crosswords	0-312-34250-0
Crosswords for Stress Relief	0-312-33953-4
Crosswords for a Brain Workout	0-312-32610-6
A Cup of Tea Crosswords	0-312-32435-9
Crosswords for Your Bedside	0-312-32032-9
Coffee Break Crosswords	0-312-37515-8
Rise and Shine Crossword Puzzles	0-312-37833-5
Coffee, Tea or Crosswords	0-312-37828-9
Sweet Dreams Crosswords	0-312-37836-X
Other volumes also available	

St. Martin's Griffin